ROYALTY IN THE NEW WORLD;

OR,

The Prince of Wales in America.

Eng^d by J.C Buttre.

H. R. H. THE PRINCE OF WALES.

From a Photograph by Brady.

ROYALTY IN THE NEW WORLD;

OR, THE

Prince of Wales in America.

BY

KINAHAN CORNWALLIS.

Long may the Prince abide,
England's hope, joy, and pride;
    Long live the Prince;
May England's future king,
Victoria's virtues bring
To grace his reign—
    God save the Prince.

NEW YORK:
M. DOOLADY, 49 WALKER STREET.
1860.

THOMAS HOLMAN, PRINTER,
CORNER OF CENTRE AND WHITE STREETS, N. Y

PREFACE BY THE AUTHOR.

My great aim in the composition of this panorama of the tour of His Royal Highness the Prince of Wales was accuracy—to convey a true idea of the progress of the greatest and most auspicious event of the age; and as I personally saw more of the scenes therein depicted than any other individual, not of the royal suite, I feel myself entitled to speak; and this I have done from my own impartial convictions, founded on those observations, and not hearsay.

My connection with the *New York Herald*, with which journal I was in constant correspondence throughout the tour, procured me facilities for observation which, under other circumstances, I could not have enjoyed, and I think it proper to mention that I have here freely availed myself of my letters so published.

That the work may be considered an acceptable addition to the literature of, not only history, but travel, is my not inglorious wish.

KINAHAN CORNWALLIS.

November, 1860.

CONTENTS.

CHAPTER XII.

CHAPTER XIII.

CHAPTER XIV.

CHAPTER XV.

CHAPTER XVI.

CHAPTER XVII.

CHAPTER XVIII.

CHAPTER XIX.

CHAPTER XX.

CHAPTER XXI.

CHAPTER XXII.

CHAPTER XXIII.

CHAPTER XXIV.

CHAPTER XXV.

CHAPTER XXVI.

CHAPTER XXVII.

ROYALTY IN THE NEW WORLD;

OR,

The Prince of Wales in America.

CHAPTER I.

INTRODUCTORY.

I AM happy to say that this is not a Blue Book, unless it happens to be so in the color of the binding. Yet it contains a faithful record of the progress of a great historical event from its inception to its termination, and to myself, at least, it will always be a pleasant *souvenir*.

When I am dead and gone, as people say in England, the visit of the Prince of Wales will be recalled in the midst of pleasant associations by hundreds of thousands who are now children, and whose present boast is that they have seen him; and when they too have gone the way of all flesh their children and their children's children will read in the history of our time the chronicle of this royal visit, and it will be equally remembered in England and America, and tend for ages to preserve and strengthen that friendship which ought always to subsist between the English and Americans, who are allied, not only by ties of interest, but by an affinity of race and language, which latter is a natural bond that can never be entirely broken, and it is to be hoped that the day will never come when it will be found weaker than we find it now.

I employed nearly the same words in a newspaper leader before the advent of His Royal Highness in America, and I think they met with a hearty response in every Anglo-Saxon breast on both sides of the Atlantic. They were quoted by the press in America, and echoed in England by the press there.

I only mention this to show the feeling which actuated me in narrating the events relating to the royal tour, of which I was an eye-witness from the first landing of His Royal Highness on the continent till his final departure from Portland.

I left New York as early as the 10th of July for Montreal, and afterwards visited Quebec, Ottowa, Toronto, and other Canadian towns, preparatory to proceeding to Halifax; and, perhaps, if I afford a few glimpses of places by the way, I may not be considered wearisome. Therefore, to begin. I left New York by the seven A.M. train for Troy, and had a delightful view of the glorious Hudson by the way. From Troy, where the passengers bound north changed cars, I was carried by that steam-horse, the locomotive, over a series of beautiful landscapes, till the sonorous voice of the conductor announced that Rutland was reached. There I succeeded in possessing myself of a sandwich and cup of coffee, upon which I dined, there being neither time nor opportunity for a more ample feast. But half a loaf is better than no bread to a hungry man, especially to one who had traveled two hundred and thirty-five miles without a previous indulgence in the customary meal of breakfast. From Rutland, till we sighted on the left the mirror-like waters of Lake Champlain, the scenery on either hand was of the most varied and fascinating character. I could describe it at a length which would satisfy the most exacting landscape painter in the world, but all the world is not made up of landscape painters, and it is possible that some of my readers would find such scrupulous detail the reverse of amusing; and as I wish my books to be of the *utile et dulce* class, I am desirous of preserving that "happy medium" of which I have heard so much in theory but seen so little in practice. It is, therefore, enough that I say the scenery was gladdening to the eye; that the sun brightened the hills, and here and there threw a shadow over the valleys; that the eye searched in vain for that monotony of feature which often characterizes North American landscapes, and that every living thing, from the young colt, that cantered across the grass land at our approach, to the dallying, bright-winged butterfly, and from the monarch of the primeval forest to the cultured rose, seemed to disport in the gladness of its existence.

Such glorious weather as thus animated the earth with its vivifying effulgence has a peculiarly inspiring effect upon my mind, when I am enabled to calmly survey nature in her placid beauty aloof from the busy haunts of men; but there is no beauty without its alloy, and in my case the alloy was chiefly made up of dust and smoke—two things inseparable from railway traveling, at least in the New World.

Late in the afternoon we crossed a couple of bridges, from which the passengers looked down into a deep and rocky gorge, at the bottom of which a stream of water coiled snake-like and stealthily, giving to the chasm an appearance of solemn, gloomy wildness, as impressive as some of the scenes pictured in the sombre pages of Dante.

The train passed slowly over the bridges, and this mournful pace gave time for reflection. Twilight soon made the distant hills grow dim, and a few broad streaks of coloring above the western horizon alone relieved the duskiness that harbingered the night.

Night had actually begun when we crossed the two-mile bridge on piles across Masisco Bay. A few minutes afterwards we crossed another of the same kind, and nearly as long, spanning Lake Champlain at Rouse's Point, where the British Custom-house officer was obliging enough to leave my baggage behind, since which time I have been under the necessity of doing without it.

By this time the weather had changed ; a heavy shower of rain came pattering against the car windows, and the darkness grew deeper. A Dutchman in the train, of the slop-built aspect, made himself ridiculous about this time by talking, in the most ungrammatical and unintelligible English imaginable, upon the slavery question.

A prisoner in handcuffs, arrested on a charge of murder, was one of our passengers all the way ; so that our society, it will be seen, was of an order more than usually varied ; but variety is not always charming, although that which has almost become a proverb tells us it is so. We must not, however, believe all that we hear, and even proverbs lie.

The train reached the banks of the St. Lawrence at a quarter to eleven, when we emerged from the cars into the now cold and damp night, the darkness of which was unrelieved by a star or moonbeam, and went on board the ferry steamer, which straightway ploughed its way across the black and silent tide to the wharf at Montreal—the Hochelaga of the red Indian, the *Ville Marie* of the French.

Five years ago I set my foot on its island shore, and did the " mountain" in a caleche, and paced the solemn aisles of the Cathedral in the *Place des Armes*. Montreal is the city of red-tiled and tinned roofs, and a birds-eye view of it is consequently not unpicturesque. It is more than half French, and this French element seems ineradicable. When you speak to a cabman he answers in a French *patois*, or with an accent which tells you that French is the mother tongue ; as you pass a group of children you hear them chattering

French; whenever you look up at the name of a street painted on the walls, the chances are twenty to one that it is French also; you meet Catholic priests in their vestments, with their heads covered with ordinary black silk hats; you read French names over the shops, and at the Custom-house and City Hall you find the names of the Departments painted on the doors in both languages; you go into your hotel and take up an entirely French newspaper, and an entirely French play-bill from a French theatre; in fact, wherever you turn, you are constantly reminded that Montreal was once a colony of France, and the features of the people, as well as of the city, confirm you in the impression.

On the following morning I took a drive through the city, the public buildings of which are, almost without exception, built of gray limestone of the granite aspect.

For the first time I now saw the completed great two-mile tubular bridge of the Grand Trunk Railway Company across the St. Lawrence. When I visited Montreal in 1855, it was not a bridge, but a mere skeleton. I therefore felt a peculiar interest in glancing over its immense span, which is supported by twenty-four piers, standing 242 feet apart, excepting the centre span, which is 339 feet, each pier being calculated to resist the force of 70,000 tons of ice at one time. Resting on these piers, and extending from abutment to abutment, is the bridge, consisting of a hollow iron tube, twenty-two feet high and sixteen feet wide. As a work of human ingenuity and industry, it is worthy to rank with the seven wonders of the world, and is decidedly one of the greatest works of engineering art in, not only America, but the two hemispheres.

I left Montreal by the four P.M. train for Quebec on the day following my arrival, and for the first time in my life passed through the bridge, which is pleasantly lighted from above by openings near the roof. The weather at this time was cold and showery, and as the evening advanced it became so chilly that a fire was lighted in the car stove. Only one first-class car was attached to the train; there was another next the tender, but it was second class, and the warmth which this wood fire emitted was very acceptable. The scenery along the road was flat and monotonous. Charred stumps of trees, and here and there a burning log, lined the wayside, which showed that those concerned were anxious to clear the land of its surplusage of timber at the earliest opportunity. A few wooden villages, and occasionally the solitary tenement of some lonely wood-cutter, enamored, perhaps, but I think it doubtful, of a lodge in the wilderness, alone gave evidence of the presence of man in this thinly peopled district.

At half-past nine we reached the terminus of the line at Point Levy, opposite the quaint old garrisoned city of Quebec. We emerged from the car shivering with the cold, and locomoted our way on board the ferry steamer, which conveyed us across the dark river, at this point about a mile wide, to the "Lower Town," a quarter inhabited chiefly by the French, or râther the descendants of the French, and about the most gloomy, unwholesome, and dirty-looking spot in all Canada. This region, which has a very antiquated appearance, is built under the cliffs, and occupies a site so low that the very wharves projecting into the river are more elevated than it. In the main street is to be seen the oldest church in the colony. It is a crumbling vestige of by-gone ages, and the plaster on its outer walls has been yellowed by the sun and rains of centuries. It reminded me strongly of the Catholic churches at Lima, and its aspect is, so far, South American.

I entered the omnibus of Russell's Hotel, and after ascending several precipitous streets we passed through the Prescott Gate, so celebrated in the history of Quebec, to which I shall hereafter make allusion, and soon reached our destination, for which I was nothing less than thankful, the cold being of raw Octoberian severity, and owing to the loss of my baggage I had been unable to effect a suitable change of clothing.

Those to whom the sight of fortifications is refreshing are likely to derive much pleasure from a visit to the gray old city of Quebec—the Gibraltar of the New World. All approaches to the city, both by land and water, are commanded by formidable batteries pointing huge black cannon, which meet you with open mouth at every turning in certain neighborhoods. The circuit of the fortifications inclosing the Upper Town is two miles and three quarters, and the total circumference outside the ditches and space reserved by government on which no house is allowed to be built, on the west side, is nearly three miles. The fortifications consist of bastions connected by lofty curtains of solid masonry, and ramparts from twenty-five to thirty-five feet high, and of an almost equal thickness, bristling with the before mentioned cannon, and diversified with round towers, loophole walls, and massive gates, which occur at regular distances. On the summit of the ramparts, from Cape Diamond to the Artillery Barracks, is a broad, covered walk, commanding a beautiful view of the country westward. This passes over the top of St. John's and St. Louis' Gates, where a sergeant's guard is stationed, and from which, at sunset, popular report informs me, a splendid view is obtainable; and I saw no reason to discredit popular report, although it is by no means always on the side of truth. I was not there at that delightful hour when nature, as it were, sinks to rest, and the sun to illuminate the other hemisphere. Phœbus is a hard-working fellow, his task is never ending and he keeps no holiday; yet he always goes his rounds, casting that pleasant, broad smile of his over the earth, as if he never knew what it was to look on the dark side of life. Happy, bright-faced luminary, whom nations have worshiped through all time as the king of the universe! Would that I were the sun!

If I had been above St. John's Gate at the hour named, just preceding that most dear to lovers, and when I sometimes find myself singing "Come into the garden, Maud," as if I really had a Maud to sing to, I should likely have taken in all the features of the landscape to my entire satisfaction. I should have seen the river St. Charles in the fleeting effulgence, either reposing with mirror-like placidity, or waving like a rye-field, according to the state of the wind; should have gazed with lingering delight and the enthusiasm of a painter upon the last touches of light and coloring resting on the spires of Lorette and Charlesbourg, and have watched them as they faded away beyond the mountains of Bonhomme and Tsounonthuan, which rear their summits dimly in the distance; while at one sweep of the eye I should have embraced every detail of the prospect, far and near, with all its picturesque variations of light and shade. But it is not yet too late, and some fine day at sunset I shall be a spectator of the scene which I have faintly traced. My eye never wearies of, but is ever eager for, beautiful sunsets and beautiful scenery, although I have seen thousands of the most splendid natural views in the world, for I have been a wanderer in my day, and there are but few climes in which I have not set my foot.

The city being defended on its land side by ramparts, is elsewhere protected by a lofty wall and parapet, based on a high natural cliff, which no troops in the world could scale. The Upper Town is founded on a rock—a very sure foundation, too, according to all authorities, from the parable downward—while the Lower Town is a wretched, populous place, built under this rock, facing the St. Lawrence. The streets leading from the Lower to the Upper Town are, as a natural consequence, very steep, and they are also very tortuous and narrow. One of these streets is named the Mountain, and the name conveys a very accurate idea of the sort of thoroughfare it is. The military history of Quebec possesses a world-wide interest, for on its fields and around its battlements some of the most courageous exploits ever attempted have taken place. Wolfe of England, Montcalm of France, and Montgomery of America died there, and their names are associated with a lasting glory in the chronicles of warfare. On the next morning I hired a wagon, as the carriages are called here, and drove to the celebrated Plains of Abraham, where General Wolfe fought and died in the remarkable battle against the French troops under Montcalm.

I drove through the St. Louis Gate, where every angle was commanded by cannon, and, leaving the citadel on the left, passed between martello-towers guarding the road, and soon afterwards reached the toll-gate at the entrance to the Plains, where ninepence of British money was demanded. This is a tax I have never paid with pleasure, and on the present occasion I did not pay it at all. I left the wagon standing, and, passing through a rude opening like a gateway, where stood a wooden shanty, which, so far as its appearance was concerned, might have been uninhabited, I found myself in one of the open and grassy fields which constitute the Plains of Abraham, and straight before me, within a small paling inclosure, stood a column surmounted with a helmet and sword, and bearing on its base the inscription, "Here died Wolfe, victorious."

Ascending an eminence a little further on, where, surrounded by a fence, can be traced the redoubt where Wolfe received the fatal wound, and from which he was carried to the spot now occupied by the column, I had a magnificent view of the surrounding country for many miles, including the cove, a little on the Montreal side of Quebec, where Wolfe landed his forces, and which has since borne his name.

According to history, which I may remark is often a gigantic lie, but not always, the English right nearly faced this redoubt, and on this position the French left rested. The French came on the Plains from the right on their way from Beauport, and not from Quebec, and after their defeat retreated down the heights by which they had ascended; they were thus entirely cut off from the city.

On my return to the highway, I saw within an in closure the stone well from which the water that moist ened the lips of the dying Wolfe was procured, and which is now looked upon by many as little less than holy.

Beyond this there is a beautiful drive as far as Marchmont, where the river widens into lake-like proportions, and exhibits a fair sprinkling of ships lying at anchor, and smaller vessels and occasionally a steamer coursing up and down, while down only immense rafts of timber may be seen to float, guided by men who, with their families and chattels, have traveled on them from the far interior of the lumber country.

Mount Hermon Cemetery lies in this direction, at a distance of about three miles from Quebec. It is thirty-two acres in extent, and slopes with picturesque irregularity down a cliff overhanging the St. Lawrence.

On my way back I visited the Citadel, which is imposing enough without, and, with its flag-staff tower, has a striking military appearance, but within presents but little to arrest attention. I found myself in a large open space, with barracks and store-houses built round it that had a worn and desolate look. I had long heard of the beautiful view attainable from the tower of this Citadel, which, from its elevation of three hundred and sixty feet above the river, set before the lingering eye a lovely panorama of the surrounding scenery, embracing mountains, valleys, and plains, and the rivers St. Lawrence and St. Charles. I, therefore, eagerly made the ascent, and well was I rewarded. The description would be monotonous, but the prospect was varied and refreshing, and I felt myself well rewarded for my trouble. I have alluded to the French features of Montreal; but Quebec is even more French than the City of the Island. Thousands of the population speak a French *patois*, and only a few words of broken English. Many of the streets have French names, and the churches of the Roman Catholics preponderate far over those of the Protestants. The former are a strong party in Lower Canada, seeing that they constitute four fifths of the entire population, and nearly all converse as often in French as in English, so that an affinity of language between the English and the bulk of the Lower Canadians can hardly be said to exist.

After returning to the city I entered the Cathedral, whose tall, tin-covered spires had attracted my attention. The interior was painted white, and over the grand altar a gilded canopy rose nearly as high as the arched roof, while round the walls were several chapels, dedicated to various saints. But the charm of the whole was by no means equal to the dim old mouldering churches of the faith in the more balmy regions of South America. Even the few kneeling figures that I saw seemed more formal, yet less fervent in their devotions than those with whose precincts I had made myself familiar on the shores of the Pacific, and there was less solemnity of aspect about the whole than belonged—yea, still belongs—to the grand old tabernacle relics of the vice-regal period of Peru—the monuments of splendid ruin in which the maiden kneels to her invisible father confessor, and the service of the mass is still said.

At eleven o'clock I drove out to the Falls of Montmorenci, which are situated at a distance of about seven miles from Quebec. The journey thither I performed in a caleche, drawn by a stout Canadian horse. After passing through a succession of narrow and declivitous streets, we emerged through a dilapidated gateway into the suburb of San Roque, and then crossed a long wooden bridge spanning the St. Charles River. The houses at the road-side were all painted white, and had a very quaint appearance. Fine gardens were attached to each, and in some of these women, dressed in short black frocks, white bodices, and broad-brimmed straw hats, were engaged in horticultural operations.

On arriving in the vicinity of the Montmorenci rivulet or torrent, which I found rushing through a rocky gorge, and just before flinging itself over a precipice two hundred and fifty feet deep—greater even than that of Niagara—so constituting the Falls, I accepted the services of a juvenile individual who exhibited great anxiety to "show" me the cataract. I now alighted from the caleche and commenced the descent over an exceedingly rugged and shelving path as far as a small ledge of rock just overhanging the Falls. After thus looking down at the tumbling waters, I descended considerably further and looked up at them. From this position I had a splendid view. The water fell in an unbroken sheet, into an oblong recess, the sides of which were almost perpendicular, and opening into the St. Lawrence, whose banks were here high, but gradually inclining. The effect of the neighboring scenery was somewhat spoiled by the too close proximity of some saw-mills, driven by water-power, on the banks of a small stream, diverted from the main channel of the Montmorenci. The spot last alluded to is remarkable for the formation of an ice cone, caused by the freezing of the spray. But as there now remained no traces of the last year's glacier, I was unable to imagine myself in Switzerland.

The Falls, although so high, and situated in a beautiful nook of the river, are not as grand as may be supposed, owing to their narrowness, fifty feet being, I should say, their greatest breadth.

The journey from Quebec to Montreal occupied by railway only five hours and a half—an arrangement very creditable to the Grand Trunk Railway Company. On the way we sighted several bush fires, which threw a lurid glare over certain parts, and covered the landscape with smoke. But to myself, who had seen the bush fires of Australia, where for miles the prospect was one sheet of flame, and where for hundreds of miles I could trace the effects of the conflagration, the scene was as insignificant as is a fusee when compared to a burning mountain. However, burning mountains are not to be seen every day, so I was content with the fusee; and as timber is a drug in this market, I did not feel as I should have done had I been gazing at a house on fire. I knew that the fire would only tend to clear the land of wood, as a great deal of human labor is brought into requisition daily for converting the saplings, yea, and the old monarchs of the forest, into firewood, for the purpose of making ready the land for agricultural and building operations.

I remained at Montreal till Monday morning, when I left by the nine A.M. train for Toronto, calling at Ottowa. In the mean time, I explored the city more than I had ever done before. The public buildings at Montreal are well worth visiting, and for the benefit of future tourists, I will make mention of a few of the principal.

The new Court House, on Nôtre Dame Street, is one of the most massive and imposing of the whole city. It is built of limestone in the Grecian Ionic style, and is seventy-six feet high, the ground plan being three hundred feet by one hundred and twenty-five. Standing immediately opposite, and contrasting remarkably with the newness of its appearance, is Nelson's monument.

The Post-office, on Great St. James Street, is a handsome building, as also is the Bonsecours Market, in St. Paul Street. Several of the banks make a very imposing display, particularly the Bank of Montreal, in the square, Place d'Armes, which is of cut stone and of the Corinthian order.

I have already made mention of the Cathedral on the opposite side of this square, the turrets of which rise conspicuously over all the other buildings in the city. There are three nunneries in and about Montreal, and Sisters of Mercy, in their unbecoming black, and with a white band across the forehead, may be seen walking through the street invariably at the one mournful pace at all hours of the day.

On the next Sunday I took another drive around the mountain—the royal one, from which the city derives its name. It is almost a misnomer to call it a mountain, for it is a mere elevated piece of table-land. The drive, however, affords a series of splendid views, although, on the present occasion, these were much hidden from my view by the clouds of dust that came whirling along the highway. I called at the Bellevue Gardens on the way, where a party of pleasure seekers were regaling themselves with such of the good things of this life as were there dispensed. Mount Royal Cemetery lies about two miles from the city, on the mountain, and is much visited, but not being in an epitaph-collecting mood, I did not stay to ponder over its tombstones. On arriving opposite the house of General Williams, I drove up one or two private roads leading to the same. I found that the General was out of town, and that the premises were being prepared for the reception of His Royal Highness. The view from the house is the most delightful on the mountain, commanding, as it does, a fine sweep of the Back River, which runs behind the city and mountain of the St. Lawrence, and the thickly wooded Nun's Island, where a large nunnery is situated ; of the great tubular railway bridge, backed in the distance by a couple of lofty hills, and with a foreground of wooded landscape, dotted with here and there a villa, while turning to the left may be seen the western end of the city.

The scenery between Montreal and the Prescott junction, where the Ottowa passengers changed cars, is pretty, but not grand. I had a pleasant glimpse of the St. Anne's River and the Lake of the Two Mountains on the way ; but the landscape partook chiefly of the character of land undergoing a transition from its natural state to that of cultivation. Just before arriving at the junction the train ran over a skunk which emitted an almost overpowering stench, so that we were obliged to close the windows in self-defense. There was nearly an hour's delay at the junction before the arrival of the train for Ottawa, distant fifty-four miles from Prescott, which latter is one hundred and twelve miles from Montreal. The line between these places disclosed a succession of dense forest, swamp and partially cleared lands, with an occasional group of shanties. Between Gloucester and Ottawa, however, a few farms were disclosed on either side of the railway, as far as the station near New Edinburg, on the left bank of the Rideau River, facing Ottawa, at the distance of about a quarter of a mile. We reached Ottawa about four P.M., when we took an omnibus belonging to Campbell's Hotel, which was the only house represented by a public vehicle at the station, and bad enough I found it.

To call Ottawa a city is ridiculous ; but it is likely to become one ; so I shall devote a few words to it. Its original name was Bytown, and it is the centre of the immense timber district of the river Ottawa, on which it is situated, at its junction with the Rideau and Gatineau. The town is intersected by the Rideau

Canal and bridge, and forms three districts, namely, that of the Lower Town on the east, Central Town on the west, and Upper Town on the northwest, all of which are on the north side of the Ottawa.

The streets are all wide and laid out at right angles, Rideau and Sussex Streets being the principal ones. The buildings are monotonously plain, and present no imposing features. The government buildings are situated on a place called Barrack Hill; but these are too insignificant to attract the attention of the visitor. Here are erected some fortifications, and the site is well adapted for such, Central Town being in the rear, while the Upper and Lower Towns are completely commanded by it on each side. In front is a precipitous embankment running almost perpendicularly to the river over a distance of several hundred feet, thus completely sweeping the river and opposite shore, at three points of the compass.

The scenery around Ottawa is varied and delightful embracing river, landscape and waterfalls, the latter being those of the Chaudiere—a Niagara in miniature. At present, they have a fall of about forty feet; but in winter, when the river is swollen, they partake more of the character of rapids. The best view of these, I was informed, could be obtained from the suspension bridge, which crosses the river close to them. Besides these, the Rideau Falls attract considerable attention. They are, however, much smaller, but present features of great natural beauty. Ottowa is pre-eminently the city of the future, and not of the present. There is a large hotel there already built, but as yet unopened. This is where the Prince resided during his stay in the place.

The new Houses of Parliament are being proceeded with very rapidly, but little more than their foundations are as yet built. The view from this position is the most delightful in the neighborhood, and perhaps in all Canada.

Leaving Ottowa by the eleven A.M. train, we arrived in Toronto at the same hour at night.

Toronto, which is the metropolis of Upper Canada, lies on the northern shore of Lake Ontario, and on a clear day is within view of the mist rising above Niagara Falls; indeed, I saw it from the roof of my hotel. It is only forty years old; yet it boasts of a university, consisting of two colleges, and several public buildings of great utility, highly creditable to the city. The site of Toronto is extremely flat, but it is nevertheless a place well worth visiting, especially by tourists on their way to Niagara.

CHAPTER II.

Enthusiastic Reception at St. John's—Processions, Levees, Presentations, Illuminations, Addresses, and Universal Rejoicings—Royalty and Loyalty Tête-à-tête—Scenes and Incidents During the Prince's Stay—The Departure for Halifax—The Halt at Sidney—A Unique Celebration.

From Toronto I proceeded to Halifax and awaited the arrival of the royal squadron there. But in order to make my narrative of the tour complete I give the following account of the ovation at St. John's, Newfoundland, compiled from the special correspondence of the *New York Herald:*

The popular idea seems to be that Newfoundland is a large, barren island, with a climate colder than Greenland's, shut off from all intercourse with the civilized world, occupied only by a few fishing stations, perpetually enveloped in the densest of fogs, and inhabited by a few hundred modern Robinson Crusoes, who live in semi-barbarous style, earning a living by catching codfish, and are prevented from holding much intercourse with each other by the heavy mists, which render navigation by land and water equally difficult and dangerous.

Newfoundland is four hundred and twenty miles in length, three hundred miles in breadth at its widest part, about one thousand miles in circumference, and with an area of thirty-five thousand nine hundred and thirteen miles. It lies just east of the river and gulf of St. Lawrence, which separates it from the American continent, and its latitude is between 46 deg. 37 min. and 51 deg. 40 min. north. The island is located upon an immense bank, its shores are broken and rugged, and its bold and lofty sea-cliffs tower like natural fortifications above the Atlantic waves, with soundings of from twenty-five to ninety-five fathoms up to their very bases. Its interior conformation presents innumerable hills, intervened with valleys, marshes, woods, and barrens, intersected by few considerable water-courses, but jeweled here and there with hundreds of lakes.

St. John's, the principal city of the colony, and the place at which the Prince was received, is situated on the extreme east of the island, and contains about thirty thousand inhabitants. Its harbor is perfectly land-locked, and is entered by a passage between two high hills, appropriately called The Narrows, since there is scarcely room for a steamship of ordinary size to enter. These hills are fortified, and completely command the harbor ; which is about half a mile in length, with deep water up to the very docks. St. John's is built in amphitheatrical form around this harbor, and rises with the hills from the water's edge. Its appearance is certainly unique, the houses being confusedly jumbled together, as if some players had been using them for dice, and had heaped them pell-mell at the last throw. The buildings in the lower part of the city are of brick, rebuilt after a large fire in 1846; in the upper part of wood; but all are of only one or two stories in height, and painted of some dingy brownish color, with roofs of black, giving the town an indescribably dull and quaint appearance. The streets, like all the roads on the island, are macadamized, but, except at intervals, do not pretend to sidewalks for pedestrians. The city covers an area of about three miles, and is very loosely and irregularly built, a few only of the thoroughfares being entitled to the name of streets, the rest being merely lanes, with as many turns and angles as the best of Boston cow-paths. The city is built upon a succession of very steep hills, and this gives all the houses upon the transverse streets the appearance of stepping up hills, and adds to the unique aspect of the place. The finest public buildings are ranged in a line at the rear of the town, are built of stone, and, excepting the Roman Catholic Cathedral, are of the most hideous styles of architecture; the governor's mansion looking more like a jail than a private residence, and the Colonial Building almost successfully contesting the palm of ugliness. The city is not a municipality, but is under the charge of the House of Assembly. There are a few policemen on duty, but they seem to have an easy life of it, and only occasionally arrest a saucy man-o'-war's man, by way of practice. The stranger who lands at St. John's is at first struck with the neatness and cleanliness everywhere apparent, and is then surprised at the apparently gigantic size of the inhabitants, who, on account of the low-storied houses, tower disproportionately large, and at the diminutive size of the horses which pass along the streets, drawing immense drays, or equally cumbersome wagons, double seated, and generally loaded with four persons. The immense number of liquor stores next attract attention, nearly every shop in the lower part of the town keeping liquor in addition to its other wares. St. John's is the seat of the Colonial Government, and almost every other person one meets is some official or other. The women are everywhere prevalent, and take the places of men in stores, in the markets, and as waiters in the hotels. During the Prince's visit the men seemed disproportionately few, the majority of them being absent at the fisheries on the Labrador coast. The inhabitants are about two thirds Roman Catholic. Along the coast, near the city, are several small fishing villages, and around the harbor are raised platforms, called "flakes," for drying the fish, from which comes an odor any thing but pleasant to unaccustomed nostrils. Beyond the city stretches away an open country, broken by diminutive hills, interspersed here and there with small lakes or ponds, and fringed with forests of evergreens. Add to these particulars a sky bright and sunshiny as that of Italy, and weather deliciously cool, and the reader can form some idea of the city of St. John's.

As soon as it was known that the Prince of Wales was to land at St. John's, and not, as had been previously arranged, to receive the addresses of the inhabitants on board ship, outside the harbor, the greatest excitement prevailed, and every effort was made to give the Prince a reception worthy of the colony. The governor's mansion was refurnished, arches of evergreens sprang across the streets, the inhabitants prepared to decorate their residences. The Queen's Wharf, at which the Prince was to land, was admirably fitted up; the various societies prepared to march in procession; a public ball was arranged, and a pavilion erected alongside the Colonial Building for the occasion; the two companies of Volunteer Riflemen incessantly practiced their drill; a company of one hundred men, in riflemen's uniform, was organized as the Prince's guard; the Newfoundland Corps, numbering about two hundred men, detailed from the British army, and stationed at St. John's, was ordered to parade; the newspapers teemed with official programmes, and the city was fairly alive with bustle and animation. The war-steamer Flying Fish, Captain Hope, one of the vessels which was to accompany the Prince, arrived at St. John's on the 18th inst., and increased the excitement. The Prince was not expected at St. John's until the 26th ; but, after a pleasant passage from England, the royal ship pushed through the fog banks which lie distinctly visible from St. John's, three or four miles from the island, and on the evening of the 23d, were signaled from the look-out at Signal Hill, which guards the entrance to the harbor.

The evening was clear and pleasant, and the sunshine dying out of the sky, left that cool and delicious half-light most favorable to marine views. Just at half-past five, the magnificent steamer of the line, Hero, with the Prince on board, entered the narrows, closely followed by the Ariadne, one of the largest and fastest war-steamers of the English navy. Instantly the fort on Signal Hill thundered its salute, the cannon of the French frigate Sesostris and the Flying Fish echoing the reports, and the Ariadne, with its heavier guns, pealing its bass to the chorus, while the reverberations of the surrounding hills repeated the salutes, like parks of artillery. Flags of every variety of color suddenly streamed from the shipping and lightened up the town with gay hues, every house displaying its decorations, and the public buildings and churches being fairly enveloped in the gaudy folds of the English ensign. Mingling with the thunder of the cannon, came the silvery chiming of the church bells, and the steady, hearty English cheers of the crowd which thronged the shore, filling up the pauses of the cannonade, and thrilling the multitude with new enthusiasm. Nothing could be grander than the spectacle presented by the land-locked harbor, covered with vessels and enveloped in dense smoke above, and beneath which the cannons of the fort and the shipping, pushed their quick, bright flashes, while every now and then, the smoke lifted and disclosed the city, gay with thousands of flags, and the wharves lined with people, in vari-colored dresses, lightened by the last golden beams of the sunshine, which touched with their magic pencil the smoke, the church spires, the summits of the hills, the many-hued flags, and lent a new beauty to the imposing spectacle. As soon as the Hero cast anchor in the harbor, Major Grant, the commandant of the garrison, with Lieutenant Coen, the aid of Governor Bannerman, went on board and submitted to the Prince the programme for his reception. The Prince announced that he would land the next morning at ten o'clock, and as soon as this intelligence became known on shore, the crowd poured back from the wharves and thronged the streets of the city. St. John's appeared fairly transformed. What had before been preparation, was now completion, and every house was decorated with flags, the principal streets were crossed by arches of evergreen, with loyal inscriptions, and thousands of people from the surrounding villages, kept pouring into the city during the night. The rejoicing was universal and enthusiastic, and every one seemed anxious to do his best to add to the *eclat* of the reception the next day.

St. John's, so gay the night before, could hardly be recognized in the sorry picture it presented the next morning, which, of all others, should have been the most brilliant. During the night, the wind had changed, the sky frowned with most gloomy clouds, and a brisk rain pelted the gay dressings of the town, as if in derision of the whole affair. Never did the town look more woe-begone and bedrenched. The flags clung to their staffs or draggled miserably along the roofs, the streets were almost entirely deserted, the dull-colored houses seemed doubly gloomy, the streets were guttered by miniature rivers running muddily along, the waters of the harbor were as dirty looking as if it were but an immense puddle, and the ships loomed drearily through the mist like spectres of unfortunate men-of-war. Ten o'clock approached. The most sanguine could discern no tokens of fair weather, and nothing remained but to postpone the landing for an hour or two, to gratify those who still hoped against hope. To this the Prince consented, and the order was issued to prepare to receive the Prince at noon. Anxious faces of ladies in Sunday finery, of volunteers in brilliant costumes, of officials excited almost to desperation at having cold water thus thrown upon a celebration which had cost them so much labor and expense, were pressed against the window panes in hopeless hope. Half-past eleven o'clock came, and still the rain came down, and the weatherwise avoided all inquiries, and could give no hopes of better things. The ladies were determined to have the celebration however, and, with umbrellas, overcoats, and pattens, trooped down to the Queen's wharf, and filled the tiers of seats erected for their accommodation. The men mustered in fewer numbers, and the military were not to be seen. Barriers had been erected across the street, above and below the wharf, to prevent a crowd of spectators, and these were guarded by policemen, who enjoyed the rain and their sinecure, and had no one to keep back or arrest. The members of the Committee of Arrangements ran about in the most deplorable frame of mind, and seriously contemplating suicide. Suddenly, at a quarter before noon, the rain ceased, a gleam of sunshine lightened up all faces, the clouds parted, and cleared away like a curtain, and in an instant the city and harbor were brilliant with glorious light, which flashed back in new brightness from the rain drops. The Queen's and the surrounding wharves rapidly filled with spectators. The roofs of the commanding buildings and the rigging of the vessels were crowded. The companies of volunteer riflemen guarded the approaches to the wharf. The policemen mustered in full force and were fully occupied in keeping back the throng and clearing the pathway for the Prince. The holders of tickets jammed the seats reserved for them. The societies with their insignia, were drawn up outside the gate with the children of the public schools. The governor, the bishops, judges, officers, civil and military members of the Assembly, foreign consuls, and the officers of the Sesostris, took their assigned positions in order of rank. Hawsers were extended from the wharf one hundred fathoms into the harbor, and along these were moored a number of small boats, loaded with spectators, and forming a lane leading to the wharf. The wharf is semi-eliptical in shape, and around it were arranged vari-colored bannerets. To the right was the landing place of the Prince, from which a raised path, carpeted with crimson cloth, led to the gateway, over which was a magnificent arch of evergreens, with the inscriptions: "Welcome," and "God Save the Queen," and the royal initials and Prince's motto, "Ich dien," *I serve.* Along this pathway were drawn up the Newfoundland Corps, as a guard of honor, the dignitaries and invited guests. To the left of the wharf were the seats for ladies, and the *tout ensemble* was most brilliant and animated. The royal salute from the Ariadne announced that the Prince had entered his barge, and in a moment after the boat rounded the Hero, and was seen pulling swiftly to the landing. Again the air was rent with the thunder of cannon, the jangling of bells and the cheers of excited thousands, which grew louder and more enthusiastic as the Prince landed, and was welcomed to St. John's by Governor Bannerman. The Prince was dressed in the uniform of an English colonel, and his appearance captivated all hearts. As he proceeded up the scarlet pathway to his carriage, the band struck up the magnificent national anthem, the cheers redoubled, the demonstrations of enthusiasm became almost frantic, and all rose from their seats as the Prince courteously and gracefully acknowledged their welcome by bowing to the right and left, as he walked on, and waved hats and handkerchiefs, and shouted huzzas and blessings in a perfect tumult of excitement. The Prince was accompanied by his suite, consisting of the Duke of Newcastle, Secretary of State for the Colonies, the Earl of St. Germains, Lord Steward of Her Majesty's household, Major Teesdale, and Capt. Grey, equerries in waiting, and Dr. Acland, the Prince's physician. Having reached the gateway, the Prince and suite entered the carriages provided for them, Gov. Bannerman riding with the Prince, and proceeded to the Government House in procession.

As the Prince passed along the street, the bishops and clergy, the judges, members of the House of Assembly, officers of the garrison, and officers of the French steamer, fell into line, followed by the three rifle companies, and societies in order of seniority.

The cortege passed through several streets, which were decorated with flags and arches of evergreens, and lined with people, who kept up an uninterrupted cheer, which the Prince gracefully acknowledged, and at length passed through a magnificent triumphal arch and entered the government grounds, the entrance to which was surrounded by an evergreen bower. The lawn was covered with people, and in front of the governor's mansion was drawn up the Prince's Guard, a company of one hundred boys, dressed in the uniform of a volunteer corps, and a number of the children belonging to the Sabbath schools, dressed in white and with wreaths of flowers. Amid the huzzas of the multitude the Prince entered, through files of soldiery, the Government House, an immense stone building, erected at a cost of over a million of dollars, and commanding a splendid view of St. John's and the surrounding country. This building is used as the residence of the governor, and was luxuriantly refitted for the occasion of the Prince's visit. The Prince took his place upon a dais in the immense drawing-room, with the Earl of St. Germains on his right, and the Duke of Newcastle on his left. Addresses were then presented from the Bishop of Newfoundland and his clergy, from the Roman Catholic bishop and clergy, from the inhabitants of St. John's and Harbor Grace, from the Council and Assembly, and from the various societies.

The addresses having been disposed of, the Prince held a levee in the drawing-rooms of the mansion, at which about two hundred gentlemen, comprising the *élite* of Newfoundland society, were introduced. These gentlemen had, according to the regulations, previously registered their names with the Committee of Arrangements, and each was announced by the equerry in waiting as he entered the room. The ceremonies consisted simply in an introduction of each gentleman to the Prince by name, His Highness bowing as each name was called. The levee, however, afforded all an opportunity to observe the *personnel* of the Prince, whose graceful affability had before delighted them.

Immediately after the levee was broken up, the Prince reviewed the Royal Newfoundland and the Volunteer Corps—the crowd cheering him wherever he appeared. In the afternoon he appeared on horseback, in citizen's dress, riding with perfect grace; and attended only by his suite, he visited Waterford Bridge, about three miles from the city. The route was lined with spectators, and the Prince seemed carried forward by unceasing waves of cheers. The houses along the road were gay with flags, and across the road were fine arches of evergreen, with mottoes and devices—prominent among which were the Prince's crest and plumes. The Prince and his suite were much gratified by the view from Topsail Road. The elements of Newfoundland scenery are very simple, but combine most beautifully. Hills dimpled with lakes, a great deal of sky, a little evergreen, and much rock—these are the components of views unsurpassed on this continent.

In the evening a State dinner was given at the Government House, at half-past eight o'clock. Arches across the streets, the churches, and public buildings, and many private residences, were most brilliantly illuminated, and all over the city fire-works were displayed in lavish profusion, the most beautiful display being given from the Colonial House. From the governor's mansion the scene was bewilderingly beautiful. The streets of the city were marked by rows of lamps, and spanned by arches of living flame, while, rising in stately columns of light, the larger edifices shut in the view, and brilliant rockets and balls of flame leaped up to the dark dome of the sky in tracks of vivid light.

Wednesday was a fine clear day, and at an early hour the population was astir to renew the festivities in honor of the Prince's arrival. The people of the surrounding villages completely deserted their homes and avocations, and flocked to St. John's, where all business was suspended. At an early hour Sir Francis Brady, the chairman of the Committee of Arrangements, waited upon the Prince, and on behalf of the people of the colony, presented him with a fine Newfoundland dog, of large size, and of the rarest breed, and wearing upon his powerful neck a massive silver collar.

The Prince said that he was delighted with his dog, and that he had been wishing for just such a one during his passage from England. He remarked that he would like to give the dog a name which would please the people of Newfoundland—some name connected with the history of the island. Chief Justice Brady suggested "Avalon." The Prince replied that this was the name of but one portion of the colony, and that he should call his dog "Cabot," after the discoverer of Newfoundland. The gentlemen present seemed no less surprised than delighted at this display of the

Prince's knowledge of their colonial history, and exchanged looks of profound admiration. The dog was sent on board the Hero, and safely secured to prevent his leaving his royal master, for whose service he seemed to have no inclination, and rejoining his more humble but older acquaintances on the south side of the harbor.

During the forenoon the Prince and suite, attended by Governor Bannerman, rode on horseback to Portugal Cove, a fishing station about nine miles from St. John's, in the direction opposite to that taken during the ride the day before. The road to the Cove is a very excellent one, and winds most picturesquely over the hills and around the mimic lakes which diversify the view, passing through bits of evergreen woods, and displaying at almost every turn some beautiful little vista or rare nook secluded among the hills. From Portugal Cove a fine view may be obtained of Conception Bay, with its cluster of islands shadowing in the distance. Indeed, the whole vicinity of this Cove abounds in romantic beauty, and was much admired by the party. The buildings along the whole route were gayly decorated; every farm-yard had its flagstaff and ensign, and the Prince was enthusiastically cheered by the residents along the road and at Portugal Cove.

Upon their return to town the Prince and suite visited the Episcopal Cathedral, a fine stone building of the Gothic style of architecture, and, after a brief stay, proceeded to the Roman Catholic Cathedral, which occupies a most commanding position upon a hill at the rear of the town. The church is flanked by convents and by the residence of Bishop Mullock, and is built of light-colored stone, in the Roman Basillican style of architecture. It was crowded to its fullest capacity upon the occasion of the Prince's visit, and as he entered the building, the magnificent organ, the fourteenth in size in the world, pealed forth the anthem "God Save the Queen," and the rich strains blended in harmonious thunder with the cheers of the populace. Upon the Prince's return to Government House, the streets along the route were crowded with people, and he was followed by hearty acclamations, which he acknowledged as he rode on, attended by his brilliant suite.

In the afternoon a regatta was given at Lake Quidi Vidi, about half a mile from St. John's, and nine prizes were contended for by oared boats. The races were not particularly interesting or well contested, but the scene around the lake well repaid a visit. The lake is small, but deep, and is delightfully located. All around the lake were groups of spectators, and booths of gay-colored stuffs flaunting rich flags in the sunshine, which flashed upon the waters of the lake its sunniest smiles. When the Prince appeared the cheering was deafening, and as he drove around the lake his carriage was followed by enthusiastic thousands, shouting the most laudatory and loyal observations. The pressure was enormous, and it was almost impossible for the police to clear a way for the Prince, who stood up in his carriage, smiling and bowing in the most approved style. "We will see him," "He's only to be here one day," "Sure, he's as safe as if in his mother's parlor," the crowd called out, the ladies being especially noticeable with their shrill outcries. The Prince soon tired of this homage, however, and the party drove off; and, at His Highness' request, inspected a fishing-station, or "room," as it is technically called, where he observed the various operations of bringing in, decapitation, splitting, salting, washing out, drying, and packing, to which the codfish is subjected, seeming to be greatly interested, and glad to learn something of the means by which Newfoundland's wealth is acquired. The Prince was not subjected to the usual boot oiling which attends a visit to these "rooms," but some of his followers were not so fortunate, and were obliged to pay a douceur for the privilege of having a greasy hand smeared across their patent leathers. A ride to Signal Hill, celebrated for many desperate combats between the English and the French, from whence a fine view of the surrounding country may be obtained, concluded the afternoon's excursion, and the Prince returned to the Government House to dine.

In the evening the grand reception ball took place at the Colonial House or Capitol. A pavilion of wood was erected as a wing to the building, and was used as a ball-room. The room was hung with alternate red and white bunting, and was neatly and tastefully decorated with flags and pictures. The Prince's arrival having occurred two days before it was anticipated, the arrangements were necessarily hurried, and the decorations fell short of what was intended, but were sufficient to satisfy the most fastidious requirement. A dais, carpeted with crimson, and with the Prince's arms above it, occupied the further extremity of the room.

The ball was a public one, a limited number of tickets being sold at five dollars each, and the attendance consequently embraced representatives of all classes and conditions. As the Prince and his suite, at ten o'clock, entered the chamber used as a reception room, the bands of the Hero and the Newfoundland Corps struck up the national anthem, and amid the wildest cheers he reached the dais at the head of the chamber. After a brief conversation with his attendants, the Prince and the company entered the ball-room, where his reception was overwhelming, and the ball was formally opened.

The Prince danced quadrilles, the lancers, polkas, waltzes, and a gallop, being upon the floor twelve times. It is almost impossible to describe this ball, for from different points of observation it presented very different aspects. Regarded as the best that the New foundlanders could do, it was certainly deserving of every praise; but regarded comparatively and on its merits, it was equal to the most ridiculous scene that ever Rabelais, Cervantes, Smollett, or Dickens imagined in their merriest moods. The Prince, dressed in the uniform of a British colonel, occupied, when not dancing, the dais at the extremity of the room. The two bands were located in niches opposite each other, and alternated their music. At first the dancing was conducted with great ceremony, but with little grace, but as the evening wore on, and supper was over, the dancers warmed to their work, and the fun began. Not one person out of twenty in the room knew anything about dancing, and the confusion at the plebeian end of the hall became almost inextricable, but was prevented from spreading over the entire room by the exertions of the Prince's body-guard of volunteers. Every few minutes the Prince would be cheered, and at every dance he selected a new partner. The Prince danced very gracefully, conversed with his partners during the pauses of the figures, and escorted them to their guardians, but not to their seats, politely avoiding the attempts made by some of the ladies, in defiance of etiquette, to take his arm.

Towards the end of the ball the stewards became less careful of those who danced in the set with the Prince, and now began the laughable *faux pas*. A tall ensign, with a very red head, insisted on blundering himself against the Prince and his partner; a volunteer danced about with the delightful idea that he was doing his duty, and unconscious that he was out of time, out of place, and out of the figure; a very tall man succeeded in waltzing his partner until she became giddy enough to fall at the Prince's feet; and bobbing up and down, over the room, were flushed, anxious faces, regarding partners who would go wrong, or who were obstinately right. The Prince could not avoid laughing outright at these mishaps, but continued to dance, good-naturedly correcting mistakes, and calling out the figures to the awkward squad before him. In these efforts he was aided by a little mite of a midshipman, a boyish sprig of nobility, who persisted in dancing with the largest ladies he could find, and thus increased the general merriment. Altogether, if the Prince did not find at the ball the refinement and the beautiful dancing to which he had been accustomed at court, he found, probably, more genuine and hearty enjoyment, and he remained very late. The ball broke up almost immediately after the young Prince had departed, followed by repeated cheers.

The next morning dawned bright and clear, and the little town, in its holiday dress, was thronged with people striving to obtain positions from which they might take a last long look at the heir apparent, who, in the meantime, was taking his leave at the Government House.

At ten o'clock the chiming of the Cathedral bells announced that the Prince was about to start for the wharf, and the streets crossing the route were thronged with people, and the various societies and corps of soldiery were drawn up upon the government lawn. When the Prince, accompanied by the Earl St. Germains and Sir and Lady Bannerman, entered the carriage, the air was rent with shouts, and darkened with hats and handkerchiefs. Suddenly a body of men rushed forward, detached the horses from the carriage, and the Prince, having graciously acceded to the wish of the people, a stout rope was hooked on, and about two hundred men, after a smart scramble for the honor of places, formed into line, and drew the carriage, at the head of the procession, to the wharf gate. The procession was the same as at the landing, and the arrangements upon the wharf were precisely similar, except that the chief officers of the British ships took their stations also at the landing steps. The Prince entered the wharf, bowing to the tremendous shouts which greeted him, and amid the thunders of cannon, the ringing of bells, the music of the bands, the cheers from ship and shore, he took his leave of Lady Bannerman and the officers of the government, stepped into the Hero's barge, and flew across the water to the noble liner which was to convey him to Halifax. A moment after, the hundreds of naval Blondins and De Laves who had been manning the yards of the men-of-war, swarmed down the rigging, the salutes ceased, the royal ensign slowly rose to the Hero's mast, and one by one the royal steamers sailed through the Narrows, and disappeared from the sight of the Newfoundlanders. As they passed out of the harbor, the Prince was greeted with a unique salute, in the form of a submarine blast, by the workmen engaged in removing the Raby Rock.

The royal fleet called on Saturday at Sidney, in Nova Scotia, for coals for the Hero. At the landing place the Prince was received by three volunteers, hastily collected, and by an old woman, who overwhelmed the Prince with garrulous blessings. Away posted the volunteers to collect their forces, and finally succeeded in getting together about thirty, in some sort of uniform, but with no two hats alike. Sidney, be it known, is probably the only finished city in the world. A place more completely used up could scarcely be imagined, and cannot be described. Around it stretch wide barrens; and as the Prince rode across these to the town, which has but a few hundred inhabitants, he encountered a tribe of Micmac Indians, the first that he had ever seen. With every indication of curiosity, the Prince dismounted, entered and examined the tents of the Indians, conversed with them, and made several purchases of moccasins. The company, with the Prince, then entered the town, where the inhabitants gave a dozen faint cheers, and the volunteers made a few disconsolate attempts at a parade.

CHAPTER III.

Arrival at Halifax—Grand Military and Civic Display—The Prince Welcomed by the Indians.

If I were asked to name the finest bay in North America, I should say that of Halifax. If I were asked to name the most miserable city in that country, my reply would also be Halifax.

The former, which is 2466 miles from Liverpool, is situated 400 miles nearer to the British Islands than any other port on the continent, and while the Canadian harbors are blocked up with ice during nearly half the year, it is always accessible. From Halifax to Quebec, through British territory, the distance is about 600 miles, and from Halifax to Prince Edward's Island, only 150 miles.

The Duke of Kent, father of Queen Victoria, was commander of the British forces in North America, and stationed at Halifax in the year 1799, and there are several now living there who remember the old gentleman, and who manifested much venerable delight at the prospect of seeing his grandson among them after the lapse of sixty years.

If Albert Edward lives to be King of England, he will not be the first ruler of the British realm who once in his life visited North America, for William IV., in his early manhood—and while the third son of his father George III., and consequently with little expectation of ever succeeding to the throne—visited several of these provinces.

The present Sir Samuel Cunard formerly worked as a carpenter in the Ordnance Department at Halifax; and Haliburton, of "Sam Slick" celebrity, was born a few miles only out of the town, in which, I may remark, murders are of such rare occurrence that no execution has taken place for fifteen years.

I will now return to the bay, the noble proportions of which would render it magnificent if the scenery in which it lies enframed was of a more stupendous character, but it lacks those classic heights which overhang Rio, Palermo, and Naples, and the prospect afforded by its shores is one of extreme baldness and sterility.

On entering it, the shores on either side are long, low, and sandy, and continue so for several miles, after which Sambro, the first signal station, is passed, and the coast becomes a little more elevated, and appears to be made up of a mass of broken rocks, between which here and there may be seen patches of furze and other hardy plants and shrubs, while the wretched wooden shanty of a fisherman, and occasionally small villages of such, in the midst of which stands a church, which is to city churches what a mouse-trap is to a hotel, rise up from the naked rocks upon which they are irregularly perched. It would be difficult to imagine anything more bleak and forlorn, especially in winter —and I have seen it in winter—than this same barren Nova Scotian *terra firma*. But, for twenty miles round Halifax, the country is almost equally rocky and uncultivated, so that the colony is by no means rich in agricultural promise. After passing the York redoubt, which is the second signal station, white sandstone and clumps of dark, stunted pine-trees distinguish the western or left-hand shore, and red sandstone and pines the opposite, or eastern one. Advancing, we pass Tower Woods on the left, which is the nearest shore, for we are sailing up the western channel, the larger of the two that lead up to the harbor, where a tower, pierced for cannon, but not in use, stands embowered in the sombre foliage of the pines.

We next come to Point Pleasant, two miles from Halifax, where a couple of batteries point their black guns as if they really meant to do us mischief. But we pass them unmolested, and are soon abreast of the Eastern Battery, so called because it commands the eastern channel, facing George's Island, which lies almost parallel with McNab's Island, the latter crowned with a formidable round tower of gray stone.

McNab's Island acts as a breakwater, and divides the harbor within immediate view of the town, which, from the water, has a very dingy, quaint, and antiquated appearance. It is backed by the Citadel, which is the third signal station, and has an aspect of the most commanding and impregnable order.

There are a few small vessels and sometimes a large one, sailing up and down the bay, and a ferry steamer plies frequently from Halifax to Dartmouth, on the opposite side of the harbor, which is to the city what Cheshire is to Liverpool. Here stands a conspicuous red brick building, which tempts the stranger to inquire about it, and his curiosity is rewarded by discovering it to be a lunatic asylum.

On landing at Cunard's wharf, a gloomy archway leads into a narrow and dusty street, which is a fair specimen of all the other streets in the town.

Those who have visited Kingston, in Jamaica, could hardly fail to recognize a resemblance between the streets of it and Halifax during the summer.

The view from the Citadel is the finest in Nova Scotia, and embraces a wide sweep of country on all sides. The wagons or caleches of the place drive up to the top of the hill, but visitors are only allowed to enter the Citadel on foot. Within, however, there is less of general interest to be seen than at the Citadel of Quebec. It is used as an infantry barrack and storehouse.

The public buildings of Halifax are neither numerous nor imposing. The Province House, where the Governor, Lord Mulgrave, resides, is a neat, but low building, inclosed within a small garden, and here an artillery soldier is always on duty, to receive passengers and cards.

The Providence Building, or House of Assembly, at the corner of Holles and Granville Streets, is the largest and best-conditioned one in the town, and is of gray stone. The Wellington Barracks, recently contructed, are handsome and durable, but the old South Barracks are wretched.

There are five tri-weekly newspapers in Halifax, but not one daily.

The colony was first settled in 1749, and its present population is nearly 300,000 a number that, considering the sterility of a large portion of the country, is surprisingly large. Halifax itself has a population of 32,000.

The reception of the Prince of Wales at Halifax was a picturesque and exciting scene, which is still in memory before me. In my mind's eye I can see the broad, heavy Hero, of 2800 tons measurement, steaming slowly past the booming guns of the York redoubt, and the smoke ascending lazily from her one huge black funnel, while Albert Edward, the hero of all heroes of the day, stands on her quarter-deck in his plain dark dress, and acknowledges the cheers of our passengers by raising his cap and bowing with a graceful inclination. The crew are gathered on the main-deck, looking on with their ordinary composure, and naval grandees in black cocked hats, red coats, and white trowsers, are, spy-glasses in hand, standing and moving about the quarter-deck. The noble form of that best of war steamers—the two funneled Ariadne—follows at a short but respectful distance in her wake. The yacht-like Flying Fish, with her two leaning, cream-colored funnels smoking like well-drawn pipes, is coming up in the rear, and more good looking gentlemen in cocked hats and white trowsers are to be seen on her quarter-deck.

The wide-mouthed guns of the batteries bid them

welcome, and the anxious multitude that stand on yonder crosstrees and on the deck of the two steamers which have come out to meet the royal squadron, and on the wharves and vessels in port, and the top of Citadel Hill, and wherever the human form is seen. Thrice welcome, say I, and the band of the steamer strikes up the national anthem, which is listened to by both men and officers of the Ariadne, alongside of which we are steaming.

It caused a pleasant thrill to hear the shouts of cheering, as the Hero passed the crowded wharves, and the rapid firing of royal salutes from the Citadel and the round tower on George's Island ; and that of Tower Woods, was an exciting demonstration, which warmed the people into exultation, notwithstanding the coldness of the weather and the depressing effects of a showery sky.

It was pretty, too, as the Hero wheeled to her moorings, rounding, as she did so, the Nile, the Valorous, and the Cossack, to see their yards manned by their brave crews, clothed in white duck and cheering and waving their hats in honor of their future king, as he stood on the broad quarter-deck beneath them ; and then looking up the bay a little further to see a fleet of twelve canoes, paddled by Indians, in their subscription clothes of blue and red, come hurrying towards us.

The squadron anchors, the drizzling rain again sets in, and again subsides, and it is now ten o'clock. The Neptune lands her passengers, and I find myself in the streets again. They are garlanded with evergreens, and thickly intersected with arches, and every house displays either illumination frames in its windows, or flowers and verdure in its front, or both. The street arches, which are all of very substantial and tasteful build, number twenty-seven. All these are constructed of timber and decorated with a heavy covering of spruce. This gives them a general resemblance ; but the devices, and in some cases the architecture, varies. It is evident that the hand of preparation has been busy, and nothing has been left undone that either the taste or opportunities of the inmates could devise for giving Albert Edward a right hearty, right royal reception.

I traversed the streets, not in the line of route, from the landing place at the dock-yard, to Government House, and I found them nearly deserted, and I knew that the shops would be closed, and they were closed. The holiday was general, and all courted it but the cabmen, and here and there a liquor dealer.

I bent my steps up to Barrington Street, through which the procession was to pass. There I found infantry in British red, and volunteers in sombre gray, lining the way on either side in long, single file, and I saw a congregation of men, women, and children outside of the barriers imposed by these, while the middle of the road was empty and in waiting for the royal equestrian and the ranks which were to follow, no vehicles being, meanwhile, permitted on its cleared precincts.

After this I retired to the quiet streets, which looked like so many avenues of green trees, and, hiring a cab, drove to the dock-yard, where I found the Mayor of Montreal, with his conspicuous chain of office round his neck, and hanging down as far as his waist. And I saw, also, clergymen in their Episcopal robes, and the Speaker of the House of Commons in his black gown, and I saw priests with white bands round their necks, and officers of the army and navy in their bright uniform moving to and fro, while the Chief Justice and Judges, the President and members of the Legislative Council, the Speaker and members of the House of Assembly, the Mayor and Corporation, the Custos and High Sheriff, the heads of Departments and the members of the Executive Municipality Committee were grouped together in the centre of the yard, near the landing steps, and in full view of the occupants of the temporary platforms which had been erected on each side.

Then, as the clock in the yard pointed to within eight minutes of the hour of twelve, I saw a slim form in military uniform step into a white-painted boat at the foot of the gangway steps of H. M. steamer Hero, and quickly following it I saw that boat rowed by brawny arms towards the dock-yard, at the foot of which the twelve Indian canoes and their Indian paddlers lay idly in waiting, while their squaws and children were grouped in a prominent position of the yard assigned to them. And now listen to that glorious chorus of the iron-mouthed guns of all the batteries and the six British men-of-war in harbor, whose yards are manned by their cheering crews, and whose rigging displays the flying flags of nations. What a glorious sight is that when combined with the scene around, and what music makes the nerves vibrate like the ringing boom of cannon. Welcome to their roar, and while I speak, glance at the multitude of anxious, eager eyes that rest upon the coming boat, whose oars now cease their play. The hero steps ashore, and there is a loud, long cheer of unfeigned rejoicing. The Admiral of the fleet and Lord Mulgrave receive him, and he is led to the central group of the local dignitaries alluded to.

The Mayor read an address. The Prince replied. Following this, he mounted a charger and rode with his suite, and a long procession of societies on foot, towards Government House.

On arriving opposite the stand occupied by the school children His Royal Highness halted, and the three thousand five hundred struck up the music of their anthem:

God save our gracious Queen!
Long live our noble Queen!
God save the Queen!

Send her victorious, happy and glorious,
Long to reign over us—
God save the Queen!

Welcome, our royal guest;
Welcome, from every breast—
From every tongue;
From hearts both warm and true—
Hearts that beat high for you,
Loudly our welcome due
To thee be sung.

Prince of a lofty line,
The virtues all be thine
Which grace the Queen.
To her we pay, through thee,
Love, faith, and loyalty—
Homage which fits the free.
God save the Queen!

The three cheers of their tiny voices given at its close, and the butterfly fluttering of their little handkerchiefs, must have sent a thrill of something akin to rapture through the heart of many a mother among the masses collected below.

On arriving at Government House the Premier of the House of Representatives read an address in the presence of all the members, which was responded to by the Prince reading another.

After this interview His Royal Highness retired to his private apartment, and at four o'clock rode in plain clothes, accompanied by several of his suite. It was fair when he started, but he was drenched with rain before returning. At half-past seven he sat down to dinner with forty-six others, the guests of Government House.

On the following morning preparations were made for a grand review of the regular and volunteer troops.

At an early hour the volunteer companies assembled at their respective barrack rooms, and at ten o'clock they were in attendance at the Pavilion Barrack Square, under their several commanders, where they were put through a variety of evolutions. Meanwhile, the "regulars" were marching from the Citadel and other military quarters towards the Common, the scene of the review. Soon after ten the commandant of the volunteers took command of the battalion, and after going through the customary duty of equalizing companies and numbering off divisions, the entire battalion directed their course to the Common, a few minutes before eleven o'clock. On arriving there they were formed into line on the left of the regular troops, and combined, they extended the whole length of the ground, and presented a most imposing appearance.

About this time—at a quarter to eleven—His Royal Highness left Government House, in his colonel's uniform, accompanied by Lord Mulgrave, in the blue and gold of his official dress, and his suite. Along the line of route of the Common he was greeted almost rapturously by the thousands who had assembled to catch a glimpse of his person. The firemen and axemen formed in open order along Spring Garden Road, and as His Royal Highness passed, they followed behind his staff.

On arriving at the Common at a few minutes past eleven, where about fifteen thousand people had assembled, he was received with a burst of enthusiasm such as never before awoke the echoes in Nova Scotia. The royal standard was then hoisted at the eastern side of the review-ground, and here the Prince and his party took up their position.

After the combined troops were formed into review order, His Royal Highness, accompanied by the Duke of Newcastle, the Earl of Mulgrave, Commander-in-chief of the Volunteers, the Earl of St. Germains, General Trollope, and the remainder of the staff, numbering in all more than twenty, rode slowly past the ranks, and was received with the usual general salute, the whole presenting arms together. This being over, the regulars and volunteers formed into open column, right in front—the regulars leading off—and marched past the royal standard, on the right of which the Prince was stationed, in slow and quick time. After this the whole formed into line and quarter distance column, and marched to the front. The regulars were then moved off the ground, and the volunteers, which included a company of negroes, facetiously called the Greeley Guard, were, in presence of His Royal Highness and staff, put through numerous evolutions by their captain. On the conclusion of the review the battalion formed into three-quarter distance column, and three cheers were given for His Royal Highness with great unction.

At this moment I saw a long line of uplifted bayonets glittering in the sun, and on the points of these the uniform caps of every man of the battalion, the variegated plumes of which enhanced the picturesque effect.

His Royal Highness then rode off the review ground in the midst of the most enthusiastic cheering from the multitude surrounding the reserved space, and under a salute from the Volunteer Artillery.

After leaving the review-ground the Prince visited the Citadel, and then returned to Government House to lunch.

In the course of the afternoon he rode out to the Common again, in plain dress, and witnessed the rural sports there going forward ; the racing and the Indian war-dance, performed by the remnant of the Mic Mac tribe, in particular attracted his attention.

The Prince dined with a large party at Government House at half-past seven, and at half-past nine in the evening he led Lady Mulgrave into the ball-room at the Province Building, which had been showily and tastefully fitted up for the occasion.

The ball-room, lined with red and white cloth, and suitable hangings over appropriate devices, inclosing Latin mottoes, and filled with the bright uniforms of military and naval officers, and ladies whose exquisite toilets were worthy of the saloons of London and Paris, presented a very gay and elegant appearance. So also did the main corridor leading from the ball-room to the supper-room, where the flags of all nations, hanging at the sides and overhead, and well lighted up, had a very pretty appearance.

The Prince, after the members of the Legislature and public service present had filed past him in the ball-room, led off the ball in a quadrille, his partner being the niece of the Premier or President of the Council.

At eleven o'clock he led Lady Mulgrave to the refreshment room, and at one to supper, when the toasts of the Queen, Prince Consort, and Prince of Wales were respectively proposed and responded to with immense cheering from the thousand guests present, who, I may remark, were without exception in strict evening dress, including a white necktie. There were twenty dances included in the programme, and of these the Prince danced eighteen, with as many different ladies, being all there were danced up to the time of his leading Lady Mulgrave to her carriage at a quarter to four.

On the following morning the Prince was up early, and after breakfast walked out in plain dress with Lord Mulgrave and his suite. He returned soon after ten and dressed in his staff uniform, that of a lieutenant colonel, and at eleven took his place in the inner reception-room and held a levee, which was attended by about three hundred of the leading men of Nova Scotia and most of the visitors at Halifax, including Mr. Lincoln, the Mayor of Boston, and the Mayor of Montreal. Of course, I was not absent on the occasion. The Prince was attended by all the members of his suite, Lord Mulgrave and the senior officers of the garrison. He looked as fresh as if he had enjoyed his usual rest on the previous night, and bowed with unaffected grace as one by one the gentlemen attending the levee were presented.

At half-past twelve he stepped out into the grounds at the back of the Government House, and with the Duke of Newcastle and the Earl of St. Germains on his left, and Lord Mulgrave and the remainder of his suite on his right, was photographed by a professional artist of the town. He stood in his uniform, and holding his hat in his right hand, under his arm, and the sun shone full on his face.

After this he partook of luncheon, and at a quarter-past two he arrived at the dock-yard in an open carriage, with Lord and Lady Mulgrave, the Duke of Newcastle, and Earl St. Germains. He there embarked on one of the boats of the Nile, in order to lunch with the Admiral on board, and witness the regatta, which had been going forward since the hour of ten. The yards of the three vessels of the Admiral's fleet were manned, and these, as also the royal squadron, fired royal salutes as the royal standard moved away from the shore. He went on board the Hero in three quarters of an hour afterwards and changed his uniform for a plain walking suit, after which he was rowed to the paddle steamer Valorous, in which he sailed up to the basin at the head of the bay, where his grandfather, the Duke of Kent, once owned a farm. At a few minutes past six the Valorous, with the royal standard fluttering at her mast-head, returned, and upon anchoring the boat was at once lowered, and Albert Edward stepped into it, when the royal standard was erected at the bow. As the boat was rowed towards the crowded wharves and landing steps the royal salutes were again fired, and the yards were manned as before.

In the meantime I had been visiting the vessels of the fleet, including the Hero, and glancing at the yachts and punts and pinnaces as they shot to and fro over the bay at the highest speed either wind or labor would carry them. To those having a taste for aquatics the scene on the bay at this time was one of the finest sights of the Halifax carnival. There was genuine good-humor among the masses that covered the wharves, and real spirit shown by the rowers.

On Thursday morning, at seven o'clock, the Prince and suite, the members of the Legislature, and a few others, left Halifax by a special train for Windsor. As the train moved away from the station a rural-looking couple jumped on to the foot-board of one of the cars, and could not be persuaded to jump back again, notwithstanding the energetic expostulations of those in charge; so they were carried to Windsor in the position of stow-aways. The Prince and suite, with Lord and Lady Mulgrave, had a car to themselves. The train arrived at Windsor at half-past eight, and the Prince passed between the ranks of a volunteer guard of honor, which had arrived from Halifax two hours previously, into the Clifton House, on the balcony of which he was soon afterwards presented with an address by the inhabitants, to whose spokesman he read a brief reply, the sun all the time shining upon his head and face. He next partook of an elegant breakfast at a large table, at which all of the special train were permitted to seat themselves. The Queen, Prince Consort, and the Prince of Wales were toasted, soon after which the royal guest left the table and took his seat in one of the carriages in waiting to convey the party to Hansport, where he embarked on board the Styx for St. John's, New Brunswick, which vessel anchored there at ten P.M., after a smooth and delightful passage down the picturesque Bay of Fundy.

CHAPTER IV.

The Feeling of the People in Regard to the Visit of the Prince—His Social Powers and Love of the Humorous—The Royal Quarters on Board the Hero—His Acquaintance with Foreign Languages—Personnel of his Suite—His Arrival and Enthusiastic Reception by the People—A Visit to the Indians.

WHEREVER I went there was but one sentiment distinguishing the people with respect to their royal visitor, and that was of admiration for the man, and loyalty to the throne, which they all hope he may at some distant day ascend.

I may say of the Prince that he is handsome, and not only that, but very pleasing in other respects. His proportions, although small and delicate, are symmetrical, while the play and expression of his features are of an order at once intellectual, refined, and prepossessing.

During the voyage from England, he was the most lively and social of all on board. He used to sit cross-legged, with telescope in hand, signaling the other ships of the squadron, alternately asking humorous questions, and returning all sorts of jocular replies.

He was slightly sea-sick during the first two or three days when the weather was rough, but afterwards he was hardly ever in his own cabin ten minutes at a time, save at meals, during the whole day. Yet he frequently passed in and out.

He had the entire use of the upper quarter-deck cabin, usually occupied by the captain, and into this none of the members of his suite ever entered, unless to dine, or by special invitation.

On walking from the main-deck, where a sentinel of marines is at all times pacing to and fro, you enter the dining cabin, which is as broad as the quarter-deck, but considerably less extensive. Right and left, on each side, you see two of the huge ninety-one guns, which the ship carries, painted white, and lashed to the deck and port-hole loops with thick, heavy ropes or hawsers, which are twisted about each of the four cannon referred to like so many coils of snakes. A mahogany dining-table stands in the centre, together with two small card-tables, and twenty two leather bottomed chairs of the same wood. The walls and ceiling are painted plain drab, and the only approaches to ornament about either, or the cabin, are a few gilt lines between the paneling. The floor is covered with a thin mottled-red carpet, which, in sobriety of look, is in keeping with everything else in the apartment. A mahogany sideboard occupies a middle position on the forward side, and over this are suspended from the roof four long silver lantern-like candle holders, which were once the property of Lord Nelson, and used by him on board the Victory, from which they were taken after the battle of Trafalgar. These had candles burning in them only once during the voyage, when the Prince gave a dinner party.

On the opposite wall hangs, in a plain narrow frame, an engraved portrait of Nelson, in his uniform, and surrounded by charts, and with one arm leaning on a table, and immediately underneath is a cabinet, which was made out of the timbers of the old Victory herself.

A doorway, facing the outer one, leads into his sitting cabin, which is a well-window lighted, and a very comfortable room, furnished with a table in the centre, and two small leather-covered sofas and chairs to match. The walls are painted similarly to those of the other apartment, and are equally devoid of ornament. Turning to the right after entering, you step into his sleeping cabin, on the right hand side of which his cot, lined with a hair mattress, was swung for him every night. On the left is a speaking-tube, which he used for summoning his servant, who entered by a doorway leading direct into the sleeping chamber, and facing the other one. Underneath a plain deal board, on which his cot rested by day, were three new-looking solid leather portmanteaus, or, as we call them, trunks, of which he carried ten in all. He arose about eight or nine o'clock in the morning, breakfasted soon after, lunched at one, and dined at five, with whoever he chose to invite, and he always invited one or more of the officers, including midshipmen, with whom, to use a familiar expression, he was "fond of skylarking." He appears to be very fond of the society of his brethren of the rising generation, for at the Halifax ball a youthful middy of, I believe, the Hero, engaged his conversation at one point of the evening more than the partner leaning on his arm.

And, while speaking of that evening, I must not omit to mention that, at dinner, being seated near the Portuguese Consul to whom he had been previously presented, he began talking Portuguese to him, a language which the consul, being an Englishman, was by no means proficient in, and was, therefore, compelled to tell the Prince, that, although the Portuguese Consul, he was anything but a Portuguese himself. "Did he speak it well?" I asked the consul. "Oh yes, so far as I could judge; better a good deal, at any rate, than I could speak it."

To return to the Hero. A plain, portable mahogany washstand, with a lid that closes over the top, stands under the speaking tube, and a small brass wire rack is fixed in the wall within reach of his cot when swung, so that he can place or take away a book or such like there while in bed.

On the deck next below, and directly under the Prince's cabins, are those of the Duke of Newcastle, and Earl St. Germains, who have separate sleeping cabins, but one sitting-room in common.

In the latter, alike with that of the Prince, there is a bookcase filled with volumes relating almost entirely to the United States and British North America, selected especially for this occasion. All the works on this country that could be gathered are on board, and have been read with avidity. Hence, to some extent, the ready information expressed with regard to places visited, historical and otherwise, in the royal replies.

The Duke is about five feet eleven inches in height, and well made. He is easily recognizable by his short-cut beard, whiskers, and mustache, which in color are sandy, with an inclination to red. His age is a little beyond forty. He stands and walks very erect, and has a fine gentlemanly bearing. He was always, when in company with the Prince, to be seen on his left; and, whenever the latter was in uniform, the Duke appeared in that of a Lord Lieutenant—scarlet, with silver facings.

The Earl of St. Germains looks more than ten years older, and his hair is gray; but he has a firm step, a quick eye, and great nobility of countenance. He is nearly as tall as the Duke, and his uniform is that of the Lord Chamberlain, which has gold work on a scarlet ground. General Bruce, His Royal Highness' Governor, is a Major General in the army, and of extremely affable and refined manners. He is nearly as tall, and a little younger than the Earl, but his hair is gray also. He wears the uniform of a General, scarlet, with gold lace. The remainder of the Prince's suite are Major Teesdale and Captain Gray, the equerries, who are both young men; Dr. Acland, physician, and Mr. Englehart, secretary, both of whom dressed in civil blue uniform, with silver facings and cocked hats, whenever the Prince assumed his, and exchanged it for plain dress as often. Besides these there were several servants of various degrees, including a steward, who, whenever on duty, was in plain evening dress, after the style of gentlemen and butlers in England, and one or more footmen, who always rode on the box of whatever carriage His Royal Highness might be riding in, and wore the royal livery.

When it was first understood that the Prince was to sail in the Hero the Admiralty prepared to take the guns out of the cabin to be used by him, and decorated the apartments in regal splendor. But an order came from Her Majesty, his mother, to the effect that everything was to remain in the same order on board, and that whatever little addition required to be made for his personal accommodation should be of the plainest kind. These instructions had, of course, to be obeyed.

In my observation of the character of the Prince I have found that he is full of genuine good-humor, which often rises into a bubbling gayety and strong relish for fun. He has a quick eye for the ludicrous wherever seen, and evidently delights in throwing off all state and acting like any common mortal.

It may be interesting either to learn or be reminded that New Brunswick extends nearly north and south, and forms an irregular square between Nova Scotia and Canada. It is bounded on the north by the Bay of Chaleurs and the Gulf of St. Lawrence, which separate it from Gaspe, or boundary of Canada. On the east it also extends to the Gulf or Northumberland Straits. A narrow peninsula joins it to Nova Scotia on the southeast, and it is separated from that province on the south by the Bay of Fundy. On the west it meets the State of Maine. It contains about 26,000 square miles of territory, which is mostly of a cultivatable character. The county of St. John's, situated at the mouth of the river of that name, occupies a long and narrow belt of land, forming the north coast of the Bay of Fundy, between Cape Eurage and Mace's Bay, being more than eighty miles in length, and on an average not more than ten miles in breadth. The whole shore is rocky, and here and there bounded by precipitous cliffs. The harbor of St. John's is safe, but not very commodious, especially at low water. The tides rise twenty-six feet, so leaving long shores at low tide. Partridge Island is situated at the mouth of the harbor, and on it there are a battery, lighthouse, signal station, and hospital. Between the island and mainland there is a long narrow bar, to be seen at low water. Eastward of the harbor there is a broad shallow estuary, terminating in a marsh, and a deep ravine that runs westward and separates the town of Portland from St. John's. The harbor of St. John's has the important advantage of being accessible at all seasons of the year. The town is built on a rocky peninsula of very uneven ground, sloping in opposite directions from a central ridge. The whole shore is lined with timber ponds, booms, and ship-yards, which receive the numerous rafts floated down the river. A little more than sixty years ago the site of the city was a rocky headland, covered with cedar thickets. It was then the refuge of American loyalists, by whose industry it was founded. Up to the year 1784 it was a part of the colony of Nova Scotia, but in that year a rupture occurred, which led to its becoming a separate province.

On the morning following my arrival at St. John's the streets were busy with the stir of human life, and the hum of voices filled the air. Most of the shop doors were open, but their shutters were closed, and a general holiday appeared to be the order of the day.

At ten o'clock I followed the crowd on foot to Reed's Point Wharf, where the landing was to take place. The Styx, gayly dressed with flags, lay midstream, opposite, at anchor, and workmen were busy erecting the stage on which His Royal Highness was to step from the boat. The guard of honor of the Sixty-third Regiment, from Halifax, lined the way nearest the water, and after them came the volunteers and the trade and other societies. The Lieutenant Governor of New Brunswick was in waiting between the ranks, as also several of the municipality of the town. On either side, amphitheatric seats of temporary construction, were crowded with thousands of the loyal and curious, who cast eager glances towards the man-of-war, whose yards were already being manned. Suddenly, and while the carpenters were still at work on the stage, there arose a general shout of "Here he comes," and true to the words, a boat with the royal standard fluttering at its peak, came bounding towards the shore. Then boomed out the glorious music of the loud-tongued cannon in a royal salute, with which the voices of the masses blended in a grand chorus of welcome. Hurrah! Hurrah! Hurrah! shouted the excited multitude in their patriotic ardor, and cheers rang again and again till the Prince had entered his carriage at the end of the wharf and disappeared from their sight, when the cry of welcome was taken up and echoed along the ranks by fresh multitudes assembled to swell the concourse in honor of their future king.

I passed from the wharf in the midst of a crowd, to which that of the Japanese ball at New York was only second, and had the felicity of joining in a foot procession as far as the house in which the Prince was to take up his abode. The long street we had to tread was very dusty, and the sun was shedding his brilliant lustre with oppressive warmth over our heads, and the carriages containing the Prince and suite stopped suddenly at irregular intervals, which had the effect of damaging the shins of those nearest, and throwing all followers back in disorder, to the entire glee of the small boys who looked on from the windows and sidewalks.

The boys and girls of the united schools threw

bunches of flowers at the carriage as it passed through the grounds of the house he was to occupy, beyond the entrance to which, none but the Prince, his suite, and the Governor were allowed to pass.

Then the procession, which included the Mayor of Montreal, who wore the same great big conspicuous chain of office around his neck that had attracted so much attention on the part of the natives of Halifax, retraced their steps over the hot, dusty street, in the direction of the Court House, where the Prince met them at half-past twelve. There he took his stand on the small platform erected for him in front of an open space of ground, where about five thousand people, with upturned faces, were assembled to look at and cheer him while the procession of trades and firemen filed past, every now and then halting to give him a hearty three times three.

"Is that all?" said the Prince, inquiringly, towards the end of the long procession, addressing the Duke of Newcastle, but the cry was "still they come."

After this he held the levee, which was attended by gentlemen in white neckties and clothes to match. It was then that the usual addresses were presented.

The Prince, having passed through this ordeal, drove home and changed his uniform for a plain suit, in which he drove to Carleton—a suburb of the town—and returned to dinner at eight. His own suite, and the Governor, and the Attorney General of New Brunswick, alone dined with him on this occasion.

At nine the next morning he was off for Fredericton. The reception there was enthusiastic enough for the place, but a mere lukewarm demonstration compared with the ovations he was destined to receive elsewhere.

He arrived at half-past six on Saturday afternoon, and landed from the steamer Forest Queen at the wharf facing the Province Building, where a crowd of about four thousand people had assembled to greet him. The Governor accompanied the royal guest to Government House, where he was domiciled while in Fredericton.

CHAPTER V.

The River St. John—Variety and Beauty of its Scenery—The Reception at Fredericton—Enthusiasm and Loyal Demonstrations of the People there—Visit to the Cathedral—Sermon by the Bishop—Visit to the Indian Encampment—Opening of a New Park under the Auspices of the Prince—Excessive Heat of the Day—Ball in the Evening—A young Lady throws the Prince a Bouquet, which he stoops to pick up—Race on the River between Indian Canoes—How the Prince received the Intelligence of his Sister's Accouchement, etc.

THE river St. John, in New Brunswick, by which the Prince traveled to Fredericton, is worthy of a fame far more extended than it now possesses. Near its mouth, at the harbor of St. John, the scenery is of a character as bold and varied as any to be found on the Hudson, and far away in the interior, over the entire length of its main stream—a distance of three hundred and sixty miles—scenes of rare picturesque beauty frequently present themselves, while in no part is there monotony or utter tameness. About sixty miles above Fredericton the river presents a series of falls, which descend perpendicularly over a depth of seventy feet.

New Brunswick gave the Prince a loyal reception, but it was second in magnificence to that of Halifax. This was as I anticipated. At Halifax there were six British ships of war, half a dozen batteries and two regiments of the line, besides artillery to thunder out royal salutes in his honor, and it being the capital, and his stay there more prolonged than at either St. John's or Fredericton, more opportunities were afforded for display than at either of the two places named. The cheering at the landing stage at St. John's was not as enthusiastic as it might have been, but I rightly attributed it to a lack of manner rather than of feeling, for I observed an awe, amounting to reverence, pictured in the faces of all I saw.

In New Brunswick every demonstration that was made was the popular outburst of patriotism and loyalty on the part of the real sinew and muscle of the country, the hard-working people, almost entirely unaided by military forces other than those of their own local organization, and these did credit to the colony. On the banks of the St. John they made their appear ance in village groups at several points, and fired a salute as the steamer, with the royal standard floating from her foremast, passed by, while the inhabitants testified their loyalty by collecting at every available spot and cheering vociferously.

Shortly before eleven o'clock on Sunday morning he drove from Government House to the Cathedral, in an open carriage. Beside him sat Mrs. Manners Sutton, the wife of the Governor, and on the opposite seat the Governor himself and the Duke of Newcastle, in plain dress, an official cap on the part of the former excepted.

On the way there was no demonstration whatever on the part of the people collectively, nor was any crowd assembled, save near the church door ; but individuals, from time to time, raised their hats to him, to which he responded by raising his own. None but regular attendants at the church were admitted till after the Prince had entered, and after that the pews were quickly filled, and many had only standing room.

His Royal Highness sat in the Governor's pew, and listened to an eloquent sermon by the bishop, with much attention. The latter made beautiful allusion to the virtues of his mother, and also his own probable career.

As he drove home again the same quiet prevailed in the streets as at his coming, and in his reply to the address of the municipality on the following morning, he made very tasteful allusion to this observance of the Sabbath. At night he strolled to the Indian encampment at the river-side.

The event of the next day following the levee and presentation of addresses was the opening of the park —a narrow walk, with a total area of only sixteen acres—and drawing the plug of a new fountain therein erected.

After lunching with Mr. Fisher, the Attorney General, I drove there, and found a large assemblage of four thousand people waiting his arrival from Government House, which stands directly opposite at a few hundred yards distance. The day was very hot, and there was little shelter from the vivid rays of the sun. Several hundred school-children were anxiously undergoing the baking process on a large stand erected for their accommodation. Everybody was complaining of the heat and wishing for the royal presence, when, at a few minutes after three there arose a cry of "Here he is," and all eyes were directed towards a small, neat figure stepping into an open carriage at the door of the Government House, in front of which waved from a flagstaff the royal standard of England.

The interest quickened, and a few minutes later a succession of cheers announced his entry into the so-called park. He was in plain costume, and on alighting was conducted under a wooden awning fronting the fountain. Here he drew the plug and a thin column of water ascended. The insignificance of the jet aroused inquiry as to the cause, when, lo and behold, it was discovered that the thirsty multitude of spectators had drank nearly all the water out of the tank which supplied the said fountain. Such a step from a sublime inauguration to a ridiculous sequel was never perhaps before witnessed, and the Prince could not suppress smiling at the *contre temps.* While this sickly jet was disporting itself in feeble play, the baking children sang the national anthem, with a puerile variation, after which they gave three cheers for the Queen, and then three for the Prince of Wales, which were echoed by the crowd.

He drove home after this, and remained there till he left in his uniform for the ball, at ten o'clock. On his arrival there he passed to a private supper-room provided for him at the extreme end of the main ball-room, between a double line of ladies, with ten of whom he afterwards danced as many dances, the first being with the wife of the Governor. There was no supper to which the company sat down, but a refreshment table was kept open all the evening. The tickets, admitting a gentleman and two ladies, were only five dollars each, so that nothing better could be afforded. The rooms, too, were consequently overcrowded, and those present were of an order less select than at Halifax, where the price was ten dollars for gentlemen and five for ladies.

The band of the Sixty-third played excellently, and to its inspiriting strains the gay throng glided through the terpsichorean mazes to their own evident delight, notwithstanding the limited space they had to tread.

When the Prince was about to step on board the Forest Queen, at half-past six on the following morning, dressed in a white hat and an Inverness cape over a black coat and drab trowsers, a young lady threw a bouquet at his feet, upon which he stooped and picked it up with alacrity, and returned her a very polite bow.

Several hundreds were collected to see him off, and they remained till eight, when, the fog having lifted, the steamer started. Meanwhile, the racing on the part of fifteen canoes, manned by Indians of the Milicelt tribe, was amusing.

The Prince had breakfasted at Government House, but he dined at one o'clock in the saloon with the rest of the passengers on board, including members of the New Brunswick Legislature, at the cost of which the steamer was provided.

The same demonstrations on the part of the people and volunteers were made along the banks of the river as during his coming.

On arriving at Indiantown, he received a telegraphic dispatch announcing the *accouchement* of his sister, the Princess of Prussia, which he read with evident pleasure. On stepping ashore, where the Mayor, Corporation, and others, were assembled to receive him, as also the volunteer companies, he was greeted with loud and prolonged cheering. He had to walk as far as a triumphal arch before reaching his carriage. When he was driven off a procession of the officials formed, and a succession of flags and evergreen decorations were passed. On arriving at the Suspension Bridge, the troops were drawn up while he passed, and a royal salute was fired from Carleton Heights. On his reaching Princess Street, where the Carleton fire companies were in waiting, the horses were taken from his carriage to which the drag-ropes of an engine were attached, and the carriage so drawn by the men, preceded by the city band.

Further on he was greeted with a shower of bouquets, some of which fell into the carriage. One of these he picked up, and bowed to the crowd as he held it.

It being a general holiday, all the societies that lined the way and joined in the procession on the occasion of his first landing were in attendance now, and the cheering was far warmer than on the previous Friday.

A stand full of school-children sang the anthem to him at a more advanced point, and during its delivery the carriage was stopped and he sat uncovered. He embarked from Rodney's Wharf for the Styx in the presence of thousands collected on the water-side, and on reaching her took his stand near one of the paddle-boxes; and answered the cheers of the crowd by raising his hat, till, at a few minutes before five, the Styx weighed anchor and receded from their gaze, with royalty on her deck and its standard at her main.

CHAPTER VI.

General Holiday and Rejoicing of the People—Appearance of the City of St. John's after the Prince's Departure—Dinner to the Representatives of the Press—From St. John's to Shediac—View of Prince Edward's Island—Facts Concerning the Island—The Way in which it was Discovered—Scenes on a crowded Steamboat—Scarcity of Hotel Accommodation—Grand Illuminations, etc.

I WILL now resume the thread of my personal narrative since arriving at St. John's. When the last echoes of the cheers that rose from the thousands of loyal New Brunswickers collected on the wharves, and casting one last, long, lingering look at the young man waving his hat from the paddle-box gangway of the receding steamer Styx, had died away, I bent my steps from the water-side into the shop-closed streets, where all of the few people I saw were idling through a general holiday, and where the triumphal arches were still spanning the streets in all the ghastliness of their decayed finery. The towns reminded me of a dining hall after the feast, a ball-room after the guests had departed. The spirit that had inspired the masses of the population with new life had gone, and here alone remained the wreck of the past. But, after all, it was not magnificent—not splendid—ruin; for there is but little magnificence or splendor of either thought or action about the slow-going inhabitants of this long-wintered colony; and it required an effort, the most extreme of which their unemotional nature was capable, to arouse them even to the tame demonstration which they made. This says nothing against their loyalty—nothing against their love of country—but it shows that their susceptibility to external influences is slight, and that what would fill a Frenchman with the bubbling gayety of extreme ardor, and make a New Yorker boil over with the excitement of enthusiasm, would upon a native of New Brunswick produce hardly any impression deeper than would be caused by the common every-day events of life.

At eight o'clock on the evening alluded to I sat down at Stubb's Hotel in company with a hundred or more to a public dinner given to the representatives of the foreign press accompanying the Prince of Wales. I can only speak of this with that sense of appreciation which such kindness and hospitality deserves. Both the viands and the wine were of the first order, and the chief men of the town were present. A torch-light procession of the firemen in honor of the guests halted in front of the hotel at about ten o'clock, upon which the dinner party adjourned to the street door, where a few speeches were made to the torch-bearers. The guests afterwards returned to the table, where toast-making was commenced and continued up to a late hour.

At eight o'clock on the next morning I left St. John's by the railway train for Shediac, thence to embark for Prince Edward's Island. This railway was only opened at the beginning of the month, when the Prince of Wales rode by it, in a car specially prepared for him, to the steamer Forest Queen, which was to convey him to Fredericton; and this car was on the present occasion reserved for the press. It was fitted up like a room, with a sofa and arm-chairs, and neatly carpeted.

The scenery by the way was here and there pretty, but of no particular interest, and Shediac was as miserable looking as most of the villages in this part of the British Provinces.

I embarked on board the Arabian steamer at four o'clock, together with three hundred and odd more, so that the accommodations for passengers were by no means of the first order. In fact the passage was disgusting to every one of any sensibility. At eleven o'clock I stood on deck and saw Prince Edward's Island lying before me as flat as a map, for over its hundred and forty miles of length and four to thirty-four of breadth, it is one almost even plain of alluvial land, without a single rock or even a pebble to harden its surface. The soil of the island is the same throughout, such being a reddish sand. The chief articles of agricultural produce are oats and potatoes; but as the latter are raised more with a view to quantity, than quality, they are not of a very superior description. Cattle of all kinds are fed upon them, pasturage being deficient. The population of the island is about sixty thousand, of which eight thousand live in Charlottetown and the immediate neighborhood. The streets are totally unpaved, but the sidewalks are slightly raised above the level of the road. The houses, being almost universally built of wood, are by no means imposing in appearance, and the only approach to a solid piece of masonry is made by the Colonial Building and the Post-office, both of which are of stone, but the former considerably larger than the latter, and both standing in an open space of ground called the Square.

During five months of winter the harbors and rivers are frozen over, and used as highroads for the conveyance of produce from the interior.

The scenery around Charlottetown presents a picturesque arrangement of land and water, but there is a scarcity of wood, which results in a lack of antithesis in the landscape.

I may, perhaps, be expected to say a few words respecting the history of this island of the Gulf of St. Lawrence, which the inhabitants tell me is in the form of a crescent.

It is not likely that neglected Columbus, or his more-honored successor, Americus Vespucius, or even that wanderer in these waters, Sebastian Cabot, ever sighted the island, which was called Prince Edward's, in honor of the late Duke of Kent, the grandfather of the royal Albert Edward who has just been gracing the ball-rooms of the New World.

It is, however, alleged by some that the island was discovered by Cabot in 1497, and subsequently rediscovered by Vedazzani, a proof that these early events are shrouded in mystery, as the records of those navigators bear no evidence of the fact.

It is, nevertheless, well known that when the French had their garrisons at Quebec and Louisburg, it was the principal source of their supplies, and this led to its being termed the Granary of North America.

In 1663 the island was granted by the French to a Frenchman, whose name it is not here essential to learn, and it subsequently became the rendezvous of French families. In 1745 it was captured by the New England forces, but restored to France by the treaty of Aix la Chapelle. But after the second reduction of Louisburg in 1758 it became permanently ceded by treaty to Great Britain, and was, up to 1770, classed as a part of Nova Scotia. In that year, however, it was constituted a separate colony, and so has remained ever since. The population at that period did not amount to more than 4000.

I will now return to myself, and the crowded steamer, from which, as soon as she touched the dark and wooden wharf, I stepped ashore. I had the happiness or misfortune, as the case may be, to be totally unencumbered with baggage—mine having been left behind at St. John's, owing to the negligence of the parties concerned. There were neither cabs, nor porters, nor lights, nor any thing alive to be seen on that long, dreary wharf, as I groped along it towards the town, which instinct told me lay somewhere ahead. I continued groping, and finally stumbled over a little, forlorn-looking boy, whom I at once impressed into my service in guiding me to a habitation. I passed through a deserted street to the chief hotel of the place, which looked like the rest of the houses in the neighborhood, with the exception that it was open and lighted, whereas all the others were shut and dark. Here a woman with a child in her arms told me that the house was full. "Aye," said she, "and these gents had to sleep on the chairs, although they came by telegraph a week ago." I smiled, and again walked out into the night to seek shelter elsewhere. I knocked at several houses, and received answers similar to that given by the woman with the child in her arms.

At length I met a tall stranger hurrying on toward a lighted window, upon which I was myself intent, and with him were several of my unfortunate fellow-passengers, who were for the present equally homeless and equally bedless with myself. This was the Mayor. "Welcome, your worship," I was about to exclaim, when his local eminence was made known to me, but I didn't. The Mayor tried all his persuasive powers upon the hostess at the house we entered, but in vain. After that he hurried away up the street, and renewed his application elsewhere. Men in night-shirts, candle in hand, unlocked doors and opened them, but only to tell us that all was full—that no more could be accommodated. At length we found a place where the host promised me a reception

—a bed—but not a room. Here the Mayor bade me good-night, and I remained in the hope of rest.

It was about an hour after this when I was introduced to a mattress, on the top of sundry chairs, in a room in which I found four other sleepers extended on as many stretchers. I lay down, but the street noises consequent on the landing of the steamer's passengers were so great that had it not been for excessive fatigue I should hardly have slept; but I did sleep; and when I awoke early in the morning and looked out of the windows I saw hundreds of my own fellow-passengers, as well as of those who had come by a subsequent steamer, crowding the streets and walking about in search of a place of rest. Alas! said I, for the pleasure-seekers (they were excursionists), for they seek it and find it not, and after so saying I dressed myself and joined the moving multitude.

The Prince arrived at Hantsport, by the Valorous, in the morning at six. He then drove to Windsor, where he breakfasted at eight. A special train conveyed him to Truro by twelve, when an address was presented, to which he briefly replied. He left at one for Pictou, where he arrived at six. At half-past eight he embarked on board the Hero, which arrived here at noon to-day, in company with the Ariadne and Flying Fish. Her Majesty's ship Valorous had arrived previously, as also the French war-steamer Pomona. At half-past one he disembarked for the landing stage, where the Governor, the Judges, the members of the Legislature, the Mayor and Corporation, the clergy and the heads of Departments were assembled to receive him. Royal salutes were thundered from all the war-ships, including the Pomona, whose yards were manned and rigging dressed alike with the others, while at her peak fluttered the British flag, the English ships hoisting the French one in acknowledgment of the compliment.

On stepping ashore he shook hands with the Governor, who was in uniform, and bowed to the Mayor, and then took his seat beside the former in an open carriage, and, preceded by militia, cavalry, and band, drove to Government House, nearly a mile distant. A guard of honor of the Sixty-second regiment, together with the local volunteers, lined a portion of the way. The Masonic and three other societies formed a double line beyond, and joined in as the procession passed.

The cheering was not very energetic, and the weather was gloomy and wet. It cleared up during the time between his leaving the ship and reaching Government House, but after that it rained heavily all day.

There were five triumphal arches erected in the town, four of which were on the line of procession.

The illuminations which were attempted in the evening did, considering the extremely wet and cloudy weather, much credit to the natives. The attempt was spirited, but the failure desperate.

On the next day there was a levee at Government House, and in the evening a public ball at the Province Building, which was well attended, and at which His Royal Highness danced nearly every dance.

On the morning following he was escorted to the water-side, as on his arrival, and there embarked on the Hero, shortly after which the squadron sailed for Gaspe.

CHAPTER VII.

Incidents on a Journey from Shediac—Crowded State of the Steamers —Appearance of Gaspe—Picturesque Scenery on the Rivers—The Ships of the Royal Squadron—Address from the People of Gaspe —Dispatches for the young Prince from his Father, Mother, and the Princess of Prussia, etc., etc.

At half-past two in the morning I wended my way in solitude through the deserted streets of Charlottetown in the direction of the wharf where lay the Shediac steamer. The night was dark, and the walk by no means pleasant, but I am in the habit of taking things as I find them, and making the best of my lot; so I did not repine.

When I stepped on board the vessel, I found her, to use strong language, terribly crowded—there being within her upwards of four hundred and fifty passengers. These crowded the decks like flies, so that there was no sitting, and barely standing room; and when I descended, with considerable difficulty, into the cabin, I beheld an accumulation of legs and arms such as I had never done before in all my travels. The packing was closer than that adopted on board an African slaver, and the ventilation less perfect. However, I had prepared myself to sail in this steamer, so I endured the "roughing," and stood and sat in a narrow compass, and breathing an unwholesome atmosphere, until the wharf at Shediac was reached, at eleven o'clock. At three in the afternoon I left in the same steamer for Gaspe, the easternmost point of Canada, in order to meet the royal squadron again. She had about one hundred and twenty passengers on board, and sailed in a roundabout route, calling at various places *en route*. The first was Richibucto, the timber port, which I shall long remember, for the reason that, in coming out of its harbor, the steamer grounded on a sand-bank, and, if it had not been for a fisherman pilot of the place, might have remained there for the night, but owing to his skill we got off after a delay of about two hours. Meanwhile, several persons on board were giving orders, and the grossest incompetence and want of discipline were displayed by each.

I succeeded in capturing a berth on this night; but the bed linen had been so long away from the wash-tub that cleanliness forbade me to do more than throw off my more external habiliments, and the shelf was so small, and the atmosphere so used up, that my repose was by no means luxurious.

The provisions served at meals were as bad as the cooking, and as we messed in the sleeping cabin, the only one in the boat, all sorts of nuisances were encountered. The waiters were as disgustingly unclean as the general arrangements of the steward, and the whole voyage was a miserable purgatory to the passengers, who had, nevertheless, to pay enormously high fares and half a dollar for every meal in addition.

Early on the next morning we called at Chatham and Newcastle, towns and timber ports on the Miramachi River. It is popularly supposed that there is a town or port named Miramachi, but such is not the case. Miramachi is a name generally applied to all the ports on the river, so called, and within the district.

In the afternoon of this day we entered the Bay of Chaleur, where the sea ran high and the breeze blew strongly, and the air was filled with mist. Our vessel, having been built for river navigation only, now pitched and rolled about in a manner anything but delightful.

The bay is ninety miles long by twenty to thirty broad, and its shores are pleasantly diversified with hill and plain, rocks and grass land. From this we passed into the Restigouche River, and landed passengers at Dalhousie. We then returned to the bay, and called at Bathurst and Paspebebita, all fishing and timber ports of New Brunswick.

After this we kept well in with the shore, which was no longer that of New Brunswick, but of Canada, and occasionally stopped to take in passengers that put off to us in boats from the adjacent villages.

The shore was a cliff of red sandstone, backed by a chain of rolling hills—a spur of the Alleghanies—pleasantly dotted with cottages and small farms. At a point named Cape Despair on the south side of the bay, I saw a cross, which denotes the spot where Jacques Cartier first landed on discovering Canada. The Duke of Kent visited this site in the Leander, which, while passing, bumped against a sunken rock, but sustained only slight damage.

The most picturesque scenery on the whole bay lay a few miles further on, in the midst of which lay embosomed the fishing village of Perce. We were pressed between the mainland and Bonaventura Island, also inhabited by fishermen. Standing at the distance of a few yards from the mainland, facing this island, is Perce Rock, a tall pillar in the form of a parallelogram, with an archway in the centre, through which, at high water, a boat may pass. On this rock thousands of seagulls were perched, and here they build their nests and keep up a perpetual chatter, so much so that the fishermen, when overtaken by a fog, ascertain their position by the sound from this natural bell-tower.

We rounded a headland after this, and then the beautiful Bay of Gaspe opened upon our view.

Beautiful hills rose on either side as we steamed into the harbor, and finally into the basin fronting the village. Here the water is almost entirely landlocked, and the hills rise to an altitude of from fifteen hundred to two thousand feet. The village in itself is insignificant, yet in the only hotel there I found the ubiquitous *New York Herald*. *Hic et ubique* ought to be its motto. It alone is universal among newspapers.

In the distance we saw the smoke of the ships of the royal squadron, which two hours afterwards anchored in the bay.

I slept on board the steamer from Charlottetown that night, but on the following morning gladly transferred myself to the government steamer Lady Head, in waiting on the squadron, where a berth had been reserved for me.

CHAPTER VIII.

Excursion to meet the Prince.

THE Lady Head steamer, by which I traveled from Gaspe, came to a full stop opposite Riviere du Loup, on the night of the 14th of August at nine o'clock, for the purpose of enabling several of the Canadian ministry, who had joined us from the Queen Victoria, to go ashore and take their places in a special train for Quebec. They went, and I with them, across the dark water in a four-oared boat to the landing slip, where lay the Magnet, bound for an excursion up the Saguenay. My object was to take passage in her, so, parting from my friends, who had a dreary, jolting three-mile ride before them, to the railroad station —a lot I by no means envied. I secured a state-room in her and retired. This is the end of Act 1.

Soon after three the paddle-wheels of the steamer began creating a sensation in the waters of the quiet inlet where she lay, and, awaking, I became conscious that she had started on her trip, which the advertisements declared to be the only opportunity for meeting the Prince in the Saguenay.

The Riviere du Loup flows into the St. Lawrence from its southern side, and away on the other side of the inlet may be seen the village of that name.

The mouth of the Saguenay is a rocky gap, situated a hundred and thirty miles below Quebec, and this gap was filled with mist as we entered. On its lower side is a barren and stony point known as L'Islet, and this divides the Saguenay from Tadoussac Bay, to the eastward of which two terraces of alluvial land deck out the distance ; while in their rear, and almost enframing them, are rugged quartz-like elevations, which might almost be called mountains, the fissures of which are filled with a growth of stunted spruce-trees.

We passed the cove and lumber village of L'Ance à L'Eau on the right, soon after entering, and caught a glimpse of the church spire in Tadoussac as we ascended higher.

People were up early on the lookout for the Prince, asking all sorts of questions about him, and appearing quite disappointed when they were told he had not arrived.

Whoever admitted to have seen him became at once an object of curiosity, and found himself watched and pursued at every corner by people anxious to learn more, till at length the man who had seen the Prince was only second in interest to the Prince himself.

Away we sped through the cold and gloomy gorge of precipitous naked rock, and over the inky flood—for the waters of the river are strangely black, and its walls look as if they had been long ago cleft asunder by some wild convulsion of nature.

Here and there occurs a narrow ravine through which a slender but foaming torrent hurries to its bed, and yonder is a sprinkling of strangely dwarfed shrubs, quite in character with the strange, sepulchral scenery around.

A thunder-storm in the Saguenay by night would be a glorious scene for the lover of gloomy grandeur; and, if I were certain of the event, I would at any time undertake the journey for the mere pleasure of listening to the ringing echoes of the thunder, and seeing those barren cliffs lighted up with supernatural radiance. The Saguenay is unique; but, save at the lofty peaks of Capes Trinity and Eternity, it can hardly be called magnificent. Like all such places of popular resort, its beauties, its wildness, its grandeur, have been exaggerated, partly by parties interested in the steamboat traffic, and still more by those who, in recounting their travels, are never satisfied to tell a plain unvarnished tale, but must ever gild the picture.

Those who are fond of exploring caves and coal mines, the Thames Tunnel, the great tubular bridge, and such other regions of shade, will like the Saguenay, for it is the most sombre river in the world. It is the best place for enjoying a fit of the blues, or melancholy, that I know of. It is an emblem of Lethe, and would pass for a channel of the Dead Sea.

It looks lifeless, but it is not so; fish abound in its waters, and its villages are the resort of anglers. There are only about three of these, and miserably small and destitute they are, between the mouth and Ha-Ha Bay—a distance of sixty miles. The average width of the Saguenay is about three quarters of a mile. In some places it narrows to a width of less than half a mile, and in others expands two miles or more. The rocks, in which it is set like a mirror, vary in height from three hundred to seventeen hundred feet, and these are composed chiefly of sienitic granite and gneiss. The water at their base is, near the river's mouth, seven hundred feet deeper than the St. Lawrence, and averages one thousand feet in depth in the main channel all the way to the Grand Bay, as that of Ha-Ha is sometimes called.

One peculiar feature of the scenery is, that wherever

there is a projection on one side of the river there is a corresponding indentation on the other, which favors the before mentioned supposition of its having been rent by the elements.

Eighteen miles above Tadoussac I had a glimpse of the island of St. Louis, a rocky mass, covered with stunted trees, and rising to the height of three hundred feet at its extreme point.

The St. Marguerite River, a tributary of the Saguenay, rolled into it from the north, and here I saw the house and tents which had been fitted up for the reception of His Royal Highness during his day's fishing there. On the opposite side of the river, another stream, called the Little Saguenay, joined the larger one, and soon after passing that we came to St. John's Bay, situated on the southern side, and twenty-seven miles from the Saguenay's mouth. Its entrance is two miles wide, and it extends two miles inland. The mountains which overhang it present some fine subjects for the hand of the landscape painter. I was told, after we had left behind St. John's Bay, that we were approaching "the best part of the river," that the lofty cape I saw before me, rising seventeen hundred feet above the water, was Cape Eternity. The very name was calculated to awe me, if I had been of a more impressible nature. I gazed with interest, yea, with admiration, on its colossal form, and my eye lingered, as the bee might linger on the flower, with a keen appreciation of the picturesque, upon a gurgling cascade that poured from its summit into the ravine on some projecting bowlder a thousand feet above me.

The river grew darker as we passed beneath, and nearly all the passengers swarmed to the right-hand side of the steamer, and with upturned faces, contemplated this handiwork of nature.

We were now in Trinity Bay, on the southern shore —a capacious estuary, semicircular in shape and surrounded with rocks, save at its mouth, which is a mile wide. Cape Trinity stands *vis-a-vis* with Eternity, and the steamer passed close under it.

Pine and spruce trees flourish in the fissures of both these lofty peaks, which stand like sentinels to guard the entrance to the bay.

Statue Point was the next great object of attention. It is a tall promontory, on which, at an elevation of eight hundred feet, is a niche of an irregular Gothic shape, supposed to be the outlet of a cave. The name originated from the fact of there having been at one time a rock resembling a statue at its entrance. The Pictures next strike the eye. They are very abrupt rocks, like the rest of the river scenery, rising to the height of a thousand feet on the south side of the river, and presenting nearly an even surface.

As we neared our destination, a young lady with a characteristic display of wonder, called my attention to another lofty elevation, known as East Cape, by exclaiming, "Oh! look at that!" I looked and saw a ragged and perpendicular cliff, the sides of which were diversified with dwarfed trees and bowlders of granite.

Soon after this we reached Ha-Ha Bay, and saw on its southern shore the village, over which floated about thirty flags, chiefly British ensigns and union-jacks.

A huge pile of deals occupied one extremity of it, and denoted the site of saw-mills, which are owned by a large lumber merchant of the district.

The steamer no sooner stopped than she became the centre around which nearly a dozen boats began to ply, some for passengers, others for the sale of poultry and blueberries, the latter being so cheap and abundant that in a few minutes several large baskets full of them were purchased by the passengers. Blueberries appeared to be every man's property, for I observed that whoever had a peck or so of them before him, had innumerable visitors, who helped themselves unceremoniously from his pile and then walked away, eating the fruits of their own coolness. French, or rather a French *patois*, is the prevailing language of the villagers, who supply the wants of nature by fishing, rearing poultry, and cultivating such scanty crops as the soil enables them.

Ha-Ha is a ridiculous name, said to have originated from the circumstance of the first explorers of the bay laughing aloud to the tune of ha ha, in consequence of their joy at finding a landing place and anchorage after the long journey over the deep channel of the river.

The steamer's passengers were not expected to go ashore, as the vessel was only to remain three quarters of an hour, and very few of them did so.

There is another small village at the extreme head of the bay, or basin, as it ought to have been called, and this, with the other, is inhabited by about four hundred people, all of whom, with two or three exceptions, belong to the laboring classes. There is a church, resembling a magnified toy, in the centre of the larger village, both of which, I may remark, are situated on the banks of a stream. Water-power is thus obtained for driving the saw-mills alluded to.

The bay is nearly circular in shape, and nearly two miles wide, with mountains as its frame-work.

The steamer arrived at eleven, and left soon after noon on her return to the Riviere du Loup and Quebec.

The weather was misty and showery, and the spirits of all were damped, for the reason that they had expected to meet the Prince, and they had not met him.

At three o'clock, however, there was a rush to the deck to see an approaching steamer. It was the Queen Victoria, and the royal standard fluttered from her main-mast. Everybody stared at the vessel in silence, but they did not recognize the Prince standing on the deck, and, as a consequence, but few cheers distinguished the event. The master of the boat, with a surprising simplicity, blew the engine whistle, as a signal for the royal steamer to stop, in order that he might deliver a bag of dispatches he had on board for His Royal Highness, and enable his passengers and himself to have a good stare at him. But, of course, the Queen Victoria, treating the whistle in question with silent contempt, passed on, to the terrible indignation of the blower.

We subsequently went alongside the Hero and delivered the bag of dispatches, and then pursued our journey to the Riviere du Loup, where the steamer was moored for the night.

CHAPTER IX.

Pictorial Glimpses of the Prince's Travels—Movements on the River Saguenay—The Prince as a Fisherman—The Scenery on the St. Lawrence—The Prince's Reception Room—View of the Citadel—Grand Show of Regulars and Volunteer Troops--Enthusiasm on the Approach of the Hero—Hearty Welcome to the young Prince —Exciting Scenes on the Landing of the Prince—Immense Concourse of People—Order of the Procession--Grand Illuminations, etc., etc.

I AM about to give you a pictorial glimpse of the reception given to His Royal Highness the Prince of Wales at Quebec ; but before doing so I will recur to the time at which I last left him.

The Prince did not, as was anticipated, remain in the Saguenay on Wednesday night ; but after proceeding in the Queen Victoria, with the Governor General, forty-five miles up the river, returned to the Hero at nightfall.

Owing to the wet and misty weather, rough clothes, including water-proofs, were in general use on board. When the steamer was near Cape Eternity, some of her guns were fired, in order that the party might be amused by hearing the echoes that rang back from the rocks around, and the effect was as fine as anticipated.

The next morning dawned more favorably than its predecessor, and the Prince re-embarked in the little steamer, and sailed again up the Saguenay as far as the village of St. Marguerite, at the mouth of the river of that name, where he spent the greater portion of the morning in fishing, alike with those who accompanied him. But, unfortunately, he had no luck, and only a few trout were caught by the united rods.

After luncheon, the entire party, taking advantage of the tide, ascended the St. Marguerite in birch canoes, paddled by French Canadians, the Prince being, as ever, foremost in this aquatic procession.

The Flying Fish, having on board many of the officers of the squadron, also steamed up the Saguenay on the same day, and as she passed the tents where the Prince's standard hung from its staff, a salute of twenty-one guns was fired by her, the echoes of which muttered in sublime accents from the neighboring cliffs and more distant hills.

Had it not been for the mishap of the Hero grounding on Bar Reef, at the mouth of the Saguenay, the Prince would have sailed up in her ; but on the occurrence of this accident—the second of the kind within two days—he transferred himself to the Governor General's steamer that was to have followed.

The boat in which I made the excursion up the Saguenay took in at Murray Bay, a point between the Riviere du Loup and Quebec, one hundred additional passengers, which resulted in a tremendous rush for the dinner tables when the doors of the dining saloon were thrown open, for "first come, first served," was the guiding rule on the occasion.

I need not describe the bright and beautiful scenery of the St. Lawrence, for the theme has been long and oft dilated upon, and, as time presses, I must hurry on. The Isle of Orleans, within five miles of Quebec, divides the river into the north and south channels, and has a very picturesque effect. It was called by Jacques Cartier the Isle of Bacchus, owing to the number of wild vines that in his day—some time during 1535—flourished over its extent. It is twenty-one miles long and five broad. Its upper extremity is near the mouth of the Montmorenci River, and within full view of the Falls of that name, a pleasing glimpse of which I obtained from the steamer's deck, as they are situated only a few hundred yards from the main channel of the St. Lawrence, and conspicuously visible to all passing.

On the north side of the highest point of land on the island may be seen the second of a chain of flag and ball telegraphs, erected by the British during the last American war, and extending from Quebec to Green Island, opposite the mouth of the Saguenay. Villages and churches may now be seen on either side of the river; and looming ahead, at the curve of the river, near its junction with the St. Charles, stands the imposing city of Quebec, situated, for the most part, on a cliff three hundred and fifty feet high, and defended on the St. Lawrence side by a citadel, and elsewhere by formidable ramparts.

Numerous vessels were sailing within view, while higher up than the city lay a fleet of merchant craft, with the frigate Nile and the Valorous, both of which had arrived at ten that morning from Prince Edward's Island, lying in the foreground.

On the morning after my arrival I drove to the Citadel, and had an inside look at the heavy cannon and square piles of cannon-balls, which are painted black in the most peaceful manner every two years. The river side of the Citadel is occupied principally by a building used as officers' quarters, and elsewhere by barracks and storehouses. The place would be hardly worth cab hire and the fee which the soldier at the lodge expects for showing the visitor round, were it not for the delightful view of the St. Lawrence and St. Charles Rivers which is here afforded.

Friday night, from the appearance of the sky, promised rain, and the dawn of Saturday was dull and showery. The streets looked like so many avenues, owing to the sidewalks being planted with spruce boughs to an extent which hardly allowed of a passage way for even one at a time ; and, as these were loaded with moisture, every one who brushed against them received a little of it. This was unpleasant, and much impeded traffic, the cartway being too muddy to tempt pedestrians.

As the morning advanced the thoroughfares became more crowded, and only then the last nails were being driven into the arches, and the last branches of evergreen matted into place. About two the current of traffic set in strongly towards the Citadel and the waterside respectively, and this continued till the time of landing. Meanwhile, the various stands about the city had been filling up rapidly, windows had become occupied, soldiers of the line and volunteer companies had lined the streets, as well as they could, and all Quebec had turned out of doors to see the landing or procession. And during this time the huge dark form of the Hero, which, since her last grounding at the Saguenay, had been making four inches of water an hour, followed by the Ariadne, and the sharp-prowed Flying Fish, was steaming up the river, with His Royal Highness on her quarter-deck, dressed in a tweed shooting suit, and looking so unlike what is expected that the eager sight-seers crowding the twenty excursion steamers in her vicinity hardly glance at him, but cheer every young officer in uniform that makes his appearance, everybody being, nevertheless, in doubt as to who's who. There is the Jenny Lind, from

Montreal, whose passengers have been peeping into the Hero's port-holes all the way up from where the squadron anchored last night, so daring has her commander been in keeping her close alongside. There are plenty of pretty girls to be seen on board of her, and these are exchanging harmless glances with those on the Hero, Albert Edward included.

There is a grand, a mighty, a swelling, a joyous chorus of welcome, filling the air as the Hero is about to drop anchor opposite the Champion Market. It comes from yonder thousands assembled on the Citadel walls, and from other thousands on the strand and wharf, and surrounding roofs, and balconies, and steamers, and ships, and river boats, and wherever else the human form can cling, and from the descendants of the French as well as the English. Welcome to their roar! And now listen to the hearty cheers of those crews manning the yards of the Admiral's fleet, which display their thousand flags, fluttering from the rigging, for Her Majesty's ships are dressed in honor of her son. A royal salute was fired from these and the Citadel as the Hero neared the anchorage ground, and there will be none now till the real hero leaves his ship for the shore.

There is no mistake about the feeling of welcome among all classes here, for on every side there are evidences of it. There is not a house to be seen without its flag or its evergreen or illumination device, and every word the people utter, whether in French or English, expresses genuine loyal pleasure at the visit of the Prince of Wales.

It is now half-past three, and the Hero drops anchor. Under a circular wooden canopy, fronting the landing steps, are gathered the Governor General and the Ministry, in their civic uniforms of blue and gold; the British minister at Washington, Lord Lyons, and his two *attachés;* the Commander of the Forces, Sir Fenwick Williams, of Kars; the Protestant and Roman Catholic bishops, and several of the Catholic clergy, all in their robes; the Mayor of the city and several of the Municipal Council, together with other officers, civil and military, and many members of the Legislature. These are in waiting to receive the illustrious visitor on the threshold of the city, and as the yards of the fleet are being manned, the chief among them step down to the water-side where the royal barge is to touch.

Minutes of suspense now ensue. The horses of the military congregated on the town side of the canopy manifest a good deal of high-blooded restlessness, and their riders are as eager in their glances towards the Hero as the crowd generally.

The time has now come. The Hero has swung round, and the Prince has stepped into the boat from the gangway, on the Point Levi side, so that while all are looking for his appearance at the one nearest, the standard is lowered from the mast-head, and a boat with another such standard fluttering from its peak rounds the ship, and appears in full view. And now the flag-ship fires the first of her twenty-one guns, which is the signal for the rest to pour forth their volleys in concert with the Citadel.

The natural cliff of Cape Diamond forms a massive and splendid background of an order the most picturesque. The Prince ascends the carpeted steps, and halts under the canopy amid renewed cheers, which he acknowledges by bowing in his usual graceful manner. His manner wins all hearts, and they hail him as a friend.

The Mayor is presented to him, and he bows; after which the former reads an address of welcome to him in French, and afterwards a translation of the same into English. The Prince listens with courteous attention, but a smile is traceable beneath the surface as he hears the address in the first language.

The Mayor has finished, and he advances and hands

copies of both to the Prince in person, who, assuming an expression of earnest gravity, receives his reply from the Duke of Newcastle, on his left, and reads it in that firm, clear manner for which his mother has been so long celebrated, and he wears the same regal yet unostentatious look as she does so.

The reply, alike with its predecessors, is well worded, and in excellent taste. He hands the copy to the Mayor, and there is a mutual bow.

There is a dead silence of some seconds' duration, when some one of the local authorities breaks it by exclaiming "Three cheers for the Prince," upon which there is a grander chorus of voices than has yet been heard. It rings from the wharf to the Citadel, and the Citadel to the wharf, and "one cheer more" is responded to with undiminished enthusiasm. The Prince, with uncovered head, bows again and again, and is then conducted to his carriage, which is drawn by four dark bays, and driven by a coachman in the reddest of livery. The Governor General, the Duke of Newcastle, and Earl St. Germain, take their places with him, and the carriage moves away in the order of procession, saluted with renewed cheers on all sides.

After this the other carriages to join in the procession came up, and moved on as fast as they were occupied. The Quebec Cavalry took up position, as an escort, to the Governor General's residence, whither the Prince was going, and the Prince's standard simultaneously waved over the landing place, the Citadel, and the house of the Governor General.

The decorations over the whole line of route were very abundant, and the cheering vociferous. Crowds lined the whole way, and every window had its occupants. Arch succeeded arch at short intervals from the wharf to the Government House, a distance of more than five miles, and nearly every arch had its motto and device.

The procession, on arriving at St. John's toll-gate,

opened files, facing inward, and lined the road for the passage of the Prince's and other carriages.

In the evening the illuminations presented from the river a long and glittering line, which was the finest sight of the kind I ever saw. In detail, however, they were less imposing, although, for Quebec, they were quite equal to what I had anticipated, and did múch credit to the city. As at Halifax, on the night appointed for the general illumination, the weather was dark and wet, and the showers which had fallen at intervals throughout the day, made the streets exceedingly muddy. Yet, notwithstanding, the streets were thronged with perambulating crowds.

I have seen much finer illuminations, but they were produced by gas jets, whereas those of Quebec were chiefly transparencies lighted with oil lamps and candles. The illumination was universal, and, as a whole, far surpassed the display of the kind made at Halifax.

CHAPTER X.

Proposed Federation of the Province, with the Prince of Wales as Viceroy—The Prince at Church—His Visit to the Falls of the Chaudiere—Description of the Falls, etc., etc.

I WILL commence my present chapter by making allusion to what I have hitherto remained silent upon, namely, a federation of the British North American provinces, with, very likely, Albert Edward, Prince of Wales, as Viceroy. This, I have every reason to believe, is not only possible, but highly probable.

The Duke of Newcastle, who has long been the chief supporter of moderate liberalism in England, is not here merely as an attendant upon royalty, but to ascertain the state of feeling throughout these colonies, with a view to the consolidation referred to in the event of such being at any time deemed desirable by the mother country; for circumstances may arise in which such a union would, not only give her strength, but insure safety to these possessions.

The feeling throughout the provinces is universally in favor of such a consolidation of England's colonial empire in North America. The inhabitants are averse to the distinctions of Newfoundlanders, Nova Scotians, New Brunswickers, Prince Edward Islanders, Canadians, and British Columbians. They wish to be all included under the one general head, and have one government in common, which, from its superior extent, would insure greater rewards and more honors than now exist among them.

There is so much petty party bickering now in existence in the North American colonies, that the system must be enlarged to avert the catastrophe of its breaking in pieces.

It is, I am certain, the political future of the whole of British America to become one, to be ruled by a single Legislature, and to have laws in common. But how soon this result will be arrived at I cannot say. Meanwhile, England is well aware of her necessity for maintaining the prestige which the possession of these colonies secures her, and the immensity of the disaster which their loss would inflict upon her political standing. A war between England and France would, under the present Emperor, probably lead to the capture of one or more of the British colonies referred to, but it is probable that were a political union of the provinces to exist, such would never occur. They would in themselves be too strong for any such attempt to meet with success.

On Sunday morning the Prince drove in an open carriage from the residence of the Governor General to the English Cathedral, where he attended Divine service. As at Fredericton, members of the congregation only were admitted previous to his arrival, in company with the Governor; his own suite, and the other distinguished personages officially in Quebec. When, at half-past ten, the party arrived, they were received at the side door by the bishop and clergy of the cathedral, who bowed most graciously. The Prince then proceeded to the Governor General's pew, which had been fitted up with crimson velvet, a throne, and sofas, for the occasion.

The Bishop preached an excellent sermon, at the end of which, he made a brief but graceful allusion to the presence of the Prince.

No demonstration was made by the people in the streets as the royal party drove past, and pedestrians were nearly as few and the general quiet as complete as on an ordinary Sunday.

The Prince remained at home during the rest of the day.

On the next morning, at a few minutes before noon, the Prince, in company with the Governor General and his suite, left the Government House for Cape Rouge, where he embarked in a boat for the opposite side of the St. Lawrence, on his way to the Falls of the Chaudiere; and this, notwithstanding the dull and rainy weather and the muddy roads—facts that left the party with a mere half dozen strangers, enterprising enough to accompany them on the excursion.

The Falls alluded to, which are situated about a mile below the railway tubular bridge, on the river from which they derive their name, are inferior in both volume and beauty to either those of St. Anne's or Montmorenci. Nevertheless, they are one of the sights which the tourist through Lower Canada is expected to visit. The distance from Quebec to the Falls is about nine miles, and the most convenient way of performing the journey is to hire a caleche, the driver of which will take you there and back for three dollars.

The ferry steamer plying between the Lower Town and Point Levi will convey horse and vehicle across the river, after which there is a good and direct road to the required spot. The time occupied in going and returning is usually about three hours.

The river at the cascade is narrower than elsewhere, being only four hundred feet across. The depth of the Falls is about a hundred and thirty-five feet, and these are divided by rocks into three currents, of which the one on the western side is the largest. These partially reunite before their broken and agitated waters are received into the basin, where the visitor looks down into a turbulent whirlpool. Owing to the shape of the rocks, a portion of the flood is diverted into an oblique direction beyond the line of the precipice, while their cavities increase the foaming fury of the hurrying stream as it flings itself wildly into the gulf, sending up meanwhile a cloud of spray, which in the sun becomes a rainbow.

The forest scenery around contrasts well with this rocky and troubled scene, and those who love the country will feel pleasure in the prospect, for it is a rural, lonely spot.

Like all waterfalls, they look well whether viewed from above or beneath, and the Prince did not miss the opportunity of scanning them from both points, for he has an inquiring, ardent mind, and likes to see everything that is to be seen. He is an observant, pleasant traveler, enthusiastic, persevering and overflowing with good spirits, and, I warrant, could write a capital narrative of his New World experiences.

The weather continued wet and dreary throughout the afternoon. At four o'clock the august party returned to Government House by the same route as on coming.

CHAPTER XI.

Closing Scenes in Quebec.

THE necessity of embracing the entire tour in a single volume compels me to compress my narrations into as small a compass as possible, which is a circumstance very adverse to excellence of composition.

The great event of Tuesday, the 21st of August, was the levee at the Province Building, upon which occasion the Speakers of the Upper and Lower Houses of the Colonial Parliament were knighted. I was present and saw the slender burnished blade of the Duke of Newcastle's sword passed to the hand of the Prince, who waved it gently from the left shoulder to the right of the gentleman in the long robe, who rose Sir Narcisse Belleau, an honor which was a few moments later shared by one of the great SMITH family, surnamed Henry.

In the afternoon, His Royal Highness and suite drove out to the Falls of Montmorenci, and afterwards walked a mile or more across some fields to the natural steps, so called from a succession of rocky shelves over which the waters of the Montmorenci River rush wildly through a gloomy gorge.

In the evening, the citizens' ball, in his honor, took place. It was attended by the *élite* of the city, and was brilliantly successful, and much enjoyed by His Royal Highness, who took part in every dance.

On the following day the illustrious scion of the House of Hanover visited the La Val University, a seminary for priests, where an address was read to him. He afterwards drove to the Ursuline Convent, where the lady inmates sang with touching effect to a guitar accompaniment, the following song of welcome in his presence:

CHORUS.

Hark! hark! a merry, merry peal
  Rings out o'er all the land;
Its echoes through the cloisters steal,
  It fires our youthful band.
Bring harp and sing; let melody,
Let joy, gush forth in numbers free!
Thy welcome Prince, is sounding still,
Thy welcome is that merry peal
  Of joy o'er all the land.

SOLO.

'Tis gladness all thy welcoming
  From Albion's isle afar;
And loyal hearts their homage bring
  To hail thy rising star;
And joyous youth their promise tell,
While tuneful notes of triumph swell!
Lo! Briton's heir deigns here to rest,
Oh! haste to greet our royal guest.

CHORUS.

Wake, wake, another merry peal,
  And let it echo long,
While wishes for the Prince's weal
  Are mingled with our song.
May every blessing on thee rest!
  Thus rings the merry peal,
And thus we hail thee, royal guest,
  Thus pray we for thy weal,
  While still that merry peal
  Rings loud and echoes long.

He also received and replied to an address from the nuns.

In the evening there was a grand display of fireworks at the expense of the Government, at which a serious accident occurred, by the breakdown of a stand full of people.

On the next morning the Prince left the Parliament House to embark for Montreal. The weather was beautifully warm and sunny, and the soldiers of the Seventeenth Regiment were stationed along the line of route, while the Quebec Cavalry acted as a guard of honor by accompanying the royal carriage.

On the wharf were collected the members of the Executive Council, the Mayor and Corporation, and the masters of various national societies.

As the royal cortege passed along, the cheers of men and the waving handkerchiefs of women denoted the highest enthusiasm. A glorious chorus of voices filled the air as he stepped from his carriage at the point of embarkation, where many thousands were assembled to do him honor, and still louder was the burst of excited loyalty and admiration as he embarked on the steamer. Then, too, the loud-tongued cannon rolled out the terrible music of a royal salute, and the crews that manned the yards of the men-of-war waved their hats and raised their voices in a grand unity of praise. From the Citadel, from the ships, from the battery overlooking the St. Charles, came the thunder and smoke of the iron-mouthed guns, and flags waved, and wavelets glittered, and magnificent was the view. But, in the midst of all this, I saw a tear course down a maiden's cheek. I had seen her dancing with the Prince at the ball. If I had been a maiden I might also have wept myself. Alas, that regrets are vain. The steamer recedes from my view. Cheers ring again and again. They are answered by a wave of the hat. Adieu!

That morning Major General Bruce had sent to the Anglican Bishop of Quebec a Bible, on the fly leaf of which was written by a royal hand, "To the Cathedral of Quebec, in memory of Sunday, August 19, 1860.

ALBERT EDWARD."

The book was exquisitely bound, and bore the arms and crest of the giver on the cover.

At four o'clock that afternoon I left the city for Montreal, on board the steamer Quebec, which had been chartered by the Government for the conveyance of members of the Legislature desirous of being present at the festivities there.

By leaving thus early in the day I enjoyed a good view of the beautiful river scenery for some hours.

A meeting was held on board, at which it was resolved that the vessel should anchor at Three Rivers during the night, and sail up with the Prince in the morning.

When we arrived at that point, at half-past ten, the whole of the water-side was beautifully illuminated, and the royal steamer lay at anchor a few hundred yards from the pier.

The Prince had landed there, under an arch and canopy erected for the occasion, at half-past six, and was honored with a salute from a corps of Royal Artillery and a company of Montreal Light Infantry. He was received by the Mayor and Corporation, the clergy, public officers, and citizens, who presented an address to him, which elicited a brief but appropriate response, after the delivery of which he returned to the steamer.

When I awoke, we were steaming up the St. Lawrence, with the royal steamer a short distance ahead. It was raining heavily, and the day promised badly. But, notwithstanding its being misty and gloomy, and wet, Montreal excursion steamers from about ten o'clock met us, with their decks crowded with thousands of men, women, and children. These steamers blew the whistle and turned back to accompany us, their passengers, meanwhile, cheering vociferously, and in one instance singing "God save the Queen."

Steamer after steamer joined us as we advanced, the decks equally crowded with people wet to the skin, notwithstanding their umbrellas, for the rain was too heavy and drifting to be escaped.

At two o'clock the Kingston stopped to await the proper time (three P.M.) for approaching the city. She was now three miles below it.

We left her behind, and, steaming up to the quay, landed. The rain had by this time ceased, and there was every promise of a fine afternoon. Nevertheless, the Mayor had issued a proclamation to the effect that owing to the state of the weather the reception would be postponed till the morning following. The tens of thousands who had prepared themselves for the event were, therefore, left to go home again.

In firing the salute in honor of His Royal Highness' approach, three men were killed on board the Flying Fish, and one on the Valorous.

CHAPTER XII.

The First day in Montreal.

THE morning of Saturday the 25th of August, broke wet and gloomy. This gave rise, I heard, to a wag remarking that His Royal Highness was not only heir apparent to the British throne, but the *Raining Prince.* Before eight o'clock, however, the rain had ceased, and the current of traffic set in strongly towards the river-side. At a few minutes before nine—the hour appointed for the landing—I drove to Bonsecours Market, and then walked through the mud between lines of citizens, kept in order by a few policemen, towards the wharf near the extreme end of which stood the triumphal arch or pavilion.

There I found the Ministry in their Third-Class uniform, members of the Upper House in their regulation steel-buttoned coats, many of the Lower House in evening dress, the Anglican Bishop and clergy and several of the Roman Catholic Hierarchy, the Admiral of the Fleet, and other naval officers, the members of the

Executive Committee, and lastly, but mightiest of all, the Mayor in his scarlet robe. He stood foremost of the group in all the pride and majesty of office, and was evidently eager to give the Prince a fervent welcome. The steamer Kingston painted white, and with the plumes and motto of the Princes of Wales painted on her paddle-boxes was only a few yards distant from the wharf, but, owing to the awkwardness displayed in getting her alongside, more than a quarter of an hour elapsed before the gangway was opened to the shore.

During this time the Prince and the noblemen accompanying him, as also the gentlemen of the suite, all of whom were in uniform, appeared standing on deck and exchanging remarks concerning the scene before them, and the yards of the Valorous, Styx, and Flying Fish were manned by crews eager for the landing and the signal when they were to cheer. The dome of Bonsecours Market, directly opposite the Pavilion, presented as pretty a background as anything short of fine natural scenery, and the thousands of people that crowded the steamers lying in the vicinity, and a few that were plying on the water, lent animation to the picture.

At twenty minutes past nine the Kingston was moored to the wharf, and the royal party stepped without delay on to the strip of red carpet leading to the steps of the Pavilion, where led by the Mayor all took their stand, the Prince on the one uppermost with the Duke of Newcastle on his left and the Governor General on his right.

The Valorous, Flying Fish, and Styx, all dressed with flags, now fired a royal salute, as also did the Volunteer Field Battery of Artillery from the wharf parallel to the landing, while the crews of the war-steamers cheered from the yards they covered and the multitude within view echoed the sound, amid the ringing of church bells, with that enthusiasm which everywhere greeted the Prince during his tour in the New World.

Our select circle on the wharf was not behind in the gladsome demonstration, for we waved our hats and raised our voices again and again in his praise and welcome.

The Mayor, after conducting the royal guest thus far, took his place on the carpeted floor, and read the usual address in English, and afterwards a translation of the same into French.

His Royal Highness then read the reply in English only. At the conclusion of this, the cheering was immense. When it had subsided, the Prince walked between the Duke of Newcastle and the Governor General to his carriage, drawn by four horses, in waiting a short distance up the wharf. As he drove away the cheering was renewed, and continued with more or less enthusiasm all along the route to the exhibition building.

The Prince arrived at the building at the appointed hour of eleven, and on alighting from his carriage passed through the horticultural tent to the reception room, where he remained only a few moments, preparatory to entering the great hall, and taking his place on the dais or throne prepared for him. He was greeted with loud cheers and clapping of hands, and by the young ladies of the orchestra singing "God save the Queen," to an organic accompaniment. The Prince stood in the centre of the official group while the anthem was being sung, and never was man more the observed of all observers. The anthem was succeeded by the Governor General leaving the Prince's right, and taking his place at the foot of the throne, where he read an address to His Royal Highness, setting forth the nature and objects of the exhibition, and praying that he would be pleased to open and inaugurate the same.

To this the Prince then replied. No sooner was this done than I heard a voice saying, "Let us pray."

It came from the mouth of the Anglican Bishop, who, clad in his robes, thereupon read a prayer, invoking God's blessing on the undertaking, the audience during its delivery listening without changing position. The royal party was now conducted over the building by the secretary of the exhibition.

Returning to the dais, His Royal Highness formally declared the exhibition opened. Upon this the Oratorio Society sang the "Hallelujah Chorus," with much spirit, at the conclusion of which the royal party retired by the door at which they entered, a farewell cheer accompanying them.

From the exhibition building I proceeded to the Grand Trunk Railway station, at Point St. Charles, from which my ticket apprised me I had to leave by special train for the bridge at half-past twelve, to witness the ceremony of its inauguration by His Royal Highness the Prince of Wales.

I entered the special train, which soon afterwards moved away in the direction of the bridge, and stopped at the entrance to it, where all the passengers alighted, in order to ascend the long wooden steps leading up to the top of the bridge, or gallery, as it was termed, where rows of seats were erected for the accommodation of those present, nearly half of whom were ladies.

We all know what women will go through when they have an object of their own choice in view, and what fatigue they will happily endure under the name of pleasure. So it was not to be wondered at that the ladies here displayed their proverbial courage in overcoming all difficulties.

When I reached the summit of the bridge, the sun was shining gloriously, and the tin roofs and spires and cupolas of the island city of Montreal, glittered like the wavelets of the river, in the midst of which, like an emerald set in diamonds, lay the green islet fronting the Custom-house.

I never before saw Montreal to so much advantage, never before took in the appearance of the two-mile tin-roofed tubular bridge, stretching from shore to shore, with such nicety of view.

On the entrance lintel of the stone parapet, above the roadway, I saw cut the following inscription:

ERECTED, A.D. MDCCCLIX.
ROBERT STEPHENSON AND ALEXANDER M. ROSS,
ENGINEERS.

One block of limestone now alone remained to be lowered into place, in order to formally complete the great practical work which has monopolized so large a share of public attention, and that block was now depending by a chain from the scaffolding over the grave in which it was to rest till disturbed by ruin.

The top of the parapet in which the stone was to be placed, was set apart for the gentlemen of the press, and this was the best possible position for them. From this point I looked down on dark masses of men assembled in the cool shade of the trackway, and who had come by a train subsequent to the one mentioned, while on either hand, forming a beautiful vista, were long rows of bonnets, with a sprinkling of hats, denoting as many ladies and gentlemen.

At twenty minutes to two, and while every one, to use a common expression, was on the tip-toe of expectation, the royal car arrived, drawn by a locomotive dressed with flags. The dark masses below formed into line on either side of the track, and there was a general cheer. The Prince jumped from the car on to the platform, and, accompanied by the Governor General, the Duke of Newcastle, Earl St. Germains, Lord Lyons, Lord Mulgrave, the members of his suite, and a few others, ascended the stairs to another platform erected a little below the level of the base the stone was to occupy. The Prince was met with renewed cheers on reaching this elevation, and here an elegant silver trowel, on which was the following inscription, was handed to him by the contractor for the work: "To commemorate the completion of the Victoria Bridge, by His Royal Highness, Albert, Prince of Wales, Montreal, 1860."

His Royal Highness then stooped and spread the mortar which had been previously placed there, after which he returned the trowel to the presenter, who, having wiped it, restored it to its case. As soon as the stone, which weighed ten tons, was lowered into place, the Prince gave it three gentle taps with the mallet. The ceremony was thus far completed, and the Prince descended the steps, and re-entered his car, in order to proceed into the bridge, and hammer the last rivet into the centre tube.

As soon as the rivet was driven in by His Royal Highness, he and his party returned to Point St. Charles, and attended the dejeuner, which was given in one of the car-shops of the railway company, decorated for the occasion. There was a gallery at the head of the room devoted to the use of the Prince and high officials accompanying him.

After a short lapse of time, the Governor General proposed the health of the Queen, which was received with hearty cheers. Prince Albert was next toasted, and afterwards "the Prince of Wales," the latter being more especially greeted with tremendous applause.

A few minutes of silence only intervened before the Prince rose and proposed "The health of the Governor General, prosperity to Canada, and success to the Grand Trunk Railway."

He waved his glass to the cheering, and evidently entered into the feeling with much warmth. The royal party left shortly after this, and no further speech-making took place.

The illuminations in the evening were the finest that the Provinces have produced, and may be said to have been universal. The ships of war in port presented a very fine spectacle, and after those the Place d'Armes wore the most brilliant aspect.

CHAPTER XIII.

The Cricket-Ground—Indian Games and Dances—The Levee and the Citizens' Ball—The Prince Encircled by Ropes—The Concert—Cornwall—In the Rapids—Lachine—The Military Review and Return—Ottawa, etc.

On Monday morning when, at a few minutes before ten, I drove to the cricket-ground where the Indian games were to take place, in the presence of the Prince, I found an immense concourse of people gathered, in a state of excitement, in front of a small door or opening in a paling which surrounded the limited territory in question.

"Keep back, keep back, you're killing these ladies," was the cry of a man clinging to the paling above the small doorway, and who kept alternately goading and soothing the crowd in their passage from purgatory to paradise.

As I walked across the smooth turf towards the stand which had been erected on the town side of the inclosure for the accommodation of the Prince and party, I saw a number of figures, chiefly Indian, in tightly fitting red and white and blue and red garments, standing here and there in picturesque groups. These were the players. Approaching nearer, I saw that the Indians wore feathers in their caps, and had their faces painted.

At ten o'clock the Prince arrived, and took his place on the stand amid loud cheering.

The first lacrosse game now commenced between sixty of the Algonquin tribe and an equal number of the Iroquois, and, after a spirited contest, was given in favor of the latter, in order to enable the Prince to witness the match between twenty-five Montreal gentlemen and as many Algonquins. Lacrosse is a game combining foot-ball and rackets, or raquets, as it used to be spelt. There is one ball in common, and every player has a racket or bat made of twigs. It is the object of the one side to keep the ball as much in one direction as possible, and strike into a space called the jail, and of the other to do exactly the reverse.

The first two games were won easily by the red men, but in the third the whites were victorious.

Now commenced the war-dance, in which about twenty painted Indians, in very warlike garb, and fully armed for battle with tomahawks, scalping knives, and other tragic weapons, formed themselves into a ring with one of their number in the centre, who engaged himself in the occupation of beating a drum and singing.

While dancing they uttered a harsh refrain, and most of them remained stooping with their hands resting on their thighs during the monotony; then yelling and changing their position for one exceedingly fierce, in which they brandished their knives in each other's faces, they assumed as many distortions of legs, arms, body, and face, as an Australian aborigine in the midst of a corrobberri.

The war-dance was the most amusing feature of the whole performance, and the Prince laughed in evident enjoyment of savage antics, the squaws in front of two or three bark wigwams beneath, meanwhile eyeing him as a being of whose position among the pale faces they would like to know more.

A race between twenty of each tribe came next, and these ran from the centre of the field up to and through tne flags, then back again through the opposite flags to the starting point. The running was not as swift as I anticipated, and the race was won by an Iroquois.

This was succeeded by a fourth game of lacrosse, in the midst of which and at eleven o'clock a shower fell, and His Royal Highness, left the grounds in the carriage by which he came, accompanied by the Governor General, the Duke of Newcastle, Lord Lyons, and his own suite. The standard was lowered on the flagstaff over the stand, and cheers followed the royal party along the moistened ranks.

The levee was appointed to take place at noon, and at a few moments before that hour the Prince arrived, in uniform, under an escort of volunteer cavalry, and accompanied by all the noblemen and gentlemen who had attended him at the levee at Quebec. He was received by the Highland Company of Rifles, acting as the guard of honor.

The levee was held in the Advocates' Library, and about two thousand presentations took place.

The next great event of the day was the citizens' ball. I went there at a few minutes before ten o'clock, and found myself among a throng of three or four thousand gathered in the largest circular ball-room I ever danced in.

It is somewhat dry work giving the measurement of such a room on such an occasion, but I will, nevertheless, descend from the poetry of the scene to the bare facts. I was in a circular room, the circumference of which was three hundred and seventy-five feet, and which had, consequently, a diameter of two hundred and fifteen feet, and a superficial space of thirty-two thousand ditto, with a gallery above, extending around the whole rotunda, where well-dressed beauty sat in pride, gazing on the festive scene.

In the centre was the stand occupied by the band, and round this was the grand promenade.

The Prince arrived at ten o'clock, up to which time

no dancing had taken place. Gas-burners circled the building in three rows, and produced a brilliant effect, for light is an important element in these grand gatherings of the *élite*. The refreshment stalls were arranged round the extreme circle, and here champagne on draught, and thick slices of cold corned beef, were to be obtained; but no sherry, or port, or any drinks of a vinous or alcoholic nature, more than the said draught champagne and some questionable claret.

The Prince entered the ball-room from his dressing-room in a secluded part of the gallery, and accompanied by his usual suite in uniform. There was a cheer, and "God save the Queen," was played by the band. The royal party was conducted to a box situated between two red ropes, meant to act as barriers in preventing other than a select circle dancing in that vicinity. Everybody was crying out against these ropes, and it would have been the most popular act that His Royal Highness could have done to have gone beyond this local boundary, but, unfortunately, he danced there all the evening, and being shut up, had a crowd around him all the time, which crowd was as solid and hard to move as a wall. The noblemen and gentlemen of His Royal Highness' suite were, therefore, unable to move about and say "How d'you?" to their friends and acquaintances, and two of them went to sleep in their chairs, and remained so during the greater part of the evening.

The only approach that has ever been made to such a ball-room, was by the Theatre Francais, at Paris, when boarded over immediately after the carnival, and used as a public *salle*; but its inferior size places it far below the great ball-room of Montreal. Yet the ball at Montreal was all show and no comfort.

The roof of the building was tastefully colored, but its supports or pillars were only parallelogramic lengths of timber, whitewashed and scantily wreathed with evergreens.

The Prince remained till a few minutes past four o'clock, and received a general cheer as he left the room through the passage way formed for his departure.

The weather was fortunately fine when, on the next morning at eleven o'clock, the Prince drove from his residence to the Grand Trunk Railway station, where he and his suite took their places in the royal car and started for Cornwall.

Cornwall is a new and by no means French-looking or French-speaking town, but pure Anglo-Saxon. It is situated about five miles from the boundary line between the United States and Canada, which runs through the village of St. Regis, inhabited chiefly by Indians, half of whom acknowledge themselves under the sway of Great Britain, while the remainder lay claim to the protection of the United States.

Cornwall has among other things a conspicuous church and court-house, and is the chief township of the eastern district, and one of the most populous and best situated of the divisions of Upper Canada, it being bounded on two sides by the broad waters of the St. Lawrence and Ottawa respectively. A canal extends from this over a distance of twelve miles, parallel with the Long Sault Rapids, at the foot of which the town lies.

Here the Prince and party on their arrival were received with much enthusiasm, and embarked on board the steamer Kingston, which had come up on the previous day in order to be in readiness for the trip down.

The St. Lawrence a little below this point expands into a lake, and presents a fine sweep of prospect. As the steamer glided away, the royal party were assembled on deck, and there they remained during most of the passage.

St. Regis Island, situated mid-channel, was the first object that was remarked upon, as the steamer sped onward towards the lake, with the royal standard floating from her topmast. The steamer on entering the lake passed between Squaw and Butternut Islands, with the lighthouse on Lancaster Shoal within easy view.

The steamer was now steered close past a floating lighthouse, and so on to Cherry Island light, with McGees' Point visible on the northern shore, and the Rapids of Coteau du Lac straight ahead.

Coteau du Lac is a small village at the foot of Lake St. Francis, and twelve miles from the Cascades. Both by name and nature its French origin is distinctly traceable.

On the right bank the shore now appeared studded with those little stone churches and comfortable farm-houses and neat farms so characteristic of the French Canadian Territory.

The Coteau Rapids were run just below the village, and then came the Cedar Rapids, extending from the village of Cedars on the north shore to that of St. Timothe on the opposite one, both sides of the river being Canadian below Cornwall.

A group of sixteen islands interrupted the navigation at the Coteau du Lac Rapids, the first of these latter being between Giron Island and the mainland; the second between French Island and those of Maple and Thorn, and the third between Prisoner's and Broad Islands, after which the steamer shot into smooth water opposite Grand Island.

This newly earned tranquillity, however, was of short duration; for the steamer was soon darting from ledge to ledge through the hurrying waters of the Cedars, the village of that name lying on the north shore and Beauharnois on the south. Emerging from these rapids, the steamer was again at rest; soon, however, to be again disturbed by the turbulent bed of the Cascade Rapids, tumbling over a chain of bars. These are situated between Cascades Point and Buisson

Point, where the St. Lawrence expands into Lake St. Louis, and the bright and rolling waters of the Ottawa mingle on the northern shore with those of the sister river. From this lovely scene the steamer now ploughed her way over the lake to the town of Lachine, on the north bank, and nearly opposite the Indian village of Caughnawaga.

Lachine is situated a short distance above the rapids of that name and nine miles from Montreal. But, although so near, the royal party preferred landing and returning to town by railway to descending these, the most swift and wild of all the rapids of the St. Lawrence; and they accordingly disembarked.

Lachine is the headquarters of the Hudson Bay Company in North America, and the residence of its Governor. A number of voyageurs were here assembled, and these manned their boats in honor of the Prince, and cheered loudly. The royal party afterwards returned to town by railway, and at half-past ten arrived for the second time at the ball-room, where all the musical talent of the country had assembled in the cause of a musical festival.

The room was crowded with a galaxy of beauty in full dress, more so even than on the previous evening. The first division was performed by the Montreal Oratorio Society. This was followed by a recess of more than an hour. Then a solo was executed by a gentleman member of the Montreal Musical Union, which consisted of over two hundred and fifty performers, all of whom were assembled on the raised circular platform in the centre of the room.

Soon after this the royal party arrived.

At its close the grand cantata, composed in honor of the visit of the Prince, was performed by the two hundred and fifty referred to. Following this came the concert by the professional artistes.

The whole concluded near midnight with "God save the Queen."

Lady Franklin was present and after His Royal Highness had retired, the chairman of the Committee of Management, conducted her to the chair vacated by the Prince, upon which she was recognized by the audience, who rose and greeted her with several rounds of applause.

The review on the next morning was a tolerable success. The companies and troops comprising the volunteer forces were assembled on the ground at Logan's farm soon after ten o'clock. At eleven the Prince arrived, when his standard was run up on the flagstaff there erected, the field battery meanwhile occupying a place on the extreme left, facing the flagstaff, and the first and second troops of cavalry occupying a position on the hill, near and to the right of the flagstaff, with the light infantry formed to the right of the cavalry, the rifles on the left, and foot artillery companies on the right of the field battery.

The line being thus formed, the battery fired a royal salute, and as the Prince rode up to the place reserved for him the brigade presented arms and the Prince's band played "God save the Queen."

The Prince at once commenced an inspection of the line, commencing with the cavalry and riding down to the extreme end, on reaching which he turned and passed slowly up the rear. This finished, the Prince led back to the flagstaff and faced the line, which broke and marched past in quick time, the salutations of the officers being returned by the Prince. The brigade marched back to the same ground, formed in quarter-distance column, and again marched by. Line was re-formed on the original ground, and the cavalry and battery retired to the rear of the cavalry supporting the battalion, which changed front obliquely to the right on the centre company of rifles. Here, at the double, two companies of rifles advanced and extended right and left in skirmishing order, after which they commenced firing, but with little effect, for the order to retire was given and the skirmishers retreated in quick time, firing as they went to their supports.

Line was once more deployed, and the companies commenced firing by platoons, the battery meanwhile loading, opened fire with two guns at either end of the line. This mock cannonading was kept up for a time when the brigade cavalry advanced from the left and charged in a very spirited manner to clear the ground of the remnants of the enemy.

Soon after this the square deployed and formed in line, and, advancing in slow time, presented arms. The royal party then left the grounds.

Afterwards the Prince and suite drove to Lachine, where they arrived about three o'clock.

The royal party embarked in four of the Valorous' boats and were rowed across to the island of Dorval, the residence of Sir George Simpson.

When about mid-channel they were met by ten canoes, each manned by a dozen Indians, who formed a double line, between which the man-of-war boats passed, to the music of an Indian salute from those on board the canoes.

His Royal Highness only remained about half an hour at the house before he went on board an Indian canoe, to be paddled round the island to the before mentioned village of Caughnawaga, and back to Lachine. This was done to the evident pleasure of England's eldest son, after which he returned to town by steamer down the Lachine Rapids.

It was a great day for the good folks of the Eastern townships St. Hyacinthe and Sherbrooke, when on Thursday morning the Prince made his appearance among them.

The royal party left Montreal at ten, and reached the former place after an hour's ride by railway, the intermediate stations being decorated with spruce, mottoes, and words of welcome.

A platform had been erected for the occasion, on to which the Prince stepped from the car amid the cheers of nearly the whole population. He was received by the Mayor and Council, and the members of the Local Reception Committee. Carriages being in attendance, he drove to the College Building through streets abounding in triumphal arches, and rich in minor decorations. Here three addresses were presented to him, after which he ascended to the roof of the building, and had a fine view of the surrounding scenery, which is of extreme beauty. On his return to the station the cheers were renewed with undiminished enthusiasm. At noon he reached Sherbrooke, and received and replied to an address from the Mayor, after which he drove to the residence of Mr. Galt under a series of arches, and amid the ringing of church bells, and the cheers of thousands, many of the fair among whom threw bouquets into his carriage. The house stood on the summit of a hill commanding a pleasing view of the St. Francis River winding through a valley beneath, and was tastefully decorated with spruce, flowers, and mottoes. The ground in front was filled with ladies, so that the scene by no means lacked animation.

Immediately after entering, His Royal Highness held an informal levee in his traveling costume, there being no restrictions as to dress on the part of those presented.

At the conclusion of this ceremony a touching incident occurred, which speaks well for the good feeling of the Prince. A gentleman who had been long residing here, was, in his youth, signal midshipman on Nelson's flag-ship, the Victory, at the memorable battle of Trafalgar, and afterwards at the battle of Copenhagen, in both of which actions he earned medals, but unluckily was officer of the watch on board the sloop of war Carieux, when, during the blockade of Guadaloupe in 1809, she struck on a rock and was wrecked. This resulted in his being dismissed the service.

His Royal Highness, on being told of these circumstances, at once, in the exercise of his prerogative, and with much show of kindly warmth, restored him to the position in the Royal Navy which he had lost. The graceful manner in which this was signified, was only second to the generosity of the act itself.

Lunch followed, during which repast the Prince displayed his usual cordiality, and when he returned to the railway car, the demonstrations on all sides were as unbounded as human nature was capable of.

In the evening the Prince and suite were present by invitation, at a people's ball in the great room at Montreal, but did not dance. Shooting-coats and bonnets were plentifully displayed by the great unwashed, who honored the event with their presence.

Early on the next morning, Friday, the royal party departed by steamer for Ottawa.

It was a matter of general regret there that the weather was so wet and the day so advanced when His Royal Highness landed that evening, for rain and darkness combined, tended very much to lessen the effect of both the aquatic and street processions, although the former was still a sight rare in its picturesque beauty. The hundred and more bark canoes manned by six times as many men all in bright red, or blue shirts, brimmed hats, and white trowsers, and every canoe looking as new and showy as the men's shirts, and with a flag at the bow and another at the stern, while the six hundred odd paddles feathered with spray played in unison together, with the royal steamer advancing in the centre of this flotilla, and several other excursion steamers following at a respectful distance, made up a picture of unrivaled interest.

There was a triumphal arch under which royalty stepped from the steamer to the shore, greeted with the thrilling cheers of thousands gathered like pelicans and penguins—men and women—on the edge of the cliffs overlooking the river, and near the landing place and wherever else a view of the fleet could be obtained from the Falls of the Chaudiere, to the promontory at Rockliffe.

The Mayor was at the landing place in his robes, surrounded by the other municipal dignitaries, and delivered the usual address, which was as promptly replied to, after which the procession groped its way to the royal quarters.

At a few minutes before eleven on Saturday morning, I drove through streets as muddy as those of Melbourne at the time of the gold mania, to witness the laying of the corner-stone of the public buildings. On reaching the gates leading to the works, in front of which, and down the street as far as the Victoria Hotel, or Prince's quarters, an immense concourse of people had assembled. It was quite an adventure passing up the inner roadway to the desired spot, so crowded was it with men, women, and children, and so encumbered with all sorts of lumber.

Being occasionally a little wiser than my neighbors, I succeeded in taking my stand among the members of the Legislature in the appointed place, my ticket being the same as their own, and so had a full view of the interesting ceremony.

His Royal Highness, preceded by his equerries, and attended by the members of his suite, arrived in open carriages and full uniform at eleven, and took their places, together with the Canadian Ministers, on the canopied platform in the northeast angle of the building, and fronting the white marble block which was to become the great corner-stone.

The Prince stood in the centre of the dais, with the Governor General on his right, and the Duke of Newcastle on his left. The Legislature occupied the front seats on either side of the platform, and in their rear were amphitheatric stands, crowded with ladies and gentlemen. Behind the block, which was suspended from a derrick by a rope intertwined with red cord, and a pulley which was gilded, stood the architects, the contractors, the Mayor, and members of the City Council, together with other gentlemen locally connected with the works. One of these now commenced laying mortar on the base it was to rest on, after which, while the block swung from the derrick preparatory to the lowering, so as to be highly suggestive of a coffin, the chaplain of the Legislature advanced, and heightened the funereal effect by reading a short prayer, concluding with that of our Lord. The Prince then descended from the dais, and receiving a chastely worked silver trowel, stooped and spread the mortar over the foundation, immediately following which the block was lowered to its grave. The royal hand gave it three taps with the mallet; the Governor General came forward, and placing his hand on it said, "Your Royal Highness, the stone is now laid;" there was a glorious cheer, repeated again and again, from the assembled multitude, whose uncovered heads were hot in the sun, and the ceremony was over.

The gentlemen connected with the works were then introduced to the Prince, after which the royal party inspected the models, and walked round as far as the cliff overlooking the river, making the best progress they could over building materials, and, having there enjoyed the view, returned to the hotel which closely adjoined, where at noon a levee was held, the attendance being very full.

A drive and a public dejeuner followed, after which His Royal Highness descended on a crib of wood the timber slide on the right side of the Chaudiere Falls. He then sailed down the river in a six-oared boat to witness some canoe races, which were conducted with spirit.

In the evening the town was illuminated.

The Prince attended the English church on the Sunday, and at eight on the next morning a salute from the Ottawa field-battery proclaimed his departure.

CHAPTER XIV.

Enthusiasm and Warmth of the People—Torch-light and Firemen's Processions, and Departure of the Prince—The Scenery among the Thousand Isles—The Trip from Brockville—Arrival at Kingston—the Preparations for the Reception—The Disappointment of the Multitude, and the Obstinacy of the Orangemen, etc.

A PLEASANT country drive brought His Royal Highness to the village of Aylmer, where a steamer was in waiting to convey him up the river Ottawa, on his way to Brockville, and a large crowd had gathered from the neighboring townships, and triumphal arches spanned the roads.

It was pleasing to see the enthusiasm alike manifested by men, women, and children, to watch the flutter of pocket-handkerchiefs, and the waving of hats in the bright, warm sunshine. Here was another of those popular outbursts of genuine good-feeling which met Albert Edward throughout his travels in the New World. Decrepit age and elastic boyhood, young maidens and grave matrons, vied with each other in the chorus of welcome to England's eldest son, who acknowledged the flattering homage in a smiling manner which won all hearts.

He embarked without delay, and the steamer started immediately for Chats' Portage, where a fleet of canoes, furnished by the lumbermen of the district, were in waiting to convey him to Arnprior. The scenery along this part of the Ottawa was very fine, and called forth expressions of admiration from all.

The Prince takes to traveling with the zeal of an old tourist; so that he enjoyed the trip exceedingly, and such enjoyment was contagious, for he puts all around him in good spirits.

Arnprior was next reached, and here arches and garlands, and words of welcome again appeared in ornamental array; and cheers arose in a prodigality of joy which touched the heart of him for whom they were meant. The scene at Aylmer was re-enacted, and the beautiful weather enhanced the festive glory of the scene.

A line of carriages was here drawn up to convey the royal party to Almonte, distant eighteen miles. Here and there along the road, spruce and pine trees were planted, and wreaths of flowers hung out, while in several instances rustic belles, who had long been waiting in anxious expectation of the royal presence, threw bouquets into one or the other of the carriages, for they were uncertain as to which was the Prince's when they saw all in plain dress, and many let the Prince go by under the delusion that he had yet to come.

At Almonte there was another warm and picturesque demonstration, which gladdened the souls of all who either participated in or witnessed it. Grave men relaxed their features, and joined in the gay and brilliant scene of rejoicing. "Lo, England's heir has come! Welcome, welcome!" was one of the public inscriptions on an archway that spanned the road at the railway station. Here the Prince entered the royal car of the Grand Trunk Railway, and receded from the view in the midst of the same waving of hats, the same fluttering of handkerchiefs, the same ringing cheers of a loyal people, as before—of a people who felt that this visit was another tie that bound them to the parent land.

At twenty minutes to eight the train reached Brockville, when the greatest crowd that Brockville ever gathered was seen at the railway station.

On stepping on to the platform the cheering prevented anything else being heard for several minutes; but when this burst of joy and welcome had subsided, the Mayor of the town, accompanied by several members of the Common Council, advanced and read an address, to which His Royal Highness replied.

The Prince was conducted to his carriage, in which he took his seat beside the Governor General, with His Grace the Duke of Newcastle on the opposite seat. A torch-light procession of the firemen and others was in waiting, and a general illumination had the effect, in the midst of the triumphal arches, and other evergreen and floral decorations, of lending a species of fairy enchantment to the scene, which was one of the prettiest I have ever seen—far more so than that of the great Japanese ball. The flaring torches in the background, the exploding rockets high above, the brilliant transparencies spanning the streets, the Chinese lanterns swinging from roofs and windows and arches, the distant bonfires, the ringing church bells and the ringing cheers, combined to make a spectacle as brilliant as it was exciting. The procession then moved forward towards the steamer Kingston, at the wharf—the firemen and other torch-bearers following in the rear, and while saluted with fire-works, that lent a terribly lurid aspect to the whole, at every point of their progress.

The display was highly creditable to the townspeople, many of whom, however, went home very much disappointed at having been unable to catch a glimpse of the royal visitor.

On the next morning the Prince appeared on the steamer's deck at nine o'clock, and, being recognized by those ashore, there was great cheering. The steamer. being anchored a short distance midstream, was surrounded by numerous boats filled with those eager to see him. At a quarter to eleven he gratified a general wish by coming ashore in a small boat, and driving through the principal streets of the town. All the resources of the place were taxed to provide carriages for the party, and with tolerable success, although there was a great want of uniformity in the size, color, and shape of the vehicles and horses enlisted in the service. The Prince took his place in an open carriage by the side of the Governor General, while the Duke of Newcastle and Earl St. Germains sat opposite. Lord Lyons and the suite followed in separate carriages. The streets were very dusty, owing partly to the crowd that ran alongside and before and behind the Prince's carriage, which was guarded by two policemen, one at either side, armed with batons. The royal party had to keep their eyes half shut for a while, but afterwards the clouds diminished both in volume and density. The drive lasted about half an hour.

At twenty minutes past twelve the Kingston steamed away, and in a few minutes afterwards was pursuing her course among the Thousand Islands.

The weather was fortunately warm and sunny, and the granite islands were seen to great advantage. Here nature appeared to have fancifully prepared a grand proscenium to feast the traveler's eye, for nothing could have exceeded in singularity the scene that presented itself. The mighty St. Lawrence—the Iroquois of the red man—here, in ages long elapsed, urged its vexed waters, before pent up in the vast inland basin of North America, against that portion of the primitive barrier which visibly extends from the granite mountains of the East over to the dividing ridge between the wild regions of Hudson Bay and the tributary waters of the Ottawa and the St. Lawrence; and here, by some tremendous effort which has evidently shaken the whole country from Kingston, at the eastern extremity of Lake Ontario, to the other side of the region through which the granite ridge pursues its northwesterly course, the river has at one time rushed over a sheet of cascades and rapids miles in breadth, but which have long disappeared under the wearing influence of time. Island succeeded island, group succeeded group, till the eye almost wearied of the succession. Most of these were beautifully wooded, and many of them so low and flat as to suggest to the mind the tranquil prospect of an Italian lagoon. Others again were split and rent into a variety of fantastic forms, forming views of peculiar wildness. A turn of the channel disclosed a new labyrinth, while we passed under a dark wall of rock, coated with moss and lichens that had likely flourished there for generations, and from whose bare and rugged top the hoary fir lifted its sombre head. Further on a lighthouse stood perched on a rock, and further still another. All was still and lonely—the cerulean vault above, the tranquil tide below, the sunshine over all. Was the poetry of the scene felt by that fair young man gazing so calmly, so thoughtfully, upon it from the deck of that steamer over which the rich tints of a Prince of Wales standard flaunted in the sun? If I were a novelist I should say "Yes."

Then another fairy picture presented itself in groves, growing, as it were, out of the water, and seeming to bar our further progress, till suddenly the sylvan curtain was withdrawn, and the eye wandered over a wide sweep of water dotted here and there with a few small rocks, and bounded by the endless forest of the mainland. Towns and villages were meanwhile passed on either shore, and once a lonely fisherman was seen practicing his gentle art in a small row-boat.

The islands extended the whole way from Brockville to Kingston, but the most compact cluster was seen in front of Alexandria Bay. Here the view was exquisite. A wide expanse of river reposed mirror-like beneath the rich autumnal sky, and this sheet of water reflected the forms of an assemblage of islets of the most picturesque, diversified, and inviting aspect; here a naked crag, there a majestic bouquet, yonder a clump of trees or a perfect island supporting a solitary stem. Such happy confusion, such an indiscriminate sprinkling of all shapes and sizes and varieties of vegetation was unique in the extreme.

As we neared Kingston, after leaving Brockville, the channel by which we advanced and which was formed by Long Island, on the borders of which were several islets, and by the mainland, Pittsburg and Kingston, gradually widened. These were well wooded, and the larger one disclosed several neat farms.

Further on appeared the strong fortification crowning the promontory of Point Henry, about a hundred feet above the level of the lake, for here Ontario and the St. Lawrence meet. This commanded a narrow entrance between Cedar Island and Hamilton Cove; and here, on a verdant slope, fronting the picturesque rocks of Cedar Island and commanding a beautiful view of the opening of the lake, stood the Garrison Hospital, built of dark blue stone, with a tin roof and veranda in front.

Advancing beyond, a prospect still finer unfolded itself to the delighted eye. The opening of the lake was observable in the distance, and the town of Kingston began to show itself on the right. Away we went past Navy Bay and Point Frederick, between which, during the American war, British frigates used to lie in waiting. Ships, powder magazines, forts, and batteries, told the tale of the past. A dangerous shoal, running off from Point Frederick, obliged us to make a large curve before entering the harbor; but this afforded a fine opportunity for observing the scenery, including the expanse of Ontario, the broad current between Long Island and the town, the fine estuary of the St. Lawrence, across which, over a distance of eighteen hundred feet in length, a wooden bridge extends; the houses, and churches, and market-place of the town rising above each other on a gentle declivity, and spreading two miles or more along the margin of the lake, the wharfs and shipping, and the distant forest on either side.

Kingston was one of the first settlements of the French missionaries on the great fresh-water seas of the New World. It was then called by its Indian name, Cataraqui, and was strengthened with a large fort, erected by order of the Governor General of Canada.

And now we were near the wharf where His Royal Highness was appointed to land, according to the original arrangement, but which consummation had been considered doubtful since the departure from Brockville, for it was there communicated by telegraph that the Orangemen were determined to take part in the procession, arrayed in all the trappings of their Order, and it had been signified that His Royal Highness would not take part in such a procession, for the reason that it was offensive to the Roman Catholic body, which had protested against it.

Immediately upon arrival the Governor General sent to the Mayor, asking the question whether or not the Orangemen intended to forego joining the procession in their robes, with the attendant banners. The answer was in the negative. The Governor General—acting likely under higher authority—then intimated that if they did not agree to dispense with their party demonstration within an hour the Prince would remain on board the steamer. The hour elapsed, the Orangemen were firm in their decision to hold out, and the Prince, as a consequence, did not land. The procession, which had been formed at great length, including all the public officers and clergy, and the volunteer cavalry of Kingston, was, therefore, left to disperse in the gray twilight. People, under the combined influence of excitement and disappointment, now stared at each other in blank wonder at the unfortunate turn of events, and after that began to speculate concerning the ultimate result.

The Prince slept on board the steamer that night, and the town was illuminated, although not as generally as if His Royal Highness had been ashore, according to original expectation. Thousands of visitors crowded the streets and hotels, unable to obtain beds.

On the following morning the Mayor and others went on board the royal steamer, in the endeavor to arrange matters so as to enable His Royal Highness to go ashore—the Orange party, meanwhile, parading the streets in full party costume, and forming a long procession. But the result was that such, under the attendant circumstances, was declined, His Royal Highness proposing to receive addresses on board the steamer instead. Thus the first shadow had fallen across the New World path of the future King of England, affording another evidence that there is no pleasure without an alloy of pain, no event in human history but is marred by some element of discord, whether individual or national. It was, therefore, hardly to be expected that the pæan of welcome would not be marred by some factional croaking, or that the cloven foot of party prejudice would not intrude among the crowd.

The following letter will explain the cause of the unfortunate difficulty:

MONTREAL, August 30, 1860.

MY DEAR SIR EDMUND,—I am informed that it is the intention of the Orangemen of Toronto to erect an arch on the line of route which it is desired by the citizens that the Prince of Wales shall take on Friday next, and to decorate it with the insignia of their association. I am also told that they mean to appear in the procession similarly decorated with party badges.

It is obvious that a display of this nature on such an occasion is likely to lead to religious feud and breach of the peace, and it is my duty to prevent, as far as I am able, the exposure of the Prince to supposed participation in a scene so much to be deprecated and so alien to the spirit in which he visits Canada.

I trust you may be able to persuade those who are concerned in these preparations to abandon their intentions; but that there may be no mistake, I hope you will inform them that, in the event of such an arch being erected, I shall advise the Prince to refuse to pass under it, and enter the town by another street; and further, if any Orange demonstration, or any other demonstration of a party character is persisted in, I shall advise the Prince to abandon his visit to the town altogether.

I have heard, but with less certainty, that a similar demonstration is contemplated at Kingston. I need not say that my remarks apply equally to that or any other town. I am, etc. NEWCASTLE.

To the Right Hon. Sir E. W. HEAD.

The Kingston left the harbor at three on the next afternoon, the occasion being distinguished by a royal salute, fired from the Market Battery by the volunteer artillery company of the town. There were not many assembled at the water-side at the time, and the cheers were of a less enthusiastic character than those given on his departure from any other place visited.

The Orangemen remained in procession in the street parallel with the water-side up to this time, although their numbers were fewer by one half than on the previous day, many having been compelled to return to their homes in the country, in consequence of the approaching harvest.

Immediately after the last shots from the battery

had died away, an indignation meeting was held by the citizens generally, who, I may remark, entertained a strong sympathy for the Orange party. I am sorry to say that the chief speaker took anything but an unbigoted and impartial view of the relations of one section of the community to another. He dragged down the religious faith of a people from the lofty standard of individual responsibility and moral influence to do battle in political and party contests. He and others were evidently disposed to revive the rancor and religious hate which long ago cast a stain upon the people of Canada. Historical recollections were revived, and the concourse was told how the Orangemen were the representatives of those who fought side by side with the illustrious William, and bled with him in the cause of a common religion and a common liberty. That banner they carried to-day had floated in triumph over the walls of Derry, and led the way when the conquerors of the Boyne waded to the neck to oppose their foes. And yet they were thus ignored. They deserved better. Was it right for the Roman Catholics in Lower Canada to assemble all their bishops from Sandwich to Gaspe to meet His Royal Highness on his first landing at Quebec, to induce him to visit their colleges and nunneries, and when the Church of England was hardly represented to allow these to gather and pass before him in all the pageantry of feudal days, and then, after such a recognition of the religion of the people in that section, altogether refuse similar privileges to the representatives of Protestantism in Upper Canada?

Then followed some rather strong language, in which the names of the Governor General and the members for the town and county were received with loud groans.

A still loftier personage interested in colonial affairs also came in for a slight share of the unpopularity caused by this party feeling.

Thus, it will be seen, the worst consequences arose from the stubborn determination of the body of Orangemen to parade the insignia of their order to the annoyance of the Roman Catholic portion of the community, and that, notwithstanding an official intimation that such a display was contrary to the wishes of the highest authorities of the crown, as well as being subversive of good order. A greater insult could hardly have been offered to the Prince and crown than was brought about by this fanatical adherence to party creed and party resolves. "You don't respect the Prince," I heard one man say to one of the gentlemen in red and yellow. "Yes, we do; but we respect Protestantism more." This is laying to their souls the flattering unction that they are something more than what they are. Protestantism, it is to be hoped, is totally independent of Orangeism.

CHAPTER XV.

The Landing at Toronto—Fifty Thousand Spectators—Four Thousand Children in Chorus—The Procession—Decorations on the Route—An Orange Arch—The Royal Party Annoyed—The Mayor in Hot Water—Illuminations—Addresses—The Prince Playing at Rackets—Reception at Osgoode Hall—The Prince Enrolled as a Barrister—The Ball—Beautiful Appearance of the Ball-room—Another Orange Outrage—Departure for Collingwood, etc., etc.

THE Orange demonstration so unwisely persisted in, which prevented the landing of the Prince at Kingston, operated with an equally unfortunate result at his next place of call, Belleville, for the Orangemen, who had paraded themselves in that town while the royal steamer remained in harbor, left by railway, to the number of about two hundred, at four o'clock on the morning following her departure, for the same destination. No sooner did they arrive at Belleville, at six, than they formed in procession, arrayed in scarf and badge, and marshaled by a man in harlequin costume, with their band playing party tunes as the vanguard.

By the cheers that met them here and there, as they passed along, it was evident that popular feeling was not opposed to them, although popular ignorance may have had a good deal to do with that. They took up their quarters at a hotel in the town, out of one of the windows of which they hung their flag. Their presence, of course, created much excitement among the populace, half of whom appeared to be in favor of the Orangemen holding out, and the other half of them giving in; but the wearers of the red and yellow were firm to their motto of "No surrender."

Soon after nine o'clock the Mayor went on board the Kingston, to acquaint the Duke of Newcastle with the resolution of the Orangemen to join in the procession if the Prince landed, as also to allow their party-colored arch, erected in one of the streets, to remain standing.

After his return from this interview, the Mayor mounted a platform and addressed the people. He said that he had seen the Duke, and heard that the Prince greatly regretted that he should not have an opportunity of seeing their town, more especially as they had gone to so much trouble and expense in their decorations.

At a quarter before ten the Kingston left the harbor on her way to Cobourg. The gloom occasioned by this event was oppressive; the triumphal arches had been erected in vain, and the loyal inhabitants were overcome with disappointment. The Orangemen returned to Kingston without disturbance, and I proceeded on to Cobourg, where I found everybody on the tip-toe of expectation. Triumphal arches, transparencies, and other devices were abundant; volunteer cavalry patrolled the streets; stands were built to accommodate sight-seers; the Town Hall had a beautiful platform and canopy in front, and was internally beautifully decorated; and all promised well, for the Orangemen of the place had agreed not to parade the insignia of their party.

Darkness succeeded daylight, and still no Prince came; but shortly before ten the royal steamer arrived, and was saluted by the Kingston Volunteer Artillery. It was then announced that His Royal Highness would land at ten, attend the citizens' ball, and sleep ashore at the house of Mr. Smith, the Postmaster General. Accordingly, soon after ten the landing took place, and open carriages being in attendance for the illustrious visitor and others, he stepped into one in company with the Duke and Governor General, when, to his surprise, the horses were turned aside and the carriage was drawn to the Town Hall by a party of gentlemen of the place in full evening costume. The cheers along the line of route were vociferous, and must have gladdened the heart of him for whom they were intended. An address was presented to him by the Mayor and Corporation, to which he briefly replied.

He then entered the ball room, which was tastefully arranged and by no means crowded, there not being more than two hundred people present. There, for the first time in America, he danced in plain evening dress, and walked about the room with his partner on his arm.

He danced every dance till a quarter to four, and then drove home.

On the following morning, at a few minutes before ten, he left the house for the railway station, escorted by a detachment of cavalry. He was in plain morning dress, and from the house to the station was enveloped in a cloud of dust.

He traveled in a special train towards Peterboro,

his departure being distinguished by the firing of a royal salute. On reaching Rice Lake, where the railway is laid across a bridge three miles long, the royal party embarked in a small steamer named the Otanabee, and sailed among a group of fir-covered islets. On the north side of the lake the Indians had erected an arch, and they had mustered there in canoes. Their chief presented a written address to His Royal Highness, signed in Indian and English, after which he tendered to the Prince a present of birch baskets full of Indian work, which was accepted. The train was then re-entered and moved on to Peterboro, where crowds had assembled at the station, and the municipal authorities of the town and county presented addresses, which were replied to in the usual manner.

The party did not remain long here before proceeding to Port Hope, where arches were plentiful and the inhabitants appeared to be in a state of exuberant joy. The Town Hall was fitted up for his accommodation, and thither he drove and received addresses from the town and county, to which he gave one reply. He then went up stairs to a public luncheon which had been provided, and at which the usual toasts of the Queen, Prince Consort, and Prince of Wales were proposed and responded to with genuine and tremendous cheers. The enthusiasm manifested at all points cannot well be described, and there was not a cloud to sully the brightness of this happy morning.

Soon afterwards the party re-entered the cars and proceeded to Whitby, where a repetition of the same glorious scene occurred. Here three addresses were read, and as many replies made by His Royal Highness, who, immediately following their delivery, drove off towards the wharf to embark on board the Kingston for Toronto. The people scampered after his carriage in thousands, and were seemingly wild with delight.

From Whitby to Toronto he was escorted by a

dozen or more excursion steamers, which number increased as the royal steamer neared the city. At a few minutes before seven the landing took place, in the presence of fifty thousand people collected on the wharf and grand stand, and amid salutes from volunteer artillery and elsewhere, and the huzzas of the mighty throng, that greeted him rapturously. A magnificent canopy had been erected on the spot, and here an address was delivered by the Mayor. To this he read his reply in his naturally clear and emphatic manner.

The procession was then formed, and the grandest sight of the kind that had yet attended his progress in the New World, was exhibited.

On entering the first street, that portion of the procession within the inclosure passed under a magnificent triumphal arch, after the Roman style.

Arch succeeded arch after this as the procession passed along the streets, attended by cheers, without a single pause.

On coming to the Orange arch, supposed to be in shape an exact imitation of the memorable gate of Derry, with a transparency on the pediment representing King William the Third mounted on a white horse, in the act of crossing the Boyne, the Prince and the Duke of Newcastle eyed it with unpleasant surprise. "Why, they've King William there," was the remark of one of them. The Mayor had assured the Duke that there was nothing of a party character about it; and here his statement was ocularly disproved.

Early on the following morning the Duke wrote to the Mayor on the subject, but this did not result in the removal of the obnoxious picture, for, to the Duke's surprise, it was alleged to be an equestrian drawing of the Prince of Wales, in the attitude in which King William is commonly represented. This, however, did not satisfy the Duke, who reproached the Mayor for a want of candor.

After a long drive by a circuitous route, the royal party reached Government House, which they entered amid a final outburst of cheers. The tens of thousands then wandered to and fro about the streets, looking at the illuminations. These were both very numerous and very fine, Osgoode Hall being a beautiful constellation, and many of the public and private buildings were gorgeously illuminated.

On Saturday morning the levee was held in the reception room of Government House, commencing at eleven o'clock, and ending at two. Thirteen addresses were here presented, but to only four of these did His Royal Highness reply. After luncheon the Prince, accompanied by the Governor General's aid-de-camp and one or two others, drove in a city cab to a public racket-court, where he threw off his coat and engaged in the fashionable game of rackets with much zest. It was soon rumored in the immediate neighborhood, and some young men procured a ladder reaching to the glass roof of the building, the doors of which were meanwhile closed to the general public. There, as the cobwebs partially screened the players from their view, they broke the windows, and the debris falling in had the effect of shortening the stay of His Royal Highness, who returned to the cab in waiting, and drove back to his residence, in front of which, during the afternoon and evening, a floating cloud of sight-seers congregated in the hope of catching a glimpse of the royal visitor. At twenty minutes past nine he left with the Governor General, the Duke of Newcastle, and Earl St. Germains, in a closed carriage, to attend the ball, or reception, as it was called, at Osgoode Hall, followed by the other members of the suite in separate carriages.

On his arrival at the building, which includes the most chastely ornamented and magnificent law courts, not only in America, but the whole world, St. George's Hall, Liverpool, perhaps, excepted, he was received by the Judges in their robes, and conducted through the corridor of white Caen stone to the central atrium, where he took his stand for a few moments on the low dais prepared for him. The dancing, which had been going forward for about half an hour previously, ceased, and there was a general cheer, followed by "God save the Queen," from the band of the Royal Canadian Rifles. This concluded, the Treasurer of the Law Society advanced, bowed, and read an address to His Royal Highness, which was replied to.

Dancing was now recommenced, but, owing to their being only one band, the Prince's set (the only one formed) was soon environed by a wall of crinoline, which hardly allowed room enough for the dancers. After the second dance, however, the throng, numbering about eight hundred, dispersed into the hall, corridors, and other rooms. Soon after this another band commenced playing in the gallery above the central hall, and here the votaries of Terpsichore betook themselves in considerable numbers. Later still, His Royal Highness proceeded there, and this had the effect of making it the most crowded part of the building, which latter looked more like courts of the Alhambra in days of yore than law courts. The whole was lighted on the principle adopted by the British Houses of Parliament, the inner roofing being of stained glass, behind which were gas jets that poured their lustre in mellow tints upon the festive scene below, illuminating the elaborately carved stone pillars supporting the galleries and roof, and contrasting with the darker shades of the tesselated pavement. It was gorgeous and unique, and, save an occasional display of choice flowers arranged in the vestibule and main hall, there was little or no attempt at any other ornament.

The gravity of the law was laid aside, mirth reigned supreme, and consulting chambers and retiring rooms, instead of being filled with papers and grave men, in horse-hair wigs and bombazine gowns, poring over old parchments, were turned upside down with crinoline, shawls, looking-glasses, and the little odds and ends of female apparel.

At a few minutes past eleven His Royal Highness conducted Mrs. Cameron, the wife of the Treasurer, to supper, which was served in the Practice Court in the west wing, and was of a very *recherché* character. Here the toasts of the Queen, Prince Consort, and Prince of Wales, were proposed and responded to with the highest enthusiasm. Dancing was afterwards resumed, and continued till five minutes past twelve, His Royal Highness having taken part in every dance during his stay.

On the next morning (Sunday) he drove to church, without passing under the Orange arch. This aroused the indignation of a few of the bigoted followers of King William, and during divine service they proceeded to their lodges and procured five of the orthodox flags of their party, with which they returned and decorated the arch. This insulting conduct aroused in its turn the wrath of a city Alderman, who forthwith obtained a ladder, and was in the act of ascending it, with a view of pulling the flags down, when some Orangemen—who had taken their stand on the top of the arch, imagining, perhaps, in their ardor, that they were defending the real instead of the imitation gate of Derry—shook the ladder till the Alderman had fallen to the ground, after which they succeeded in breaking the ladder itself. A master of a lodge then interfered, but with an equally fruitless result. The flags remained flying when the Prince came out of church, and within view of the royal party. There was a large crowd assembled, and a good deal of excitement and disorder prevailed. One Orangeman conducted himself in a riotous manner, and was taken into custody, upon which another of his party attempted to rescue him. The object of this was to create a disturbance favorable to forcing the royal carriage to pass under the arch—a proceeding which some of these wretched blackguards had openly talked about while the flags were being put up, and as the Prince emerged from the church. Had there been the slightest practical attempt at carrying out this design there would have been bloodshed, and the Battle of Toronto would hereafter have occupied as conspicuous a place in the pages of the future historian, as the recent conduct of the Orangemen in Canada will, notwithstanding.

In the afternoon the Duke of Newcastle, Earl St. Germains, and the Governor General, after visiting the University, walked down to inspect the objectionable arch, and, being recognized by some of the Orange party, they were hooted and followed in a rather threatening manner.

On the following Monday morning at a few minutes before nine, several thousands had assembled in and around the amphitheatre at the railway station for the purpose of witnessing the departure of His Royal Highness for Collingwood, ninety-four miles northward from Toronto. These greeted him with loud cheers as he appeared in view and stepped into the open car, decorated with flags, embossed crowns, Prince's plumes, imitation maple leaves, and ottomans, which had been provided for the occasion by the Northern Railway Company of Canada.

Davenport was the first station arrived at, and the train passed slowly, in order to give those present an opportunity of seeing the Prince, and *vice versa*.

At Richmond Hill there was a few minutes' stoppage, to take in water. A neat arch here spanned the track, and a large concourse stood gathered, uttering vociferous acclamations, to which the Buffalo band on board the train joined "God save the Queen."

At Aurora there was a stoppage for wood. Two arches were erected across the track at this point, one of which was Masonic and the other Orange. There, was some excitement and annoyance displayed, here, owing to the presence of the Orange arch. However the royal car passed under it, and, arriving at Newmarket, stopped a few minutes. The crowd was here very dense, amounting to nearly three thousand persons. A large stand or platform was filled with ladies, gentlemen and children of an agricultural aspect. A salute was fired, and an address presented by the local authorities.

At Bradford a stoppage of ten minutes occurred. The concourse was here greater than at any former place, and the preparations more extensive. A handsome dais occupied the centre of an amphitheatre, and to this His Royal Highness was conducted to receive an address. Two large arches were erected within view, and three companies of firemen and two bands of music were among the other attractions. The municipal authorities and leading men of the town were in full evening dress. An address was presented, to which the Prince read a reply. Cheers rang again and again after this.

Women put their butterflies in motion, or rather their cambrics into a flutter, and said "Where is he?" "There he is!" and lifted their children on to the shoulders of men and seemed wild with delight, while the heroes of the plough and lords of the stubble opened wide their mouths with sheer curiosity. Young ladies endeavored to make themselves as conspicuous as possible, and threw bouquets into the royal car. The Prince smiled, bowed, looked happy, and pleased all.

Craigville was hurried by, and Barrie, the county town of Simcoe, was reached, where the train stopped another ten minutes, and the Bradford scene was more than re-enacted. A handsome pavilion, commanding a fine view of the town, the bay, and the lake, stretching away further than the eye could carry, was erected near the track in the rear of the station. To this pavilion His Royal Highness was conducted, passing under on his way a tastefully built agricultural arch, surmounted by a Prince of Wales' plume made of sheaves of wheat. The firemen and Barrie Volunteer Rifles were present in full force, a band discoursed pleasant music, and seven or eight thousand people cheered. The County Council and Magistrates presented addresses respectively, which were separately replied to.

Angus was passed slowly, during which a gun was fired. Here, as well as at the two next stations—arches were erected, and near one of them a gentleman, with bare legs and a peculiar wag of the head, was indulging in the pastime of playing the bagpipes, to the intense delight of some small boys.

Collingwood was next reached, and here the reception, although warm enough for the size of the place, was second to that of Barrie. In the number of its arches, however, it surpassed Barrie, but they were of less imposing appearance. A pavilion stood near the station, and in this two addresses were presented to His Royal Highness, to which he returned separate replies. Some hundreds of school children then sang two verses of the national anthem, at the conclusion of which the band struck up the same, and the Prince proceeded to the steamer Rescue—only a short distance removed—and which sailed immediately after the royal party had gone aboard, on a trip on Georgian Bay, an inlet of Lake Huron. Luncheon was at once served, and after a sail of an hour and a quarter the party returned. Two other excursion steamers escorted the Rescue, and they were crowded with cheering masses. The Prince engaged himself in conversation with those around him during the time thus spent, and impressed all who saw him with the same favorable opinion as he has earned among all ranks elsewhere. The scenery around Collingwood is not very inviting; but "anything for a change," as the play says.

His Royal Highness and suite returned to the train shortly before three, and arrived in Toronto at half-past six.

A display of fire-works took place between eight and nine in the area of the amphitheatre; but a poorer exhibition hardly ever called together twenty thousand people. A torch-light procession of the firemen followed immediately afterwards.

Tuesday was a busy day for His Royal Highness, and equally so for those who, like myself, went over the same ground with him.

It was a pitiful sight, although under opposite circumstances it would have been a fine one, to watch the thousands that crowded the streets between ten and eleven on that dreary morning—to see them all making for the one point, and that one point the amphitheatre near the water's side. There were school children marshaled in long lines, and dressed in a dozen varieties of costume, the girls with wet frocks and dirty stockings—for before many of them reached the desired spot it began to rain—and the boys with their trowsers turned up at the feet. There were citizens and folks from the country of all descriptions, and Sons of Temperance carrying banners, and rifle companies in sombre garb.

These assembled by the hour of eleven, in a dense mass, in and around the amphitheatre adjoining the royal pavilion, and remained in eager waiting for the arrival of the Prince. But it was not till nearly a quarter to twelve that the open carriage, with the hood over it, drawn by four horses, passed under the triumphal arch into the inclosure, where the twenty or thirty thousand were congregated. Then there was a long and glorious cheer, which did the heart good to listen to, and His Royal Highness alighted, and taking his stand in the pavilion, listened to an address from the officers and members of the Royal Canadian Yacht Club, all of whom were in their uniform standing on each side of the pavilion.

He then walked to the rear of the structure, where a wide sweep of the lake was commanded, with the fourteen first and second class yachts that were to run together drawn up for starting in the foreground. He went as far as the water's edge to give the signal for starting, but owing to some mismanagement a delay occurred, and His Royal Highness, preferring shelter to the storm, retired under the railway station. At this stage of the proceedings the crowd broke through the lines of the policemen and rushed in disorder around the royal suite. Meanwhile, the wet school children were singing two verses of the national anthem, and the royal suite were anxious to be off; but His Royal Highness was resolved to see the start notwithstanding the uncomfortable surroundings. One man pushed his way forward with an old umbrella, which he held up, possibly with the best intentions, and addressing the Prince, said, "Will you take my umbrella, sir?" His Royal Highness turned away with a smile, and the favor was declined.

In a few moments after this the signal for the start was fired. That instant the jibs and foresails of the yachts were hoisted, and, veering round, they all went off well together towards the first buoy, near the eastern entrance. Out they stood, with a full spread of canvas, and the heavy breeze bending them freely over. The thousands lining the esplanade shouted, the children sang, the disorder ashore became greater, and His Royal Highness, expressing regret that he was unable to await the result, entered his carriage and drove away, followed by a tremendous outburst of cheering.

It spoke well for the enthusiasm and loyalty of the people that the rush to the Park after this was equal to that at the amphitheatre, notwithstanding the rain.

The St. George's and St. Andrew's Societies and the Highland Brigade were present in the neighborhood of the canvas-covered stand erected near the foundation stone of the Queen's statue in the grounds fronting the University.

Thousands held umbrellas in the background.

At half-past twelve the Prince arrived, and this was the signal for a salute from the field battery. He was received on alighting from his carriage by the Mayor and Dr. McCaul, the President of the Univeristy, and by them conducted over a carpeted pathway to the stand, passing on their way a couple of Russian guns captured by the British at Sebastopol, and presented to Toronto by the Queen.

The cheering was immense during this time. Silence having been restored, Dr. McCaul read an address to His Royal Highness, asking him on behalf of the inhabitants of the city to lay the foundation stone of a pedestal for a statute of the Queen. A silver trowel was then handed to him, and he at once proceeded to spread some mortar on the stone. The builder completed the trowel-work, and the stone was lowered by a pulley. Royalty then applied the square and plumb, and giving the stone three gentle taps with a mallet, pronounced it laid, and the Park inaugurated.

A review of the active volunteer force followed. The several corps were drawn up eastward of the stand. The evolutions commenced by the troops presenting arms, while the bands played the national anthem, His Royal Highness, meanwhile, having advanced to the east front of the platform. They next shouldered arms, and forming fours right, marched past him in quick step to the music of the "British Grenadiers."

His Royal Highness then drove to the University, where he was received by the Chancellor, President, and others, and conducted to the Convocation Hall. A large number of ladies and gentlemen were here assembled, and the students lined a passage through which the Prince passed to the dais at the head of the hall, on which a throne had been erected.

The Chancellor, Justice Burns, then read an address of welcome, which was graciously replied to by the Prince, after which the former proposed the enrollment of His Royal Highness as a student of the University. The motion was carried amid loud cheering, after which the Registrar presented the college book to the Prince, who at once signed it.

The Prince was next conducted through the Museum and class-rooms, but not on to the roof, as originally intended, owing to the state of the weather.

After this he drove back to Government House. At three, the weather having moderated, he re-entered his carriage, and proceeded to the Botanical Gardens.

A large amphitheatre or rustic pavilion had been erected inside, with a reserved place in its centre for the royal party. To this they were conducted, and here an address from the Directors of the Horticultural Society was read to His Royal Highness. In his reply he said, "I shall be content if the tree which I am about to plant flourish as your youthful city has already done." The tree alluded to was a maple, and after it had been lowered into its place, a few spadefulls of earth were thrown about its roots by royal hands. He then walked to the tents, where some flowers and fruits had been placed for exhibition, and after a short stay returned to the gateway, in the midst of a disorderly crowd that gathered round, and stared at and followed him to his carriage, making it a matter of considerable difficulty for him to work his way through, and still worse for his suite behind. His exertion reddened his face; but he laughed heartily, with the Governor General, when he reached the carriage.

The Normal School, to which he drove next, was less than half a mile off; so many of those who had gathered in and near the gardens scampered after him to have another glimpse of the royal face. Here an address was presented, a song was sung, and bouquets thrown; "Albert Edward" was also written in the visitor's book.

Knox's College was afterwards visited, where a similar scene occurred, after which His Royal Highness returned to the Government House. Meanwhile, the two or three hundred composing the Belleville deputation were walking about the streets with their badges on their breasts.

The deputation, which included the Mayor and nine members of the City Council, had been received by His Royal Highness at two o'clock, and in reply to their expressions of regret, and invitation to return, in which case nothing should occur to mar the harmony of the visit, the Prince said that it pleasedh im to see them, and he was convinced of the loyalty of the people, and that the doings of a certain party were against the wishes of the majority. He would blot all unpleasant recollections from his memory, and on returning home assure Her Majesty of the loyalty of the citizens of Belleville; but prior engagements would prevent his visiting the town, otherwise he should have been happy to do so.

The ball in the Crystal Palace was the next great event of the day, and presented a magnificent spectacle; but there were several drawbacks attending it. The room was built in the form of a parallelogram, and tastefully decorated with flags. It was provided with full length galleries down each side, and a separate division on the ground floor for supper.

The Prince did not arrive till a quarter past eleven, and as dancing did not commence before, he opened it with the Lady Mayoress as his partner. Those who had come early found the time drag on very slowly. Moreover, the whole building was uncomfortably cold and draughty, and remained so during the whole evening. So much was this felt that blue noses, attenuated features, cold hands, and occasional shivers were general. Ladies pronounced it the most unbecoming ball they had ever attended, and the complaint was universal.

The Prince was dressed in his uniform, and, with his usual penchant for dancing, took part in every dance till the programme was exhausted, soon after four. Then a general scramble for hats, caps, and coats took place, which resulted in nearly everybody carrying away somebody else's garments instead of their own, despite their being ticketed.

At eleven o'clock on the next morning the royal guest left by special train for London, calling at Guelph and other places *en route*. He was loudly cheered on his departure by several thousands assembled in the amphitheatre and its vicinity. Brompton and Georgetown were the first stopping places, and at each a large portion of the inhabitants had collected to give England's heir a welcome.

Guelph came next, and here a splendid reception awaited him. He was escorted to a pavilion fronting the Town Hall by the Mayor and other functionaries, who were in full dress. A salute was fired, nearly a thousand children sang "God save the Queen," and addresses were presented from the town and county respectively. A handsome arch was erected within view, and other decorations abounded on all sides.

The royal party returned to the cars in the midst of rapturous cheering.

At Petersburg an address was presented in German, and an impromptu reply returned to it by His Royal Highness, an incident which delighted the Germans. At Stratford another address was presented, and a salute fired from logs pierced for cannon, there being no metal guns in the place. Truly, necessity is the mother of invention.

St. Mary's was passed slowly, to the music of a thousand cheers, and at a few minutes past four the royal train reached London. Here the reception was very enthusiastic, and the display creditable to the town. The royal party stepped into their carriage and drove without delay to a pavilion, where addresses were read by the Mayor and Warden of the county respectively, to each of which the Prince read a reply. Cheers were then given with much gusto, and the Prince re-entered his carriage; the moment after which a rude brute lifted His Royal Highness' hat off, and said "Let's have a look at you." This outrage was borne with excellent temper by the Prince, who gracefully retook his hat from the fellow.

There was considerable disorder just now, the crowd rushing in on all sides, in the midst of which the royal carriage moved away, and took its place in the procession. At one point the horses drawing the royal carriage were stopped, and several halts occurred through the people blocking up the way.

The cavalry force of the town acted as the guard of honor, and their patience was severely tested. However, he reached the Tecumseh Hotel in safety, and dined there at half-past seven, after which he retired early.

CHAPTER XVI.

The London of America—Its Features and its Differences—Sarnia—The Indians and their Eloquence—Presentation of Medals—The Prince's Journey to Niagara—Fort Erie—Arrival at Niagara—Illumination of the Falls, etc., etc.

I AM writing of the city of London, situated on the banks of the Thames, in the county of Middlesex. The London of the New World is a Lancashire village, compared with its namesake of the Old World. It is a rural-looking semi-civilized spot, with a clownish population, for the most part, that have none of the wit or discipline of a London mob in England.

The city has only been incorporated fifteen years, yet it boasts of two daily newspapers, which speaks well for the tastes of many of the community. The population is about twelve thousand, the great majority of whom are Protestants.

London, which is also called the Forest City, is the centre of an extensive agricultural district. The streets of the city cross each other at right angles, and the shops and houses are chiefly of one or two stories, although there are several fine buildings and many averagely so. There is no doubt that London will eventually become a fine city, but the absence of shipping will always operate against it. As Cuzco was to Peru, so will London be hereafter to Western Canada. I strolled round the city on the night after the reception, to see the illuminations. I passed through Pall Mall and Piccadilly, and had a good look at Westminster Bridge, and after that at Blackfriars Bridge, both spanning the Thames, which is here less than two hundred feet wide. But I saw in them no splendid thoroughfares, no monuments of stone-work or triumphs of engineering skill. Wood, not many years hewn from the forest of Windsor, which environs the city, was the material of which both the bridges, and the Pall Mall and Piccadilly houses were built, and the contrast between the things of the old London and the new became more and more marked. Verily, I said, this is London only in name. I meet nothing familiar here. There is nothing to remind me of the great city of the world but so many names that appear before me as if in mockery. But go on and flourish, thou young giant, fresh from the primeval forest. The surest way to reach a mark is to aim beyond it.

With these reflections, I walked on, my path lighted by the reflections of gaseliers shaped into Prince of of Wales' plumes and words of welcome. The illuminations were creditable. Arches lighted with gas jets here and there crossed the streets, but at longer intervals than at any other town where the Prince remained to attend a ball. I glanced at cottage and house and store windows, and I saw rows of burning candles, and occasionally my eye rested on some bright transparency. Once in the distance I saw a bonfire casting a lurid glare around, and once a procession of firemen and others bearing torches in their hands, arrested my attention. "Are you the man as shook hands with the Prince," said one rough fellow to another, jocularly, within hearing, after the procession had passed with its accompaniment of blaze and Roman candles. It was a joke founded on fact, for I am sorry to say that one of London's horny-handed citizens had the audacity to seize the hand of His Royal Highness, and shake it like a pump-handle, as he sat in his carriage, during his progress from the pavilion to the hotel. The trip by railway to Sarnia, on Thursday, was a very pleasant one. The Prince left London at nine o'clock in the morning, and rode through without stopping, the scenery being one of primeval forest the whole way. The tints of the foliage looked rich and mellow in the autumnal sun, and the primitive aspect of the scene was refreshing. Among the four thousand assembled at the Sarnia Railway Station were two hundred Indians from the Maniboulin Islands, who sat on long benches, with the St. Clair River at their back, and the white cottages of Port Distinguishable on the opposite shore. The red men in question had all the characteristics of their nature apparently unaltered by intercourse with their civilized brethren. Their faces were painted red and black, and their heads wreathed with hawks' feathers and squirrels' tails. They wore rings in their noses and moccasins on their feet, and were otherwise appareled in true Indian style, while, to complete the *toute ensemble*, they were armed with battle-axes. The chief of these, Kanwagashi, or the Great Bear, by name, advanced towards His Royal Highness, after the municipal authorities had presented their addresses, and himself uttered an oration to his " Great Chief" in the Indian tongue.

What Demosthenes would have said of such an outburst of native eloquence, I cannot say, but all who heard it were prodigiously amused. At the close of each sentence or part, the red man folded his arms and paused while it was being translated into English. The harangue reminded the Prince that the sky was beautiful, that it was preordained that Albert Edward and himself should meet and that his heart was glad of the event. He hoped the sky would continue fine for both those of the white and those of the red skin, and that His Royal Highness would remember the red men when he came to the throne.

The Prince smiled, said he was grateful for the address, and hoped the sky would continue beautiful. He would never forget his red brethren.

The yells of delight which issued from the throats of the aborigines as this was translated to them, caused involuntary mirth among the pale-faces.

The chiefs, in addition to being ring-nosed, painted, and moccasined, had buffalo horns on their heads, and snake skins around their waists, thickly set with porcupine quills or colored grass. To these His Royal Highness presented medals nearly as large as the mouth of a tumbler, while to the Indians of lower rank he gave medals of smaller size, and these bore the likeness of the Queen on one side and the royal arms on the reverse. The Indians felt flattered, and returned the compliment by giving him a present of tomahawks, wampums, pipes, bows and arrows, and bark work.

After driving through the town and lunching at the Grand Trunk Railway Station, the prosperity of which the Prince proposed in a toast, he embarked on the steamer Michigan and sailed up the St. Clair River to Lake Huron—which appeared dotted with sails—and back again.

An hour and a half later I saw men in ill-fitting garments bobbing to His Royal Highness at the levee in the Town Hall, London, and that evening I saw him dancing with the worst-dressed, worst-looking, worst-dancing partners he has had in Canada. Between two and three hundred attended it, and the Prince danced from the Alpha to the Omega of the programme.

At ten o'clock on the next morning he left by special train on the Great Western Railway for Paris, on his way to Niagara.

The car he rode in was built for this occasion and furnished like a drawing-room, with the walls painted white, with gilt lines. Enviable railway traveler! We honored a crowd at Ingersoll by waiting a few moments while they were letting off the steam of their loyalty, and then proceeded to Woodstock, thirty miles from London, where all, save the Duke of Newcastle, who was unwell, undertook an exceedingly dusty drive to the residence of the Mayor, where a dais was erected under the veranda, to which the Prince was conducted. Here no less than four addresses were read, to which replies were promised by mail.

The weather was beautiful, and the ladies, dressed in white, with blue sashes, gathered round His Royal Highness, and sang "God save the Queen," in a manner rather embarrassing to the Prince than otherwise. A collation was spread in the dining-room, to which the party afterwards adjourned for a few moments, preparatory to their return through the dusty streets.

Woodstock is a quiet spot in the centre of an agricultural district, and has a population of about five thousand. Its hedgerows and fields are suggestive of English country scenes, and haystacks and hotels are almost equally common within its precincts.

When we arrived at Paris a rifle company had formed as a guard of honor, and a thousand of loyal Canadians were assembled to welcome their future King. An arch, crowned with a Prince of Wales plume, made of wheat-sheaves, stood in the rear, and a landscape of hill and dale filled up the background. The inevitable address was presented, and we stepped from the Great Western to the Buffalo and Lake Huron Railway, where another State car was in waiting for the Prince.

A rapid ride brought us to Brantford, where His Royal Highness walked to his carriage under a handsome arch, and between a double line of school-girls, in white frocks, who, while singing the national anthem, threw bouquets at his feet, so that his path was literally strewed with flowers.

A group of Mohawk Indian chiefs met him at the end of the platform, and one of them delivered into his hand an address, upon which there was a mutual bow, but no exchange of words. The red men of Brantford were dressed in as full and gorgeous costume as their brethren of Sarnia, but the squaws, that stood crouchingly aloof, looked wretched.

Another address from the pale-faces, and another dusty drive succeeded, before we reached the Kirby House, where a public luncheon was served, presided over by the Mayor, who, as soon as the royal party had sat down, rose and said, "Now, then, you must all keep quiet—I must have it. I can't allow any remarks to be made while we're here."

The Prince smiled, the Governor General looked angry, and everybody else felt either amused or annoyed at such an uncalled for lecture. The Mayor was a rough, farmer-like man, and was evidently under the influence of strong waters. He rose again, after a short interval, and made another observation of the same kind, notwithstanding the remonstrance of Sir Edmund Head, which occasioned much merriment throughout the room.

Danville was the next place of stoppage, and here an address was presented in the royal car, and a negro attracted general attention by his rapid loading and firing of a cannon. He fired about twenty shots from the one piece within a quarter of an hour. Such fellows as him would astonish the enemy in a sea-fight, and would have made Pizarro grow pale, and Cortez tremble.

At half-past four we arrived at Fort Erie, after passing through twenty miles of uncleared land. Carriages were in waiting to convey the royal party to the ruins of the fort, which, in years gone by, had been a stronghold of the British. It stood at the distance of half a mile from the station, with its two towers pierced with embrasures and partly overgrown with ivy, distinctly visible. The city of Buffalo lay immediately facing us on the opposite side of the Niagara River, here about two miles wide.

The historical recollections of His Royal Highness and suite were revived as they stood gazing upon the spectacle of decay, just as people might in an old graveyard upon the tombs of their ancestors.

On their return, the Prince embarked on board the steamer for Chippewa, and received a salute of twenty-one guns from the United States battery fronting the railway terminus as he passed. The scenery here was delightful, and the weather equally so. The river was as tranquil as an Italian lagoon, and the sun sinking with lurid radiance shed a flood of brilliant many-hued light across the still bosom of the river. It was such a scene as would have fascinated the eye of Turner, who was grand upon sun and sunset views, and very prodigal of his paint into the bargain, as all who have been through the Turner Gallery cannot fail to have remarked.

It was dusk when we entered the narrow inlet at Chippewa, between two huge bonfires blazing on either bank, and crowds in their vicinity looking spectral in the glare. A torch-light procession enlivened the landing scene, and a temple, illuminated with Bengal lights, at a point nearly half way between the railway station and the Clifton House, in which the usual addresses were presented, had a very theatrical effect.

That evening the Prince dined at his residence, formerly known as Mr. Zimmerman's. It stands, surrounded with lawn and garden ground, within a pistol shot of the Clifton, but is hidden from the view by trees and shrubbery. Thus His Royal Highness at length found a sequestered spot where he could beguile existence as calmly and pleasantly as he pleased.

Two or three hours after his arrival the Falls were illuminated with Bengal lights, which had a very unique and splendid effect. This was done by Mr. Blackwell, of Montreal, Director of the Grand Trunk Railway, to whom the public are indebted for so original an idea. One of the lights was placed under the Table Rock, and burned there with varying intensity for nearly half an hour, meanwhile revealing the foaming waters of the Horseshoe cataract as they hurried wildly to the gulf, their whiteness shining in clear contrast with the surrounding darkness. The reflection of other lights fell full upon the American fall, that had all the lustre of snow in the first rays of an Arctic sun, and all the charm of vitality, for those waters seemed to live as they disported in their strength, and spoke in their voice of thunder.

The play of the changing light across a scene of such natural grandeur was sublime in the influence it worked. The imagination of Dante never conjured up anything so singular as existing in the dreamy regions of which he wrote as this night scene at Niagara. The mist and spray might have been likened, in the language of Spurgeon, to smoke from hell or steam from boiling waters, so much did they appear in character with the lights which shone like huge fires.

If the moonbeams had been playing upon the face of nature, then the illusion would, to a great extent, have been lost; but that darkness, which was necessary to give it full effect, was there to enhance a spectacle, the like of which was never seen before. A display of rockets and illuminations ashore aided the fiery grandeur of the tableau, and gave unto men the transitory look of imps.

It was a grand sight thus to see the proud waters of the greatest cataract in the world rushing to their gorge under an aspect so entirely novel, and the spectators gazed in admiration till the fleeting effulgence had passed away, and night once more in darkness reigned supreme.

CHAPTER XVII.

The Falls and the Prince of Wales—Farini crossing Niagara—Blondin and his Exploits—Description of his Performances—Crossing on Stilts—The Prince in the Spray—Illumination of the Falls—The Prince in the United States, etc.

If I were to write a description of the great cataract of America in modern Greek it would be somewhat new to the people of Athens; if I were to do the same in Arabic, it would carry freshness with it to the subjects of Abd-el-Kader; if in Hindostanee, it would be read with curiosity by the Mohammedans; but if I were to do it in English, French, Italian, or German, it would appear but a barren repetition, for the theme is well worn. Thousands have exhausted their stock of similes and power of language in the endeavor to bring clearly before the mind's eye the one famous waterfall of the world—Niagara. And, strange to say, no two descriptions have an exact affinity to each other, for, perhaps, no two men have formed exactly the same judgment upon them or viewed them with the same feelings, and this diversity has been heightened by the various aspects under which the Falls may be viewed, both as regards point of view, weather, season, light and darkness, and other local influences. There are the sublime, the sentimental, the eloquent, the pictorial, the artistic, the fanciful, the topographical, the technical, the statistical, the practical or matter-of-fact, the poetical, the legendary, the hum-drum, and the bombastic styles of describing Niagara, and each style has had its votaries. It would be interesting to the student of Niagara—for the task would amount to a study—to read all the descriptions of the great cataract ever written. How Niagara would alternately smile and frown, and knit its brow, and finally burst into a roar of laughter, if it had a personality and intelligence of its own, and could only read these specimens of descriptive skill, and how he or she would laugh at me into the bargain for setting myself up as a critic over all, when, at the same time, I am no better than my neighbors.

After this I can hardly venture to say more of Niagara without finding some good excuse. But, happily, I have one in the visit of the Prince of Wales. He is standing on Table Rock on this pleasant morning, and the warm September sun is shining full upon him as he looks down at the glittering flood of foam, with its many hues, from the diamond to the emerald, through shades of green and yellow, brown and purple, red and blue, above which wreaths of vapor float from the bed of the gorge lightly tinted with the rainbow. The roar of the cataract is sublime, the sky beautifully blue, the forest rich in foliage, the shore tranquil.

Five years ago I stood on the same spot in the midst

of a storm. The sky was then dark and gloomy, and contrasted deeply with the fleecy whiteness of the Rapids. The lurid streaks of lightning, the roll of thunder, the rushing of the wind, the roar of the leaping waters, lent an awful grandeur to the ordinary magnificence of the scene.

His Royal Highness gazed upon the graceful curve of the eighteen hundred feet span and hundred and fifty-eight feet depth of the Canadian fall, with an evident appreciation of its beauty. The thirty feet broad middle fall and the cliff of Goat Island divided the American cataract, with its fringe of foam and its steady torrent and its thickly wooded shore. Here was antithesis of the rarest order. I might say more, and become grandiloquent, metaphorical, eulogistic; but I prefer preserving the happy medium, and delight not in exaggeration.

I am not depicting an unsubstantial pageant, but a reality of the most probable character; therefore it behooves me not to give rein to fancy and write as if Niagara were to be seen pouring out of a tinted cloud, surrounded by thick darkness, a mile or two above the point of view, while looking at which spectators were shaken off their feet by the see-saw trembling of the earth under the falls, and deafened for life by the roar of the waters. I write in the knowledge that a storm or hurricane at sea is as much more terrible, sublime, and awful to the senses than Niagara, as Niagara, is in comparison with a running brook.

Shortly before five o'clock in the afternoon of the same day I saw a sight the like of which I never saw before. It was Farini crossing the Niagara River, about half-way between the Falls and the Suspension Bridge, on a tight rope. He had started from the American side, habited in a red jacket, and was advancing quickly, with the balance-pole in his hand. The river here was much wider and the cliffs higher than below the bridge, where Blondin was to perform his feats, and the work of walking so far, under such circumstances, must have required enormous courage, endurance, skill, and presence of mind, especially when the rather high state of the wind was taken into consideration. Yet the remuneration derivable from an occupation involving so much peril seemed quite inadequate, for the number of spectators was small on either shore.

His Royal Highness passed on horseback at this time, and uttered an exclamation of wonder as he watched the stealthy progress of the actor in a part so thrilling.

As soon as the Prince and party arrived in Blondin's inclosure, that genius of the rope set out from the American side, and came on slowly towards the opposite point. Huge rocks pointed their naked heads three hundred feet below, and boiling rapids plunged onward in their wild vexation. But Blondin was as composed as if he had been striding on *terra firma*, although he advanced warily, for one false step would have hurried him to perdition. He rested two or three times in his passage over, and also turned several somersaults, and, with his hands grasping the rope, hung down at length, and then, gathering himself up, turned round and round like a squirrel's cage. It was by no means a healthy sight, and the Prince and many others withdrew their eyes from such a terrible display of hardihood. "I felt my heart in my mouth all the time," was a remark I heard after the performance was over.

He had twelve hundred feet to walk between the two shores; but he accomplished the task easily, and arrived unexhausted in his shed, where the royal party were assembled, in less than half an hour from the time of starting. The Prince and others shook him by the hand and congratulated him on his safe arrival, and the spectators on the other side of the river cheered. There were about two thousand present in all.

Blondin is a man of slight but wiry frame, with sandy hair, small gray eyes, sunken cheeks and dried-up, sallow-looking features. He is about five feet six in height, and wears a mustache and imperial, but no beard or whiskers. He is thirty-six years old and a native of Calais, and has practiced tight-rope walking since he was four years of age. He resides with his wife and children in the town of Clifton, Niagara. In manner he is quiet, almost subdued, yet when spoken to has all the cordiality of the Frenchman. He speaks very good English, and expresses his intention of visiting England in a short time. I remarked, as a set off to his very slight frame, that the muscle of his arms, though small, was freely developed, and that his chest was large for his size.

He was now about to perform a feat far more perilous than that just described. This consisted in carrying a man on his back across the same rope. It may seem strange that any one could be found to put himself in this position, and upon whose presence of mind Blondin could depend. However, one Harry Colcord —the same that he carried across on the two former occasions of his performing a similar feat—placed himself on the back of Blondin, to whom he acts as agent, and forthwith Blondin started with him. I may mention that, in order the more steadily to secure the rider, there were stirrups depending from Blondin's shoulders, into which the other inserted his feet. They rested twice or thrice on the way, and Colcord had to stand on the rope till Blondin gave the word for him to mount again. On one of these occasions I saw the balance-pole swaying violently up and down, and Col cord striving, but ineffectually, to get his right foot into the stirrup. People could look at the spectacle no longer, and sought relief in turning away their eyes. That evening Colcord told me that he was seized with cramp in the thigh. "Yes," said he, "we were nearly getting into a scrape to-day. I thought I couldn't go any further. But it would never do to get frightened, because it would throw him over in a moment."

Never was one man more dependent upon another for his life than either of these acrobatic pilgrims across the Niagara River during the twenty long minutes of suspense which elapsed between their passage from shore to shore. Several times the hardy walker seemed to falter, almost stumble, under his load, and anxious eyes that had followed as he had gradually lessened to the view were withdrawn in the fear of an impending catastrophe. Then they were reassured again as they saw him making his way steadily towards the opposite point; but at frequent intervals the irresistible anxiety would be increased by a staggering movement or the act of resting. "I was more frightened than Blondin," said an officer of the rifles after the destination had been reached in safety. Everybody present felt a weight removed as this was accomplished, and they once more breathed freely.

A pause of about a quarter of an hour ensued before the dangerous experiment of walking across on stilts was attempted. This was an entirely new feature in Blondin's career, and was put forward as the great event of the day. He stepped on the rope and advanced towards us with lofty strides. This, I afterwards found, was owing to the stilts being hooked at the end in a shape resembling the feet of a bird. The stilts were short and fastened to his legs, so that he had only to be careful to step fairly on the rope and preserve his balance with the pole. Once he dropped rather suddenly on to the rope, and women uttered ejaculations of horror, but it was soon found that he had only sat down to rest. How he got up again was a puzzle to many. He came in with rapid bird-like and measured step, and was once more cheered and congratulated by His Royal Highness and those near.

I shook his hand and found it naturally warm, while his features betrayed no excitement or exhaustion.

The royal party and the spectators generally now retired, and Blondin, with his balance-pole and stilts across his shoulder, walked home in his skin-fitting merino undervest and drawers, with a wreath of feathers on his head.

The Prince, after this, rode down to the ferry, where, in company with the Duke of Newcastle, Earl St. Germains, the Governor General and his suite, he embarked on the small steamer Maid of the Mist, which at once steamed towards the Falls. The royal party each took down one of the hooded oilskin coats from the pegs in the cabin, and soon re-emerged upon deck, the Prince laughing heartily at the strange figure he cut, being entirely enveloped in the huge Mackintosh, which the falling spray now played upon most musically, at the same time drenching the deck like heavy rain.

The view of the Falls—looking upward, as the steamer suddenly swept round at the Horseshoe curve, heaving as she went on the verge of the descending waters—was beautiful, magnificent, sublime. There was a solemn grandeur in the wildness of those foaming floods that thrilled, and a majesty in their immensity and far-resounding voice that awed, inspired, and fascinated all who from that deck beheld them.

Receding from the cataract, the vessel steamed down the still and silent river, hemmed in by the steep and giant cliffs that forcibly remind one of the scenery of the Saguenay. Indeed, the remark was made on board.

The steamer returned to her starting point within half an hour from the time of her departure, and then, after signing their names in the visitors' book, the party remounted and rode up the steep to the residence of His Royal Highness, which was a beautifully situated two-story villa, standing in park-like grounds, commanding a view of the Falls. It was neatly furnished with cherry and walnut wood furniture, but the accommodation it afforded was so limited that all the suite had to reside at the Clifton House.

At ten o'clock in the evening the Falls were again illuminated with Bengal lights, which gave to the plunging waters the same spectral appearance as I faintly pictured in my last. Visions of liquid amber, pearls, molten metal, a storm in the Alps, and much beside, might have arisen before the mind of the spectator of a scene so strange.

Sunday dawned wet and windy, and continued so throughout. The Prince attended the village church, and remained at home the rest of the day.

On Monday morning the weather broke dry and clear, and the sun shone brightly on Albert Edward of England, as he was rowed in a small oared boat from the Canadian to the American side, landing at the foot of the two hundred and ninety wooden steps, leading three hundred and sixty feet up the cliff from the water-side to the summit. These he ascended and was soon standing on Prospect Place, within full view of the rainbow and the flood. Near him he surveyed the nine hundred feet span and hundred and sixty-four feet depth of the American fall; and while looking over the vast body of water rushing down in rapids at his left, and rolling wildly over the brink of the precipice at his right, into the yawning gulf beneath, his vision embraced the even more picturesque curve of the broad torrent separated by Goat Island.

Here now, for the first time in his life, he stood in United States territory, which had once been British. The fact recurred to him, but he felt none the less happy.

The contrast between the troubled rush of the waters, before reaching the precipice, and their tranquil flow after plunging over, was striking. Walking on eastward, along the river-side, where the rapids rushed tumultuously over a succession of rocky shelves, he reached the point where the river is divided in the middle by the intervention of the island, and where the long wooden bridge extends around the agitated waste from that to the mainland. He advanced half way over this, and then paused to take in the magnificent view of the Rapids that presented itself. On sped the raging torrent, its wild wavelets leaping over the shelving bed and sending their foaming crests into the air, showing themselves in their whirling fury against the background of the sky, or upheaving themselves into sporting billows, ever changing and gleaming in the brilliant sunlight as they hurried madly to the gulf.

Why should I launch into a peroration—why further attempt the description of Niagara after my prefatory remarks? It is enough that it is an enduring reality which all who come can see, and there is no natural wonder of the world better worthy of a visit, at least once in a lifetime, than Niagara.

CHAPTER XVIII.

Departure from Niagara Falls—Brock's Monument and its Corner-Stone—A Magnificent View—St. Catharine's and the Prince's Reception there—Grimsby—Hamilton—Enthusiasm of the Populace—Description of the City, etc.

On Tuesday morning at ten o'clock the Prince and party left Niagara Falls, under a salute from the Volunteer Artillery, and traveled by special train to Queenston Heights, distant seven miles. There they scaled the "Mountain," an elevation three hundred and forty-six feet above the level of the river, and approached the lofty monument under which lie the ashes of the brave General Sir Isaac Brock and his aid-de-camp.

The arrival was signaled by the firing of a royal salute and hoisting the Prince of Wales standard on the flag-staff at the foot of the monument. A company of the Canadian Rifles acted as a guard of honor, and nearly a thousand people were assembled in the vicinity of the platform, built at one side of the column.

This monument has only been erected three years, and then by subscription, the original one having been blown up with gunpowder, placed there by some malicious hand.

The object of this visit was to inaugurate the monument and receive an address from the Veterans of 1812, one hundred and fifty of whom were now present, including Sir Allen McNab and Sir John Robinson, the oldest of the survivors. The address was read by the latter gentleman, to which the Prince returned a very feeling reply.

From this lofty point a magnificent view was afforded of the gorge of the Niagara, and beyond of forest and field, mountains and hills, backed, far as the eye could carry, by a wide sweep of the blue Ontario, while beneath and at the back of the village of Queenston, which has a population of five hundred, stood under the solemn cliffs a solitary tree. There fell Brock in the arms of victory. I might descant for hours upon a scene so picturesque and full of interest, but time presses, and my book has limits.

To this tree—a venerable thorn—His Royal Highness repaired after replying to the address. Near it an obelisk had been built, and the top stone only required to be lowered into place. This stone was inscribed with letters which told the melancholy history of the man. He died on the 13th of October, 1812, while advancing to repel the invading enemy.

A silver trowel was handed to the Prince, with which he spread the mortar under the stone, and then the stone was lowered like a coffin to its grave, and this ended the ceremony.

His Royal Highness and suite immediately after this proceeded in row-boats to the steamer Zimmerman, and, embarking, sailed down the river to the village of Niagara, which, in 1792, when the Duke of Kent landed there, was not only the metropolis of, but the only town in, Upper Canada. Several neat and handsome arches here lent a festive aspect to the scene at the water-side. The Corporation and Magistrates presented addresses, to which brief replies were read in the pavilion built for the occasion.

After this the steamer ploughed her way into the wide but tranquil lake, passing the American fort at the mouth of the river on her way. It was soon discovered that some of the servants had been left behind, and for these the boat returned. Then she sped forward again, and before her arrival at Port Dalhousie, the terminus of the Welland Canal, lunch was served on board. The three-mile carriage drive from the latter place to St. Catharine's was very pleasant, owing to the absence of dust, the rural quiet of the road and the beautiful sunny weather.

The Prince was then conducted under a handsome pavilion, when a Corporation address was read by the Mayor and replied to in the usual manner. St. Catharine's presented a very pretty appearance, both architecturally and in its display of volunteer troops and numerous decorations. One of the arches was unique and better-looking than might be supposed when I say it was built entirely of flour barrels.

St. Catharine's is pleasantly situated on an open plateau above the valley, through which winds the Welland Canal.

It is distant twelve miles from Niagara Falls, and has a population of about seven thousand.

It is becoming a trite remark to say that His Royal Highness had an enthusiastic reception from the inhabitants, that the cheering and waving of handkerchiefs were energetic, and that bouquets were here and there thrown across his path; but it will apply to this visit as much as to any other made by the Prince in North America.

From St. Catharine's to Hamilton the journey was performed by the Great Western Railway, the line of which here runs for the most part through beautiful park-like scenery, reminding one of the landscapes of Devonshire and other parts of England. The train stopped at Grimsby, on the way, where a platform and dais were erected at the station, which was gayly festooned with evergreens, and crowded with an eager multitude. The invariable address was here presented, after which the train moved on, followed by the rejoicing shouts of a thousand.

Hamilton, or "The Ambitious City," as its inhabitants delight to call it, was soon reached after this, and here, for the size of the place, the proceedings were exceedingly lively. The Hamilton Field Battery fired a salute, the dogs barked, and there are unfortunately plenty of such in the Ambitious City; the people hurrahed from the hills and the level ground, boys scampered and jostled old women while in the act of shaking their pocket-handkerchiefs in the air for the gratification of eyes that did not see; the Roman Catholic Bishop and his clergy walked away in high dudgeon because no particular position was assigned to them in the procession; the half-broken horses of the volunteer cavalry cut sad capers under their riders; the members of the Abolition Society, composed entirely of negroes, stood in waiting like so many animated blocks of India-rubber; those of the Temperance Society looked thirsting for beer; the officers of the Sedentary Militia had all the appearance of theatrical soldiers; the Canadian Order of Odd Fellows were certainly true to their order, and the Mayor would persist in exposing his bare head to the sun. The platform at the station overflowed with a crowd of both sexes, intent upon squeezing each other.

In the centre of the platform was erected a dais, surmounted by a canopy, to which His Royal Highness stepped on alighting from the car. Here the Mayor, with his head in the sun, read an address to the Prince, who, with more wisdom, kept his in the shade, and endeavored, by saying "Come out of the sun," to induce that worthy to study his health more.

To this a reply having more than ordinary significance was returned, it being the last of the kind he would make in the provinces. It ran thus, and was uttered with marked emphasis and feeling:

"Gentlemen,—This is the last of the very numerous addresses which have flowed in upon me from the municipal authorities, as well as other bodies throughout the Queen's dominions in North America, which I have now traversed from east to west, and I can say with truth that it is not the least fervent in its declarations of attachment to the Queen, nor the least earnest in its aspirations for the success and happiness of my future life, and in its prayers that my career may be one of usefulness to others and of honor to myself. You cannot doubt the readiness with which I undertook the duty which was intrusted to me by the Queen, of visiting in her name, and on her behalf, these possessions of her crown. That task is now nearly completed, and it only remains for me to report to your sovereign universal enthusiasm, unanimous loyalty, all-pervading patriotism, general contentment, and, I trust, no less general prosperity and happiness. I can never forget the scenes I have witnessed. The short time during which I have enjoyed the privilege of associating myself with the Canadian people, must ever form a high epoch in my life. I shall bear away with me a grateful remembrance of kindness and affection, which, as yet, I have been unable to do anything to merit, and it shall be the constant effort of my future years to prove myself not unworthy of the love and confidence of a generous people."

Hamilton was well favored by the elements. Its triumphal arches and other evergreen decorations, its ten thousand flags fluttering in the sunlight over the housetops, its illumination devices, its men and women in holiday attire, its natural scenery—all were seen to the best advantage in the bright and rosy light of day.

The city, which was so incorporated in 1847, is built on a gentle slope, backed, like Montreal, by a hill called the "Mountain," on the southwestern shore of Burlington Bay, an inlet of Lake Ontario. Its streets cross each other at right angels, and it can boast of many substantial stone and brick buildings, and, what is better, few wooden ones, the houses being chiefly of the former materials. It has a population of about twenty-eight thousand, and publishes two daily newspapers.

The procession moved forward in the midst of a dense multitude; the progress was thus impeded, and there was much of that disorder always inseparable from a country mob. The line of route extended for about a mile and a half through the principal streets to the residence prepared for His Royal Highness on the "Mountain." This is a pleasant mansion, standing in its own grounds, and from its elevation commanding a full view of the city and bay. A similar house stands near, which was made ready for the suite, while others of the royal and official party were provided for at the Royal Hotel. Both of these residences had been given up by private citizens, now abandoned for the use of the Prince and suite.

After passing under numerous tastefully decorated

arches, and being sung to, at one point, by a large platform full of school children, to whom he smiled and bowed with his customary cordiality, tired though he was, Albert Edward, at six o'clock, arrived at his destination.

In the evening a general illumination and a firemen's torch-light procession contributed to keep up the excitement, but the latter was singularly poor. At ten o'clock His Royal Highness arrived at the Mechanics' Institute, where a grand concert was being given by the Hamilton Philharmonic Society.

As the royal party entered the box prepared for them, preceded by a flourish of trumpets, the audience, by no means a large one, rose, and the performers, numbering more than a hundred, commenced singing the national anthem, all present taking part in the chorus. The Prince only remained a short time, and then drove home.

In the morning, before holding the levee at the Royal Hotel, he visited the Central School, where a lot of anxious children that had lain awake half the night thinking about him, were assembled at their desks. After the levee he visited the exhibition building. The latter is situated on an elevation at the western end of the city, where the view is as fine and extended as from the so-called Mountain. It is an industrial and agricultural exhibition, with the addition of a cattle show.

On His Royal Highness' return from the contemplation of pigs and ploughs, oxen, sheep, and horses, he lunched with the chief men of the city at the hotel, and soon after three drove to inaugurate the Water Works.

The Prince had a four-horse carriage, but his suite rode in vehicles that would have done credit to Donnybrook Fair, and these were so crowded as to necessitate one man sitting on another's knee. Away they went, helter-skelter, through the cheering crowd..

The Prince was received by the Sheriff of the county, who conducted him to the engine-house grounds, where the watermen—or rather, Water Commissioners—the Mayor, and other local dignitaries, were assembled. These, at the hand and mouth of the Chairman of the Board, presented an address, to which a brief reply was given. His Royal Highness then started the engines, and a salute was fired in honor of the event. The ceremony being now ended, the party returned to town.

The citizens' ball given in the evening was, in one or two respects, the worst offered to the Prince of Wales in the British Provinces. Owing to the hurried manner in which the room was built, none of the arrangements were complete. There was not even time enough left to allow of the floor being washed. It was, therefore, spotted with tobacco juice, like a bar-room, when the company began to assemble. Moreover, there was a most offensive odor, which was at first said to be gas, but afterwards admitted to come from a sewer, rising in pestiferous puffs through the boarding, and when the Prince and party arrived, at eleven o'clock, this stench had become almost unbearable, and everybody complained of it, while some went home in consequence.

The room was large and square, and draped with red and white baize, so that its appearance was light and airy; but, owing to there being at no time more than six hundred people present, the general effect of the ball was meagre.

His Royal Highness remained till a quarter to three, when he left, in the midst of a general cheer.

The illuminations in front of the public offices, banks, and stores, were, meanwhile, almost as general as on the previous evening.

The hotels were uncomfortably crowded, and many sat up all night in the hall and reading-room seats, unable to obtain beds. Soon after noon on the following day His Royal Highness drove to the exhibition and formally opened it. There was an immense crowd in the grounds adjoining, and these hooted the Governor General in a manner which must have produced anything but a delightful effect upon that venerable head of the Canadian Government.

The public were debarred admittance to the interior of the building during the royal presence, and, as a consequence, they pushed each other about outside in a manner which betrayed anything but refinement. Immediately after the inspection of the horses and carriages, cattle and pigs, sheep and farming implements, the party drove to the railway station, and left by special train at two o'clock, under a salute from the volunteer battery, and cheers from the crowd assembled. Farewell, "ambitious city!"

CHAPTER XIX.

The Grandeur of the Prince's Reception at Detroit—Immense Turn-out of the Populace—The Coup d'Etat of the Prince to reach the Russell House—His Royal Highness takes a Drive through Detroit—His Departure for Chicago—Demonstrations of Welcome—Immense Turn-out of the Chicagoans—The Prince makes his Appearance on the Balcony of the Richmond House—Enthusiastic Cheers of Welcome by the Populace—The Royal Party proceed on a Prairie Shooting Excursion.

THE night scene at Detroit on the occasion of the entry of the son of Queen Victoria into the United States was one long to be remembered by all who witnessed it. The glittering line of steamers on the river and the illuminated shores had a beautiful effect, and so also had the six hundred torches of the firemen, that threw a lurid glare upon the heads of the immense and densely packed multitude from the water-side to Jefferson Avenue.

Unfortunately, however, the crowd was too great to be comfortable, and it was with some difficulty that even the lines of the boat were fastened to the snubbing posts. It became a still more difficult matter to attempt the formation of the procession which had been planned. The military and firemen were wedged here and there in the general mass, and endeavors to get them into order were utterly useless. The carriages were jammed in immovably, and could not be approached from the steamer. Half an hour was thus passed, during which the cheers that had greeted the illustrious party had given place to a Babel of sounds, a noisy enthusiasm, expressive of the bubbling ardor and curiosity which swayed the congregated thousands. It was amusing to watch the unflinching perseverance with which delicate women, in spite of crushed bonnets and flattened crinoline, struggled in the midst of all for a place near where the Prince was likely to pass. Such heroic fortitude deserved a better reward than it met with. It was fortunate that only one of the crowd was pushed into the river, and that he was rescued immediately afterwards.

The police by this time had succeeded in clearing a passage to the nearest carriage, which was a close one; and no sooner was this done than His Royal Highness, accompanied by two of his suite, quietly entered it without being recognized by the people, who had expected to see him land surrounded by a phalanx of attendants. As soon as the carriage had forced its way through the crowd it was announced that the bird had flown, and immediately there was a grand rush towards the Russell House, where it was known that apartments had been secured for "Baron Renfrew" and his suite. But the carriage arrived there before the pursuers, who were left outside to vainly speculate on the possibility or probability—which they did—of that regal gentleman making his appearance on the balcony.

Meanwhile, the procession, which those concerned had succeeded in stringing together, was advancing by Jefferson Avenue and Shelby Street towards the hotel, and with it came the carriages containing the remaining members of the royal party.

Although there was an entire absence of triumphal arches and evergreen decorations, and, by necessity, a lack of that pageantry which had attended his progress through the British provinces, the eagerness to have a glance at royalty was even greater than that manifested on the other side of the border; and since the days when Detroit acknowledged the rule of the great grandfather of the present Prince of Wales, it has been said by competent authorities that such a general turn-out of its population was never before witnessed. And it was not mere curiosity that brought about this result, but a sincere desire to show their admiration of Victoria and Victoria's son and the British nation, with whose people those of the United States felt allied by the ties of consanguinity, language, and commerce.

The people were bound to see His Royal Highness if such were possible, and although their efforts to do so detracted from the effect of the reception, the results were hardly to be regretted. There was a great people's demonstration in honor of the Prince's arrival, and it was by the feeling of the people participating in that demonstration that we must judge.

After breakfast on the next morning, the party took their places in open carriages, and, under the guidance of the Mayor, drove through the principal avenues for about half an hour, and then turned down to the Michigan Central Railroad Station, where they arrived at a few minutes past ten. The crowd had, by this time, deserted the hotel, and formed there to the number of five thousand and more. The cheering was as energetic as Americans are ever wont to indulge in, and the excitement ran high.

At every station, as the train progressed, there was a crowd proportionate in its size to the population of the place, and a rush to the car steps by those hopeful of a glimpse of the royal countenance through the windows. But disappointment followed, for the windows were curtained.

The party paid for traveling the usual English special train rates, namely, five cents per mile for each person.

On nearing Chicago we saw several houses and one of the large lakeside hotels beautifully illuminated. The railway had run parallel with the southern shore of the Michigan for more than sixty miles, although its waters were frequently shut out from our view.

We reached Chicago at eight o'clock and found about fifteen thousand people assembled within the railway terminus, but kept back from the platform by a stretched rope. These gave a hearty cheer as the heir apparent walked hastily, in company with Lord Lyons, to the carriage in waiting for him, in which he was conveyed to the Richmond House, where the necessary apartments had been prepared for his reception.

As soon as he passed, the crowd broke beyond the rope, and rushed down the platform like a torrent and followed the carriage to the hotel, which closely adjoined the station. The scene at Detroit was thereupon re-enacted. The royal party dined, slept, and on the next morning Baron Renfrew, happening to make his appearance on the balcony, was loudly cheered. At ten o'clock he entered his carriage in the midst of a shower of bouquets from the lady boarders of the house, and together with the Mayor, the Duke of Newcastle, Lord Lyons, and others, drove to the Court House. Here the celebrated Mayor Wentworth, better known as "Long John," conducted the party into his office, and, producing his ledger, asked the favor of their autographs for his future delectation. This request having been courteously complied with, the giant of Chicago led the way up the spiral staircase to the summit, where a fine view of the city and the lake was afforded. Owing to the perfect flatness of Chicago, it must be seen from a lofty elevation. The top of the Court House is, therefore, the great resort of strangers.

There is no doubt that the son of Queen Victoria was made fully familiar with the short history of the City of the Wigwam; how, when it was incorporated in 1836, it had a population of little more than five thousand, while now it could boast of more than a hundred and five thousand, and some of the widest streets and finest stores and warehouses in the Union, and a commerce that outrivaled—well, I had better leave that to conjecture; and what results still greater it might have achieved, but for the last three years' depression, that had thrown a mantle of sackcloth over the whole of the West, cities and villages alike.

From the Court House the royal party, headed by the sagacious Mayor, visited the different points of the city. They returned to the hotel to luncheon, and afterwards drove down Michigan Avenue, which was lined with spectators, on their way to Bridgeport, where they inspected the hydraulic works, preparatory to leaving town by special train, for Dwight station, distant eighty miles, in order to enjoy a couple of days' shooting on the prairies.

No sooner had the party arrived at Dwight than they proceeded, with the necessary dogs and guns, into the field; but the gathering twilight was unpropitious to their sport, and they bagged no game; nevertheless the canine pack displayed points that augured well for their future usefulness, and the Prince said "they'll do." He and the Duke of Newcastle, General Bruce and Dr. Ackland, were comfortably domiciled in the house of a Mr. Spencer, while the other members of the suite were quartered in the other two houses, which, with a few wooden additions, compose the village.

On the next morning His Royal Highness drove with his suite to the old-school Presbyterian church, where divine service was performed.

On returning to the house it was found that a special engine had just arrived from Chicago, bringing a special messenger with dispatches from the Queen and Colonial Office. The result of this was that all remained at home during the entire afternoon, reading and replying to their correspondence.

The wind blew almost a gale the whole day, and it was impossible to avoid draughts and gusts of air, even indoors. The prairie presented a beautiful sight at this time, for the sun shone with that radiance peculiar to dry, windy weather, and lighted up the restless waves of green with incomparable effect.

Notwithstanding that the breeze thus whistled its stormy song, and a few drops of rain that came in with the night pattered ominously against the window panes, His Royal Highness resolved, if the weather moderated, to rise at half-past five o'clock, breakfast, and start off to shoot prairie fowl, reserving quail for the morrow.

By this time the wind had subsided, and the dogs and guns were brought into requisition. The Prince started in shooting costume in company with his equerries, Mr. Spencer, and two others. The gray light of dawn and the vapors of the morning were soon dispelled by the rising sun. Far away in the East streaks of crimson and gold, mellowed by all the tints of the rainbow, presaged the advent of the glorious orb that gradually appeared before the vision like a ball of fire. Now the streaks melted away slowly before the bursting effulgence. The sky was a mighty vault of dim uncheckered blue, so unrelieved by cloud that the eye almost ached in surveying its vastness. A cool fresh breeze gave a graceful sweep to the long grass, and made the few trees that bordered the open land sing their rustling carol.

In upward flight the bright wings of the morning fast spread awide. Rich, vivid, and inspiring hues decked the eastern horizon, and the bladed desert was bathed in a flood of silver radiance.

It is not advisable to descend to the minutiæ of the day's sport, for His Royal Highness came here to be, to a certain extent, free from observation. I will, therefore, content myself by saying that the party were delighted with the prairie and the country generally. During the day the entire suite were out with "his lordship," who could point a gun and bring down his bird as well as any one of them. Notwithstanding that the birds were very wild, tolerable success attended their shots.

The sportsmen returned home when the day was far spent.

I would advise all who have the taste, money, and leisure, to visit this great and unique landscape feature of Illinois. Here, although nature presents to the eye but little antithesis, she has given in the great unvarying flower-sprinkled plain a prospect which, for sublimity and grandeur, is equal to many of those sights in which she appears most fantastic.

On the morning of Tuesday, the 25th September, at half-past seven His Royal Highness and the entire suite left Dwight by a special train, for Stuart's Grove, where there is good quail-shooting to be had, owing to the prairie-clearing in that vicinity.

His life, since leaving Chicago, had been one of unmitigated pleasure, and already his naturally healthy look was enhanced by a robustness and flow of animal spirits before unknown to him. He never before enjoyed anything so much as this shooting on the prairies. He entered into the sport with all the zest of his ardent nature, and few can compare with him in his genuine relish for outdoor amusement and adventure.

The cottage which was his temporary residence has become an object of considerable interest, both in the village and abroad, and will likely be a sort of Mecca to a certain class of pilgrims. It is a pleasant two-storied, white-painted, eight-windowed habitation, with a veranda in front, where each night the game brought home by the party was deposited. The Prince took great pride in the birds shot by himself, and took a candle with him to have a look at them after dinner.

He slept in the largest bedroom, situated in the second story, with a dressing-room adjoining. The apartment of General Bruce was at the opposite side of the house, and between the two was the chamber occupied by the Duke of Newcastle.

The cottage is named the Prairie Home by its owner, Mr. J. C. Spencer.

On Saturday night the Prince went to a cottage on the same farm to look at the quarters occupied by his equerries. He was accompanied by Mr. Spencer, who pointed the way up a ladder-like flight of steps to a small room—the only one—which was shared by the gentlemen in question. The Prince had his coat covered with whitewash by the time he reached the top, where, meeting with those he was in search of, he had a hearty laugh at the adventure. When he came down stairs he saw the horny-handed host, who, little suspecting who he was, said, addressing Mr. Spencer, "Where's the Prince?" "Well, if you must know," was the reply, "this is the Prince standing beside you."

The man thought there was an attempt to "sell" him, and with a look of the most sublime skepticism ejaculated, "Well, if that's the Prince, all that I can say is, that if old Abe Lincoln was here, I'd say you'd go to the White House." Albert Edward went off in a roar.

Lord Lyons was accommodated in another cottage,

and Lord Hinchinbrook and the Hon. Mr. Eliot, private friends of His Royal Highness, recruited exhausted nature in a railway sleeping-car. Pleasant recollections of a day spent in driving over and shooting on the grand prairie and visiting in the village crowd upon me, and I write as one in love with his subject.

I set out early, and drove across the grassy plain by a mere path, and started flights of prairie birds, and saw the horizon sparsely dotted with farm-houses, surrounded by fields of Indian corn. Mile after mile I continued my journey, and still the scene remained the same—farm after farm, undulation after undulation. Once I met a herdsman in charge of some cattle; but he was the only specimen of humanity I saw in my long drive through these vast solitudes.

Six miles below the village I came to several groves that looked like islands rising from the sea of green. These denoted the presence of water. One of them fringed Gooseberry Lake, in the vicinity of which the Prince passed the whole of Monday. Into its shade he retired for luncheon and partook of some potatoes baked for him on the spot, and then lighted his segar at the fire, which soon afterwards accidentally ignited a tree.

The Grand Prairie is a hundred and seventy miles long by twenty-five to fifty broad, and is more or less settled over its entire extent. Hardly any one could fail to venture a supposition that this vast tract of country was once the bed of a lake, or that it will eventually be as densely populated as the adjacent regions. In the meantime the extreme fertility of the soil, which is a dark stoneless loam, is a source of sure wealth to the farmer.

The Prince returned at half-past seven from Stuart's Grove, after a day's successful quail-shooting. The Prince's own party consisted, as on the previous day, of the Duke of Newcastle, Mr. Spencer, and Captain

Retallack. The latter gentleman, who is aid-de-camp to the Governor General of Canada, organized the whole affair, he having previously visited this neighborhood for sporting purposes. The other members of the suite shot on their own account. The result of the day's sport was as follows: The Prince, thirty head of quail; the Duke of Newcastle, twenty head of quail; Mr. J. Clinton Spencer, ten head of quail; Captain Retallack, twenty head of quail.

On the previous day the Prince shot fifteen brace of prairie fowl; the Duke of Newcastle, twelve brace; Captain Retallack, five brace; and Mr. Spencer, two brace. The excess on the side of His Royal Highness may be accounted for by the fact of his having always the first shot.

Dwight is a village of fifty houses and six hundred people, and has had an existence of only four years. It will doubtless receive an impetus from the royal visit, and we shall likely hear of a Renfrew Hotel at some future time.

CHAPTER XX.

Trip from Dwight to St. Louis—Origin of St. Louis—Its Early History and Progress—Presents from His Royal Highness—The Journey to Cincinnati.

It was a little before one o'clock in the morning when I traversed the silent prairie village of Dwight, in the direction of the railway station. The oscillation of the train which carried me thenceforward to St. Louis exceeded anything of the kind I had before met with. It was a perpetual jumping reel, which made the bones ache. Moreover, the pace was so slow—about twenty miles an hour—that it was past noon when we reached the terminus on the banks of the Mississippi, and there, owing to the absence of a ferry steamer to carry us across, nearly an hour's delay took place before we reached the city.

I was unceremoniously shaken out of my sleep at daybreak, alike with the other occupants of the sleeping-car, by an ebony-faced individual, wishing to know if I wanted breakfast. He received anything but a calm reply from some of those disturbed by him. However, I was amused as he was walking away by hearing some one call out to him, "Bring me a cup of coffee on a waiter."

"On who?" was the darkey's responsive query, and he chuckled as he spoke. I imagine his thoughts recurred to a waiter in human form, for he seemed to enjoy the idea amazingly.

The view of St. Louis from the opposite, or Illinois side of the river, is very fine. In its river-side warehouses it may be likened to Liverpool, while the vicinity of the State House reminds one, when seen afar off, of Lisbon. But no sooner does the traveler land than the resemblance is no longer recognized, and the scene hardly suggests comparison.

The site of St. Louis was selected by Laclerc, who named it in honor of Louis XV., of France, on the 15th of February, 1764. It was afterwards used as a trading station for the western trappers. At this period the population varied between fifteen hundred and two thousand, half of whom were usually absent, leading the semi-wild life of *voyageurs* and trappers. The population experienced no rapid increase, for as late as 1820 it numbered less than five thousand.

Meanwhile, and in the year 1768, Spanish troops had taken possession of it in the name of Her Catholic Majesty, and these retained it till its transfer to the United States in 1804. Then its real progress began. In 1813 wood first gave place to brick in the construction of houses. In 1817 the first steam-boat ploughed its waters. Immigration from Illinois succeeded, and its population in 1840 exceeded sixteen thousand. Ten years later the census declared it to be nearly seventy-eight thousand, and now it is a hundred and sixty thousand. These figures tell their own tale of advancement, and as they are unfamiliar to many even of the American public, I have thought their introduction not entirely without use. It has become too much a habit with us to neglect home, and look abroad for information. But now that the Prince of Wales has invested the places of his sojourn with a more than common interest, it is well to revive old recollections, and impart whatever there is new concerning them. The present royal tour has been the text for the promulgation of much general knowledge relating to the British provinces, and the centre from which has radiated a light by which those regions and our neighbors, their inhabitants, ought to be seen in a clearer and truer manner than ever they were before.

St. Louis is situated on the right or western shore of the Mississippi, below the mouth of the Missouri, and above the mouth of the Ohio. The city is built on two limestone elevations, twenty and sixty feet above the level of the river. The upper terrace widens into a plain, from which a fine view of the surrounding scenery is obtainable. St. Louis is at either extremity somewhat straggling in appearance, and extends seven miles along the curve of the river.

It may or may not be generally known that General Bruce transmitted three hundred dollars on behalf of His Royal Highness to Blondin, of tight-rope notoriety, and that Mr. Sanderson, the steward, who attended to the royal *cuisine* in Canada, was presented with a gold watch bearing the Prince's crest, and that similar favors have been elsewhere bestowed under like circumstances.

The Prince and suite left Dwight at eight on Wednesday morning. I am told that before leaving the cottage, he planted an elm in the garden, and named the place " Renfrew Lodge."

The train arrived at Alton, its destination, on the Mississippi, twenty miles above St. Louis, at three o'clock, without the occurrence of any special incident. The royal party then embarked on the steamer City of Alton, where they were met by Earl St. Germains, who had come from St. Louis to meet them, upon which they started for that city, and arrived at half-past five o'clock, under a salute from a solitary cannon. The upper deck was alone reserved for the Prince and suite, the lower part being occupied by excursionists.

There was hardly any crowd as the vessel steamed up to the wharf, but before the disembarkation, a quarter of an hour afterwards, a few thousand people had gathered near the landing place.

The Prince was received with a general cheer as he stepped ashore and entered one of the carriages in waiting, but the curiosity of some of the " roughs" led them to commit the indiscretion of running close alongside of the carriage and staring at the occupants through its closed windows. The other carriages containing the suite drove off in an opposite direction, in order to divide the crowd, which impeded the progress of that containing His Royal Highness. However, within less than ten minutes the whole party had reached the hotel and taken possession of their quarters.

The nature of Albert Edward, Prince of Wales, is of a highly sensitive order, and there is a timidity about him which makes him shrink from contact with a large and tumultuous crowd, such as that which surrounded his carriage on the occasion of his landing. He is of delicate organization, the temperament most allied to genius, and to him the paths of peace are most welcome. The turbulent manifestations of a mob, however well meant or dictated by good feeling, could not fail to grate harshly upon one of so much natural and acquired refinement. Therefore, the lower strata of the democratic element may have proved somewhat uncongenial to him. But I am happy to say that the people of the United States generally, and the superior order particularly, studied his comfort, pleasure, and wishes with a delicacy dictated by that good sense which is their prevailing characteristic, that has not failed to impress him and his suite with a very favorable idea of American consideration and courtesy. There was a universal desire to pay him respect and do him honor, and the affections have been widely enlisted in his welfare. The enthusiasm was even greater than that displayed by the people of the British Provinces.

His Royal Highness and suite left the hotel in carriages on the next morning at eleven o'clock, for the purpose of visiting the principal sights of the city, including the fair.

The committee of leading citizens, headed by the Mayor, accompanied His Royal Highness.

On arriving at the fair-grounds the party were cheered, to which the Prince, as usual, responded by bowing and raising his hat. He accepted the invitation into the pagoda in the centre of the amphitheatre, and inspected the stock on exhibition, the gaze of the forty thousand being meanwhile full upon him.

The party, at the invitation of the committee, afterwards partook of luncheon in a reserved portion of the building. The sight of the immense multitude on the grounds was during this time very grand, and the enthusiasm ran high.

The drive around the city was resumed a little later, amid prolonged cheering from the citizens, and it was near six o'clock before the illustrious visitors returned to the hotel, much pleased with their day out.

The peculiarities of St. Louis consist in its red brick houses, its smoky and ill-paved streets, its large German population, its hotel life, and the "Western men" who centre in it.

The houses and smoke give it an English aspect; the streets remind me of Cape Town and Melbourne as they were seven years ago; the Germans and German bookstores suggest recollections of Munich; but the hotels and the men are incomparable. They are of the West Western.

The notices posted in every room and passage of those houses of entertainment constitute the best index of the nature of their guests. I see several around me now. One is—"Gentlemen are requested not to spit on the walls or scratch matches on them." Another announces, "If gents throw their boots and shoes into the public hall it must be at their own risk." A third I will not mention. The fourth gives notice that "Gentlemen without a sufficient guarantee of baggage will be required to pay in advance;" that "One gentle pull of the bell is sufficient;" that "Gaming is expressly forbidden," and that "If you leave your light burning after going to bed, it will be the duty of the watchman to inquire the cause." Further, "Guests are requested not to ring after twelve o'clock, nor unnecessarily disturb the quiet of the house during the night," to send the money when they order liquor to their rooms, and if they have meals there, not to place the dishes in the public halls. That all these and more such notices are considered necessary, speaks very poorly for the refinement of the floating population of St. Louis.

Those who want to see the restless and fast-eating propensities of the American character will find them here in their extreme degree.

I need not enumerate the many railways from the East that centre at the city of which I speak, but the 282 mile long line from Kansas, and the 206 mile long line from the direction of the Rocky Mountains, as also the southwestern lines, are worthy of special mention. Yet new threads will soon be added to this giant net-work of railways, and the city, which is now the great starting point from civilization to the wilderness—to Kansas, Nebraska, and Utah, and the rugged wilds of the Rocky Mountains leading to the Territories on the Pacific—will itself become the centre of a vast civilized region, a region which as yet is included in savagedom.

The river fronting St. Louis is about a mile wide and seventy feet deep. Its waters are usually more or less muddy, and stumps of trees may be seen floating quickly onwards in the swelling current, midstream, to the ocean. Sand-banks, barren and dreary, here and there border its shores for several miles beyond, and but little of the picturesque meets the eye. Further up, however, the scenery changes; verdure crowns the elevations, and silver-stemmed birches and green maples, with an occasional clump of huge dark pines, are to be seen.

When the Prince and party returned from their drive they proceeded to the balcony in front of Barnum's Hotel, and witnessed the working of one of three steam fire-engines, which throbbed aloud in quick pulsation as it threw a couple of heavy jets high into the air. The engines were a few minutes later driven under the windows of the royal apartments, where they gave in chorus three excruciating cheers from their steam-pipes, the force of whose sound half deafened the assembled crowd, many of whom would have sacrificed a month's wages rather than have missed a sight of the Prince. He appeared at one of the windows and acknowledged the compliment thus paid him by the firemen, and the people went home satisfied, and new faces took the place of old ones.

His Royal Highness and suite left St. Louis soon after eight.

When I arrived at the railway station in Cincinnati, at ten, I found it crowded with people, who were all in a state of anxious expectation. For the last hundred miles of the journey the stations had been more or less filled with the same eager expectants of the approach of royalty. I had, however, ascertained two hours previously that, owing to the break down of a freight train, the progress of the royal one had been impeded, and that the illustrious party were waiting at Vincennes, the place at which it had been arranged that they were to lunch, till the track was cleared.

A dispatch was received at the hotel at ten, announcing that the royal train would not arrive till two A.M., and at that hour it arrived accordingly.

To me "Porkopolis" is as the face of an old friend; for, years ago, I traversed its streets, and sailed down the bright and rolling waters of the swift Ohio. With its two hundred and sixty thousand inhabitants, it is the largest capital of the Mississippi region, the grand emporium of western commerce, and the fifth in importance and extent in the whole Union. I have ascended the hills that environ the three-mile valley in which the city is situated, and there gazed upon its spires and domes and the pleasant scenery of Kentucky on the opposite shore of the river. I have witnessed the unpoetical operation of pig-killing in its water-side slaughter-houses, where the swinish herd were converted into barreled pork by steam in a space of time almost shockingly short. And I have otherwise explored the ins and outs of the big town which, less than eighty years ago, was a mere village in the wilderness, with a white population of less than a hundred. It is, perhaps, a work of supererogation to say that swine were, and still are to some extent, to Cincinnati what dogs are to Constantinople and buzzards to Lima—namely, very useful scavengers. These wandering pigs are the remnants of droves or "acres," and being considered municipal property are allowed to wallow about the suburbs till the time comes when, according to periodical custom, they are sold by auction, caught, and cut up.

On the next morning, Saturday, the Prince and suite, escorted by the Mayor, left the hotel in open carriages and visited the chief points of interest in and around the city, the drive culminating on Clifton Heights where the party alighted at the residence of Mr. R. B. Bowler, who is not only sole proprietor of the Kentucky Central Railroad, but a gentleman celebrated for the unique and costly splendor of his mansion, which may be called the Vathek of America. Here Mr. Bowler had the honor of entertaining the illustrious travelers at luncheon, after which the drive was resumed.

In the evening there was a ball at the Opera House, the less I say about which the better it will please those concerned.

St. John's Church was the centre of attraction on the Sunday, and I am afraid the eyes of the congregation wandered from their Bibles to the face of Albert Edward more than could have been justified.

Early on the following morning the "Baron" and his friends left by special train for Pittsburg, and arrived there on the same evening. They were received by the Mayor and a committee of citizens at the railway station, and conducted across an illuminated bridge to the Monongahela House.

CHAPTER XXI.

From Pittsburg to Harrisburg—Over the Mountains—Fast Traveling of the Prince—A Mistake—His Royal Highness in Harrisburg—The Ladies and their Affections—The Arrival in Baltimore—The Enthusiasm—The Reception in Washington—Republican Simplicity, etc.

After the four hundred torches had died out on the bridge, the Prince was serenaded by the Duquesne Grays, who had met him on his arrival at Alleghany City. The front of the hotel was at the same time illuminated with gas jets, and the crowd of spectators numbered several thousands. The cross of St. George and the stars and stripes swayed to and fro from lines spanning the street, and notwithstanding the wet the enthusiasm of the people was very great. The popular expectation ran in favor of His Royal Highness presenting himself to the admiring audience on the balcony, but the expectation remained unrealized, for the future King of England wisely partook of dinner and went to bed at an early hour.

At half-past eleven the entire party entered a long file of carriages, and drove by a circuitous route to the Pennsylvania Railway Station. The crowd near the hotel was as large as on the previous evening, and the streets through which the cortege passed were lined with spectators, who cheered and shouted as the procession passed. It was a source of much disappointment to some of the citizens that His Royal Highness did not visit the rolling-mills, at Birmingham, on the opposite side of the Ohio, the coal mines, and other places of industrial interest.

On arriving at the station, the Grays, who were ready to receive the party, cleared a passage where the Prince alighted.

As the train moved away there was a grand rush through the broken lines of the Grays, and the five thousand surged alongside and over the platforms of the cars with semi-frantic enthusiasm, cheering and shouting and waving their hats as they went. The Prince, meanwhile, stood on the rear platform, bowing to the salutations and smiling at the tumult.

The weather, although not rainy, was dull, and the ground wet. But the worst feature of all Pittsburg was the smoke, which filled the streets and everybody in them. The city may well be called the Birmingham of America, which is the dirtiest town in England.

The two hundred and eighty miles' ride from Pittsburg to Harrisburg was one of much interest, and occupied nearly ten hours in its performance. The beautiful scenery of the Alleghany Mountains refreshed the eye mile after mile, hour after hour, as the iron horse careered on its way. There was a pleasing blending of the rugged and the smooth. The finest view lay on the left, till we passed with a rumbling rush through the 3612 feet long tunnel, which has been bored through the solid rock. We were at this time two thousand two hundred feet above the level of the sea. The Juniata River, a tributary of the Susquehanna, and a lengthy stretch of canal, kept us company over a portion of the line, and varied the aspect of the majestic prospect. The mountains now lay on our right, here and there streaked with the rays of the sinking sun; but a gathering mist soon hid them from our view, and, night following quickly after, entirely shrouded the glorious scene. Give me a bright sunny day in spring for a ride through the Alleghanies. Gloom and darkness become them not.

There are as beautiful spots in the Alleghanies as the White Mountains, but they are less known to fame, and the wants of the traveler are here but little attended to, which is in itself a formidable drawback in the eyes of even the most devoted admirer of romantic beauty in the world.

Fertile valleys with a mountain background are ever fine landscape features, and the valleys of the Alleghanies are pre-eminently so.

At the village of Gallitzin, beautifully secluded in a small recess of the Mountains, the train stopped, the door of the Prince's car opened, and that illustrious scion of the reigning family of England emerged therefrom, and, accompanied by his equerries and two or three others of the suite, ascended the locomotive.

No sooner was this done than the train was once more set in motion, and away over the summit of the mountains flew the fire-fed monster, rounding the rapid descent at Kittaning Point, and revealing at every bend some new feature in the magnificent prospect for the delectation of its riders. The moon shed her placid beams upon the delicious and tranquil scene, and as the steam-horse plunged down the valley of the Juniata the view was one of the highest fascination. The river glistened like molten silver, every tree stood out in bold relief on the hill sides, the crags looked naked, the grass green, the foliage sombre, the elevations grand, the steeps lovely, and insensibly the poetry of the hour worked its influence upon the mind of the spectator.

At Altoona the party alighted and re-entered the cars, and so this pleasant incident ended.

It was no joke, but real hard work, this traveling with the Prince. In this respect he may be considered about the fastest young man of the age, and presents a singular contrast to the torpidity of some of his masculine ancestors, who, if it were possible to awaken them from their graves and tell them the history of Victoria's eldest son, would return some such answer as "You may tell that to the marines, but the sailors won't believe it," for before those fellows died, steamers and railways were undreamed of, and the winds of heaven and the sinews of horses were alone trusted to in the performance of a journey. But time works changes, and history proclaims the rest.

I will glance at Harrisburg, where at the hotel I resigned myself to slumber, and awoke to find a large crowd in front of my room window. I drew aside the curtain, when, lo! a thousand voices exclaimed aloud, "There he is!" and fingers were pointed like bayonets at my diminished head—for what could it be but diminished after that, and what better could I do than hide it? I did so, and proceeded to dress, reflecting meanwhile upon the circumstance of my having been, for the moment, mistaken for the gentleman in the next room but one, who at some future period (God willing) will ascend the throne of England and become the nominal ruler of a great people.

At nine o'clock the Prince and suite, having previously breakfasted, drove in open carriages to the State House, from the roof of which a splendid view of the city is obtainable. There you see the silent Susquehanna, coiled like a serpent in a garden, and spotted with flowery islets. You have that pleasant antithesis afforded by an intermingling of hill and valley, mirror-like glimpses of water, verdure, forest, and a town with eleven thousand inhabitants, and after the survey of the prospect you return to *terra firma*, feeling well repaid for the trouble incurred in ascending the steps.

The Mayor, crowned with a hat contrasting in its shallowness with the shiny length of the "stove-pipe" sombreros worn by the royal party, sat beside the Prince, and opposite them sat His Grace the Duke of Newcastle and Lord Lyons. The committee of citizens followed the suite in other carriages.

There was great anxiety manifested by all to get a sight of the British lion, and a hot pursuit of the carriages was the result. This made the way cheerful and dusty, and enabled the illustrious guests to overhear the remarks of the people as to their appearance and the like, which, however, only tended to convince them that they were all good-looking fellows, particularly Albert Edward, with whom all the ladies appeared to have fallen desperately in love, notwithstanding the improbability of that love being ever returned.

At twenty minutes past nine ("Bless me, how exact you are!" exclaims my conscience,) the vehicles found their way to the railway station, and the royal party into the cars of the special train of the Northern Central Railway Company, which started immediately afterwards, in the presence of three or four hundred spectators, who cast one last, long, lingering look after us as we—that is to say the train—receded from their vision.

The scenery after starting, embracing the Susquehanna River, which looked like a miniature lake of the Thousand Islands, was very picturesque, and so were two young women in short frocks, who stood on a hill-side waving towels or pocket-handkerchiefs for the gratification of royal eyes, which saw and sparkled as they glanced.

At every station there was a crowd proportionate to the number of inhabitants, notwithstanding the slender hopes of seeing the object of so much popular curiosity and esteem. Baltimore, however, dimmed every preceding daylight ovation in the States. Along the track on either side, the ground was packed with human forms, but in front of the platform where the car wheels ceased their revolutions, the concourse was as dense as pushing could make it.

A capital brass band played "God save the Queen," and followed up the performance with several other tunes as His Royal Highness stepped from the car, and exchanged a shake of the hand with the Mayor of the city, the British Consul, and the members of a committee of citizens, amid the cheers of the assembled thousands. Everybody seemed disposed to climb on somebody else's shoulders as the Prince, the Duke, Lord Lyons, and others of the suite stood conversing and smiling with those who had just welcomed them to the city. The fineness of the weather enhanced the pleasure of the spectators, and lent a radiant beauty to the picture, natural though it was, and free of everything *bizarre*.

After a few minutes' delay, it being now a quarter past one, the party entered the carriages in waiting—the police, meanwhile, having great difficulty in keeping the multitude even partially in check, so as to allow of a passage sufficient for an individual to struggle through.

The Mayor sat beside the Prince, according to invariable usage, and the cortege drove to the Camden Station of the Baltimore and Ohio Railroad. The thoroughfares through which the carriages passed were lined with citizens, and thousands followed behind and alongside, cheering and waving hats, caps, and newspapers; while ladies, with fluttering pocket-handkerchiefs, eyed the great hero of the day with intense delight, which subsided into regret as he disappeared from their view. Alas! that these young ladies should have been born to wish for what they could never have.

The crowd at the other station was very large as the royal party alighted from their carriages and took leave of the Mayor and citizens till their return, after which the special train moved onward towards Washington, where we arrived, without incident, at four o'clock. General Cass was on the platform to receive His Royal Highness, and, on being introduced by Lord Lyons, shook hands with him very warmly. He then welcomed him to the United States in a few words, and introduced the Private Secretary of the President, Mayor Berret, Mr. Ledyard, and a few others, with each of whom the Prince exchanged a cordial greeting. He was then conducted to the President's carriage, in waiting, in which General Cass took his seat beside him. The suite having been seated in other private equipages, all drove away towards the White House.

The sides of Pennsylvania Avenue were thickly studded with men, women, and children, and in the road fronting the White House there was another large gathering.

He was received at the threshold of the White House by President Buchanan, who looked as composed as usual. He shook him by the hand in the most fatherly manner imaginable, and like one who knew his guest well. It was just such a hearty welcome as a rich old bachelor uncle would give to the nephew he intended to make his heir. There was, consequently, no mistake about its sincerity.

Of course, it was not long before he introduced his niece, Miss Lane, to his illustrious guest, and the blush of beauty stole across her features as she echoed the old man's greeting, more inwardly, however, than aloud.

In the course of an hour after this, the grounds of the White House presented a gay scene. The President, with the Prince and suite, and nearly a hundred ladies and gentlemen, composed of the *élite* of Washington society, were out walking and enjoying the pleasures of fresh air, a fine view and cheerful conversation. Meanwhile, the boys and girls from the back streets were enjoying their part in the world's great show, by grinning at them through the gate railings and other places in the distance, which latter, no doubt, lent enchantment to the view.

Dinner followed at the Presidential mansion, the company, in addition to the royal party, consisting of Cabinet Ministers and their wives, Lord Lyons and his first Secretary of Legation, and two or three others.

It was about eleven on the next morning when the Prince, accompanied by Lord Lyons, Secretary Floyd, and others, drove up to the eastern front of the Capitol, where he was received by the architect and chief engineer of the public works, and by them conducted over the building. First they visited the library, from which they passed by a private staircase to the Senate Chamber and the committee-rooms, and thence to the rotunda, where the beautiful paintings hung round its magnificent interior attracted their especial attention. The history of Pocahontas was inquired into, and even the "Surrender of Lord Cornwallis" became a theme of pleasant conversation. From this they proceeded through the old hall of the House of Representatives to the new hall of the House, where the sides occupied by the administration and opposition members were pointed out, and much general information afforded in answer to their queries. The Speaker's room was next entered, then the Agricultural and other rooms, the Naval and Military Committee apartments and offices of the Senate. The party then viewed the Capitol grounds from the portico of the east front, and, descending the steps after half an hour's stay, drove back to the White House, where, at noon, the doors were thrown open for the President's reception in honor of the Prince of Wales.

I went in with the crowd of ladies and gentlemen, nearly all of whom were in their usual morning dress, a few military and naval uniforms excepted. Such a flutter of crinoline never was seen in the Presidential Mansion before, such a glistening of bright eyes, all having the one object in view; such a busy murmur of women's voices, all bearing upon the one theme, and that theme the Prince of Wales, who stood almost within hearing in the east room, and on the right of the President.

I need not mention how Mr. Buchanan was dressed, for he was perhaps never seen either at breakfast, dinner, or supper, in any other costume than a black dress suit and white necktie; but I may say that the Prince appeared in the same colored clothes that he wore during the morning.

It was evidently wonderfully new to His Royal Highness to see such familiarity between ruler and subject as he did on this occasion. It was contrary to his ideas of a levee for ladies to attend, especially when they all came up smiling in their bonnets, and said, "How are you, Mr. Buchanan?" at the same time extending their hands for the old gentleman to shake, which he did with his usual warmth and frankness, so much so that if he had exclaimed to those he knew best, "Bless me, Betsey, how well you're looking," it would have created but little surprise on the part of Albert Edward.

The host of the White House stood on the eastern window side of the room, but not far from its centre, and very soon the apartment, extensive as it is, became uncomfortably crowded, and the Prince showed signs of weariness of the reception before it had progressed half an hour. Many of the ladies and some of the gentlemen extended their hands to him after exchanging a cordial shake with the President, and this His Royal Highness evidently felt to be a great bore, although politeness compelled him to submit to it with a show of pleasure.

The reception did not last an hour, and many that arrived at one o'clock were too late for presentation, although most of them succeeded in obtaining a glimpse of him standing near the central window of the mansion, where he engaged in conversation with Mr. Buchanan and his suite.

After luncheon the Prince and party, including Miss Lane, drove to the Patent-office, where they inspected the Japanese collection, the autographs of celebrated persons, and other curiosities, in addition to the models, plans, and such like, for which the building is mainly intended. From this the lady of the White House took her royal guest to—what will his mother and the people of England say?—a young ladies' academy, where he, the future King of England, played ten-pins for two hours with Miss Lane herself and her friends. This was a fine afternoon amusement, certainly, and no doubt will long be remembered both by the Prince of Wales and all the young ladies present on the occasion.

At half-past six, thirty-five sat down to dinner at the White House, the guests being chiefly the foreign ministers at Washington. In the evening about six hundred ladies and gentlemen were present by invitation, and at half-past nine the much-talked of fire-works began, and lasted hardly half an hour. The sky pieces were very brilliant, notwithstanding the misty atmosphere and a drizzling rain that fell. Fountains of flame played without intermission for more than a minute in the air, and floods of crimson and golden light were let loose in the heavens with a result that was gorgeous in the extreme.

Five sixths of the population of Washington and its suburbs were on the ground when the last piece—a frame-work device, including the arms of England and the United States, with symbols and mottoes, and the figures of Columbia and Britannia—blazed out upon the view with a splendor not to be depicted in words.

During the whole time of this pyrotechnical display the President and his royal guest, together with as many of the six hundred as could find standing room under the rear portico, were witnesses of it.

When the last lights had died away there was a tremendous rush towards the gates leading into Pennsylvania Avenue, and down that wide thoroughfare there poured, for more than an hour, a torrent of human beings, carriages, and omnibuses, such as the Federal Metropolis never saw before.

CHAPTER XXII.

The Prince's Visit to Mount Vernon—The Trip of the Royal Party and Hosts down the Potomac—Arrival at Mount Vernon—The Prince evinces a deep Interest in the History of Washington—He Plants a Tree in Commemoration of his Visit—He Pockets some Horse-Chestnuts, which he intends to Plant in Windsor Park—The Return Trip—The Quarter-Deck of the Revenue Cutter Devoted to the Disciples of Terpsichore—The Prince at Richmond, etc.

THE most interesting event connected with the Prince of Wales' progress through the United States was the visit, with President Buchanan to the Tomb of Washington, of which it has been truly said:

There rests the man, the flower of human kind,
Whose visage mild bespoke his nobler mind;
There rests the soldier who his sword ne'er drew
But in a righteous cause, to freedom true;
There rests the hero, who ne'er fought for fame,
Yet gained more glory than a Cæsar's name;
There rests the statesman who, devoid of art,
Gave soundest counsel from an upright heart.
And, Oh! Columbia, by thy sons caressed,
There rests the Father of the realms he blessed,
Who no wish felt to make his mighty praise,
Like other chiefs, the means himself to raise;
But when retiring, breathed in pure renown,
And felt a grandeur that disowned a crown.

The party, in addition to Mr. Buchanan and the Prince and suite, consisted of Miss Lane, Mr. Cass, all the heads of departments and their wives and daughters, and several others of less official note. The steamer in which they made the excursion was the Government cutter Harriet Lane. Only those of the royal and official party were admitted on board, not excepting the gentlemen of the press, for the worthy host of the White House had said, in reply to a question bearing upon them, "No; the press is to be suppressed on this occasion."

As the Prince and Miss Lane were passing from the carriage to the steamer, which lay at the foot of the Arsenal, amid the boom of a national salute, one of the officers of the establishment stepped forward and presented her with a bouquet, upon which she mirthfully feigned to believe that it was intended for her companion, and offered it to him; but Albert Edward, with his usual gallantry, laughed, and assured her that the flowers were for her, and she accepted the assurance and the bouquet accordingly.

Then, at eleven o'clock, and all being on board, the paddle-wheels flew round, while the last notes of "God save the Queen" were being played by the Marine Band on deck. Another national salute was fired, and the flags with which the rigging was dressed fluttered gayly in the sunshine and the breeze as the vessel glided through the glistening waters of the Potomac towards Mount Vernon.

The beauty of the weather enhanced the yet rarer beauty of the scenery, through which the winding stream coursed so calmly that hardly a ripple broke its mirror-like surface. On either hand the dark green foliage of the woods enframed it, save where the spires and chimneys of Alexandria rose on the right. Some small steamers and sailing craft lay at its wharf, and were dressed in honor of the passing guest. Conversation filled up the time during which the sixteen miles from Washington were run, and the Prince declared it a delightful sail. The steamer anchored. The party went ashore in small boats, and were met on the platform by Mr. John A. Washington, who conducted them to the tomb, on arriving at which the band played the dirge "Trovatore," the solemn and impressive strains of which added a singular effect to the scene.

All present felt they were standing on hallowed

ground. Around them was the deep wooded dell in which venerable oaks spread their brawny arms over luxuriant shrubbery, extending to the water's side. Before them was the mausoleum—an arched vault, surrounded by a brick wall, with a pointed arch and double gates of iron railings opening into the outer chamber, in which were two marble sarcophagi, on each of which rested a slab; the one to the right bearing the inscription, "Within this inclosure rest the remains of General George Washington," and the other, "Martha, wife of Washington."

The Prince made several remarks appreciative of the glorious character of the man whose death was deplored by his country and whose deeds and history are imperishable. He expressed a willingness to plant a tree on the spot in commemoration of his visit, and, some horse-chestnuts having been handed to him, he stooped down and placed them in the earth. He afterwards put a few more in his pocket with the intention as he said, of planting them in Windsor Park on his return home as another memento of a visit which he should ever regard with feelings of peculiar interest.

From the tomb the company bent their steps towards the house of Washington—a long, two-storied wooden building facing the river, and with two wings standing at right angles to it and connected with the main part by open corridors, while the entrance in the court, formed by the wings, was flanked by a row of negro huts and other out-buildings in the rear. This was only thirty yards distant, and approached by a path across the grounds.

For more than two hours the illustrious visitors continued their stay, during the whole time of which they were occupied in visiting and inquiring into the surroundings of the interesting spot. They then returned by boats to the steamer, where a *dejeuner* was at once served; after which, by general consent, there was a dance on deck, the speed of the vessel being reduced at His Royal Highness' suggestion, in order to prolong the pleasure.

Then flying feet tripped to the swell of music, and eyes looked love to eyes which spake again, as Byron said of the ball at Brussels.

It was more than half-past five when the Harriet Lane touched the wharf at the Navy Yard, where private carriages were in waiting for the fortunate few.

A salute was fired in honor of the return, and soon afterwards the cortege created a sensation on Pennsylvania Avenue, which attracted long lines of spectators. A crowd on foot, on horseback, and in vehicles, also kept pace with the procession in the middle of the road.

At eight the Prince and suite, the Marquis of Chandos, and others, dined with Lord Lyons at his residence, and on Saturday morning His Royal Highness took leave of the President, his niece, and others, with regret and many assurances of the pleasure he had derived from his stay at the Federal Metropolis and White House.

He then left Washington, accompanied by the members of the Cabinet, on board the Harriet Lane, at a few minutes past ten, under a salute from the Arsenal and amid the cheers of crowds collected at the riverside.

After a sail of fifty-five miles down the picturesque stream, he landed at Acquia Creek, on the Virginia shore, from which he proceeded by the special train in waiting to the capital of the Old Dominion.

The multitude that congregated at every station on the way was surprisingly large, but Richmond itself, in the eager demonstration of its assembled thousands, eclipsed every other place the Prince had visited.

The Mayor and a committee of citizens were in waiting to receive him at the Fair Grounds Railway Station, two miles out of town, on his arrival, which took place about six; but owing to the immense crowd at the Exchange Hotel, where he quartered, it was seven o'clock before he entered his rooms, and then only after struggling through a swaying mass that, not only filled the adjoining streets, but all the approaches to his apartments. It was not till some hours had elapsed that curiosity abated sufficiently to clear the neighborhood of the multitude anxious to see the heir apparent to the British throne, when all was as tranquil as usual in this quiet-going old city.

Like good Christians, the Prince and his suite went to St. Paul's Church on the Sunday, and I occupied a pew next—but twenty-one—to His Royal Highness. The congregation was large and fashionable, and, of course, there was the usual display of crinoline, kid gloves, and pretty bonnets, and the usual flutter among the ladies of the Old Dominion. Indeed, the lady members of the congregation were in a delightful state of excitement from the arrival to the departure of Albert Edward of Wales, who has been the object of many of the most endearing expressions I have ever heard, from cradledom up to the present moment. But let me not tell tales. I have no wish to be an eavesdropper.

The crowd that escorted him to church by following his carriage afoot was only exceeded by the crowd that pursued him thence to the Capitol after the conclusion of the ordinary service. He was accompanied at this time only by the Duke of Newcastle, Lord Lyons, and the Mayor of the city.

They were received on arriving by the Governor of the State, who conducted them, first, into the Hall of Delegates, where an old arm-chair, formerly that of the Speaker of the House of Burgesses, while this country was a British colony, was pointed out to them; also the full length portraits, in oil, of the Earl of Chatham, in a Roman toga, and Thomas

Jefferson, which were originally bequeathed to the county of Westmoreland, and by the county given to Virginia. Here the crowd surrounded the royal party, and it was with difficulty that the few composing it passed into the rotunda, the multitude surging after them in their exuberance of good feeling.

The marble statue of Washington, by Houdon, in the centre of this, first attracted their attention.

A marble bust of Lafayette filled one of the eight niches of the surrounding wall, the other seven being empty.

The Senate chamber was next entered, a stream of men and boys pouring in at the same time. They then descended the steps to the portico, from which, owing to the Capitol being situated on an elevated plain near the summit of Shockhoe Hill, a wide and picturesque view presented itself. The course of the James River was there traceable for miles, and a complete panorama of the city, with all its hill and dale, riveted the eye.

From this point Richmond had a far more imposing effect than as viewed from any other portion of the city. The approach by river, however, commands a still finer prospect; but this vanishes like mirage as the vessel draws alongside the wharf, where all is prosaic black and white. And now His Royal Highness stepped a hundred yards into the Governor's house, where several of the family and friends of the latter were presented.

Ten minutes elapsed before the visitors drove back to the hotel, followed by a rushing mass of people.

After luncheon, the Prince, the Mayor, and several of the suite drove to the Holywood Cemetery, a mile out of town, where, at the monument erected over the grave of Monroe, the party halted in silence.

They subsequently visited St. John's Church, where Patrick Henry and Richard Henry Lee once declaimed in front of what is now the communion table. A suburban drive followed, and they returned home to dinner.

The Prince and suite drove to the railway station, accompanied by the Mayor, at nine o'clock on the next morning, and left by a special train.

Soon after the royal party had taken leave of the Mayor and committee, and the train was set in motion, a violent rain-storm set in, accompanied with vivid flashes of lightning, which had the effect of thinning the number of spectators along the road. By the time the train reached Petersburg, the birth-place of Washington, sixty miles from Richmond, the rain had ceased, and the day promised fair again. Sixteen miles further on was the Acquia Creek Terminus, where the party alighted, and, after a short delay, embarked on the steamer Powhatan, which had been specially chartered for this service. Owing to several inlets, the waters of the Potomac here assumed a lake-like spread, and this, with the many indentations of the wooded shore, had a highly picturesque effect, and the eye lingered long in contemplation of its beauty.

On went the steamer, an Irishman on the wharf exclaiming to the Prince as she started, "May luck go wid you. And, bedad, I only wish I'd an ould shoe to fling afther yez, for its not the likes of yez as come here every day."

A glimpse of the house at Mount Vernon, almost embowered in foliage, was succeeded by a full view of Fort Washington.

The special train which conveyed the party from Washington to Baltimore, arrived at the station shortly after eight o'clock. They were met by the Mayor and some of the committee, who accompanied them to the Gilmor House, under an escort of the City Guard and Independent Grays, the bands of which executed some spirited music by the way, commencing with "God save the Queen."

A large concourse had assembled at the station, and

there was much enthusiastic shouting. Thousands followed the procession to the hotel, where another great crowd had been long in waiting.

Dinner followed, then a serenade and sleep.

CHAPTER XXIII.

The Departure from Baltimore, and Arrival at Philadelphia—Enthusiasm of the People—Quarters of the Prince at the Continental—He occupies the same Rooms as did the Japanese Princes—Incidents, etc.

SHORTLY before eleven, His Royal Highness and party left the hotel in open carriages, accompanied by the Mayor, and enjoyed a pleasant drive on their way to the railway station. Among the objects of interest they passed were the two hundred feet Doric column of the Washington Monument, on Mount Vernon place, and the marble column of the Battle Monument, in memory of those who fell while defending the city in 1814.

A fragment of the great crowd that had gathered in front of the hotel, ran after the carriages for a considerable distance. Passers-by halted, and so lined the streets as the carriages were seen approaching, and the curiosity of the people was only equaled by their evident respect.

On reaching the railway station, where several thousands had assembled to see the party step from their carriages—the general public being debarred admission inside—His Royal Highness was received by a guard of honor of the Independent Grays, the band of which struck up "God save the Queen," with much spirit.

The Prince and noblemen and gentlemen of the suite, having taken a kind leave of the Mayor and members of the committee, to whom they expressed the pleasure their visit to Baltimore had afforded them, entered the royal car, which, preceded by one containing the attendants, moved away towards the Quaker City, in the midst of enthusiastic cheering from those on the platform. The numbers gathered at the wayside stations were few, compared with other places I could name, and even in Philadelphia itself the popular demonstration was slight; but this was all the more agreeable to His Royal Highness. The Susquehanna River, which was crossed on the usual ferry steamer, revived recollections of Harrisburg where it was first sighted. The weather was fine, and the journey devoid of more than ordinary incident.

On the arrival of the special train at the station, soon after four o'clock, the Prince was met by the Mayor, who welcomed him to the city in a few words. The members of the suite were severally introduced after this, when the Mayor conducted His Royal Highness to one of the carriages in waiting, and taking his seat beside him, with Lord Lyons and the Duke of Newcastle opposite, the party drove directly to the Continental Hotel.

All was quiet till the arrival at the hotel, where a large crowd had collected. Owing, however, to the royal carriage having been driven to the Ninth Street entrance, instead of the private one on Chestnut Street, as was expected, very few became aware of its arrival till the occupants had entered the house.

There was a general feeling of disappointment after this, and the multitude remained for hours gazing upwards towards the windows of the apartments occupied by the distinguished travelers.

These were the same that were devoted to the use of the Japanese Ambassadors. The Prince's bedroom was the one in which that bamboo-complexioned individual, Simmie Boojzen No-Kami, reclined his weary limbs, and the smallest and plainest of the entire suit.

Those who suppose that His Royal Highness and suite dressed for dinner every day are mistaken. There was little ceremony observed in this respect, and the only peculiarity about the royal dining and sitting rooms was in the long, red, white, and blue wax candles which were invariably to be seen burning on the tables during the hours of gaslight.

The chief event of the next morning was a drive, and this proved to be a very long one.

Mayor Henry accompanied the party, and visit number one was paid to Girard College, where a large crowd had collected, and they were received by the President and the Directors. The schools were in session, and the scholars hard at work, as at the time of the visit of the Japanese. But the boys and girls did not lose the opportunity of enjoying a good look at the illustrious visitors, and particularly one of them, as they passed through.

The Prince smiled and displayed his usual affability, while to several he addressed a few words of congratulation. From the school-rooms they were conducted to the front of the President's house, where that estimable functionary made the best of the occasion by presenting some horse-chestnuts to His Royal Highness and asking him to plant them ; " for," said he, " a tree so grown may serve to tell the recipients of the bounty of Girard of your visit."

The future King of England complied accordingly, with the assistance of a gardener, who, as it happened, marched in the procession in London in honor of the coronation of Queen Victoria. This was told to the Prince, who crammed it into his mental bread-basket, along with many other similar incidents which have occurred during his present tour.

Of course, in visiting the College, they could not omit its roof, for from that point of elevation a panorama of the city unfolds itself, with the Delaware and the country around visible in the distance.

With this end in view they ascended a succession of narrow and dimly lighted steps, and finally put their heads out into clear daylight at the top.

The roof was broad and nearly flat, and formed of squares of stone lapped over each other after the fashion of tiles.

Unfortunately, as the party were admiring the view, the wind, which blew rather fresh at the time, lifted the hat off the royal head and sent it flying from stone to stone, till it fell over into the garden beneath. This was awkward, but the young man bore it calmly, and when somebody near (it was one of the committee) offered the loan of his own in its place, Albert Edward gratefully accepted the favor, and became the wearer of the borrowed hat till his own was brought up from the regions below.

I consider this last incident as quite a feather in the cap of the eldest son of Mr. Buchanan's "good friend," and she is good, which is more than we can say of all crowned heads.

From the College the party went to the Eastern Penitentiary, a building from which radiate seven wings, in which the cells are built. The central building was crowded with ladies and gentlemen, who had come in anticipation of the visit. Many of these were introduced to him by the prison authorities, upon which the usual hands-shaking took place.

The party were afterwards conducted through the wards, during which the Prince inquired after the cell alluded to by Charles Dickens, in his "American Notes," as having been entirely and beautifully painted by a German sentenced to five years' imprisonment for larceny. Dickens had an interview with this man, whom he described as the most dejected, heart-broken, wretched creature it would be possible to imagine.

Before leaving the institution the party inscribed

their names in the visitors' book, the Prince simply signing Albert Edward, in a small, neat hand. No sooner had he turned his back upon the writing than there was a rush of ladies, anxious to scan the "dear fellow's" penmanship, which, as a matter of course, they pronounced exquisite.

Still another corridor was visited after this, and there the Prince entered into conversation with one Judge Vondersmith, who deported himself with the utmost nonchalance. He was a miserable-looking man, in a tight-fitting suit of blue woolen, and as he stood in his gloomy square cell both his position and prospects afforded a striking contrast to the young man with whom he conversed. Alas! that society should present such inequalities.

I saw one of the unhappy creatures there incarcerated burst into tears as the Prince took his departure.

The party then went to the Asylum for the Insane, where one of the lunatics danced a jig in celebration of so unusual an event. From this to the Park was but a short drive, and here the lovers of the picturesque enjoyed a refreshing view, embracing a beautiful extent of timbered and grass land, with the Schuylkill River winding in the foreground and a glimpse of the city and the Delaware to the right. The weather was clear and sunny to a delightful degree; and as the cortege neared the main building or hotel fronting the race-course, where a temporary platform had been erected for the accommodation of a more than ordinary number of visitors, in consequence of this anticipated visit, the scene was enlivened by the presence of thirty thousand people scattered about the course, but more particularly near the grand stand—if I may so call it.

No sooner did the carriages appear in sight than a swarm set in around the building, and the uproar of voices filled the air. The men were equally eager with the women to get a glimpse of England's hope. On alighting the visitors proceeded, in the midst of a warm display of curiosity on the part of the collected thousands, to the northern part of the building allud ed to, where they were gazed upon by a battery of bright eyes from the opposite or southern point.

Albert Edward's natural modesty recoiled before so embarrassing a spectacle; but, eventually recovering, His Royal Highness beguiled the flying moments by turning a segar into smoke. At half-past two, general attention was diverted from the contemplation of the Prince of Wales to the races, which were the ostensible cause of so great an assemblage of the brave and fair. There was a sudden cry of "They're off!" and then there was one minute and forty-seven and a quarter seconds of suspense before the race was decided by "Rosa Bonneur" flying past the winning post, pursued by her competitors in a manner highly suggestive of that celebrated neck and crop race once run by Johnny Gilpin, of Cowper notoriety. The single mile handicup was won, and the winners were left to chuckle—for those may laugh who win, says the old song.

The band, which had played on the arrival of the grandees, now struck up again, and a transplanted Irishman exclaimed, as he looked towards what had once more become the centre of attraction: "Arrah, bedad, and there he is," which was a fact.

The Prince and party then stepped down to their carriages and drove away, a few cheers following them as they went.

It was near six o'clock when they returned to the hotel, where a large crowd had gathered to see the lions, and many saw and felt rewarded for their toil.

At five minutes past eight, His Royal Highness, the Duke of Newcastle, the Earl St. Germains, Lord Lyons, General Bruce, Major Teesdale, Captain Gray, Dr. Ackland, Lord Hinchinbrook, Hon. Mr. Eliot, Mr. Englehart, Mr. Warre, and Mr. Jenner, accompanied by the Mayor, entered their boxes at the Academy of Music. These boxes were two in number, and on opposite sides of the stage. Over the royal, or north proscenium balcony box, externally, were the arms of the United States and England, and the stars and stripes and union-jack, tastefully arranged. These were the only visible decorations of the royal box. But those in the boxes fronting it, had a glimpse of a vase of flowers and a silver ice pitcher, standing on a table with a marble top, in a luxurious divan lighted with a mellow radiance, which allowed fine scope for the imagination.

As the royal party took their seats, the curtain rose, the band rose, the audience rose.

The house, lighted by the hundred jets, sparkling in the glassy chandelier, had a brilliant appearance, so also had the stage, with its group of theatrical villagers, foremost among whom stood Patti and Formes, the shrill soprano of the one breaking out with a sudden thrill, to which the deep bass of the others was as thunder to lightning, the silence of the latter element excepted.

Formes came in at the second part with the verses in honor of the Prince, composed for the occasion.

The others joined in a grand chorus, the curtain dropped, and all sat down, while the gaze of the assemblage fell upon the royal box, the occupants of which were in plain evening dress.

The curtain again rose, and now upon the opening scene of Flotow's grand opera of "Martha."

In the *entrée acte*—the interval between the end of "Martha" and the opening of "La Traviata"—the Prince and other occupants of the royal box removed to the front seat of the first tier, which had just been vacated by the Marquis of Chandos, and friends. His Royal Highness beckoned to the others of his party in the opposite box, and they joined him. The curtain rose on a scene which rivaled the appearance of the finest ball-room of its size in the world. But what was the scene compared with the actors, and one especially, Madame Pauline Colson? She was bewitching, and to my taste, she rivaled Piccolomini. There was a voluptuous grace about her acting, which carried with it fascination; there was a melody in her song which was irresistible and carried away all hearers. Welcome, Madame Pauline Colson! Violetta has no choicer impersonation than thou. Signor Errani, as Alfredo, did well, and the masculine swell of his voice sounded well in response to the warbling music of Pauline.

But what was all this to the scene itself—the chiseled arms, the beaming faces, eyes included; the costumes, grand in the abstract, but faulty in detail; the mass, the lights, the cause of all this—the Prince—the illuminated crimson of the proscenium box? Everybody can imagine such a scene for themselves. Therefore, adieu. All ended well, and at the conclusion the Prince retired, well pleased with the performance.

CHAPTER XXIV.

New York's Glorious Welcome to the Prince—A Million on Broadway and Fifth Avenue—Splendid Military Spectacle—The Review on the Battery and in the Park—Five Miles of Human Beings—Housetops, Brick Piles, Lamp-Posts, Windows, Steps, Awning-Posts, Doorways, Carriages, Boxes, Stages, Carts, Iron Railings, and Trees, from the Battery to Madison Square, Covered with Men, Women, and Children—The Diamond Ball—Grand Procession of Firemen, etc., etc.

ON the morning following the Opera, His Royal Highness and suite left Philadelphia by a special train for Amboy, where he embarked on board the U. S.

steamer Harriet Lane, which the President had dispatched for the purpose. There he was met by many of the New York Committee of four hundred citizens, who accompanied him to the city. Salvos of twenty-one guns were fired from Fort Hamilton and the other batteries, as the steamer passed, and on nearing Castle Garden salutes were also fired from the shipping, while the cheers of tens of thousands swelled in a joyous chorus of welcome, and great was the waving of hats, the flutter of handkerchiefs, and the display of bunting.

On stepping ashore at half-past two, His Royal Highness was received by Mayor Wood, who welcomed him cordially to the commercial metropolis, and after a little delay, introduced him to Major General Sandford, commanding the First Division of the New York State Militia, who invited him to review the same, to which the Prince assented. He shortly afterwards made his appearance on horseback in full uniform, accompanied by his suite and the staff officers. He was received with all the military honors, ruffles, colors drooping, arms presented, and band playing. The troops numbered more than six thousand, and presented a splendid appearance. The review was made by brigades numerically in succession, and as they were formed on different lines, the Prince had a fine opportunity of watching their entire movements.

At the close of the review His Royal Highness entered his carriage, which was drawn by six horses, and in company with his suite and the Mayor, preceded by a military column, was driven slowly towards the City Hall, followed by the troops in regular order. After alighting, they ascended a carpeted platform, and the troops marched past in the prearranged order. All, however, had not passed at ten minutes past five, by which time it was dusk. It was, therefore, thought advisable to cry "Halt!" and the carriages of the royal party were soon moving up Broadway, the

Prince reviewing the troops formed in line as he passed. The acclamations that, thenceforward to the Fifth Avenue Hotel, rent the air, as the royal cortege passed mile after mile between lines of human beings, surpassed every other demonstration that ever took place in America. No grander ovation to the representative of the elder branch of the Anglo-Saxon race, was possible. Here the *entente cordiale* with England was proclaimed to the skies by hundreds of thousands of freemen, who hailed the coming and showered hearty blessings upon the head of the son of that peerless Queen, whose virtues shed a halo round the throne of England, and constitute the pride and joy of all where England's tongue is spoken and England's honor loved —of England our mother country.

In moral significance, as well as in the material fact, the spectacle was one never to be surpassed, while the entirely spontaneous and hearty homage was imbued with a peculiar interest from the antecedents of the two nations.

It is unnecessary for me to enter into the minutiæ of the day's proceedings, after the idea I have already given of the whole. But had I the necessary space, I might fill a volume merely with descriptions of scenes *en route*, for the mighty masses of men, women, and children that lined the way, and looked down from the housetops, trees, and lamp-posts, and wherever else the human form could cling, are still in memory vividly before me, and every detail of the imposing pageant I can summon to my recollection.

To convey an idea of the crowd, which, next to the Prince, was the great curiosity of the day, is difficult. It was huge, immense, enormous, exaggerated, stupendous, infinite, and indefinite. It was a multitude countless as the leaves of the forest—one of those crushes which are perfectly bewildering to the senses. Below, a stratum of humanity was so wedged in and Macadamized together that to move one individual was to stir the whole mass; while above, every window-sill was a rough frame, within which the faces of beautiful women and smiling children made up an attractive picture. Every opening, every story, every roof, was a parapet, from which constantly played a battery of bright eyes. Every available place was occupied, and where circumstances naturally failed to provide accommodations, ingenuity brought into requisition boxes, benches, chairs, tables, and any other appliance that would effect the desired object.

Those who could not enjoy the privileges of a window were content to take to the street, and the quantity of well-dressed ladies and children, mixed in with the not over fragrant crowd of unscoured publicans and sinners, was painfully amazing to behold. Once in, it was almost impossible to get out, and the poor females were compelled to endure the pains of purgatory to gratify the curiosity they couldn't help. Even the side streets were made available, and vehicles of various kinds were pressed into service and speedily crowned with an array of human beings. To the boys the lamp-posts and iron railings were a godsend; and though now and then by looking up, the spectator might see tattered integuments fluttering in the breeze from points of the human corporosity, little attention was paid to these freaks of nature and accident. On the whole the crowd was altogether unobjectionable, except to its individual components. Occasionally there would be an eruption of highly oxygenated adjectives that would make a man's ears tingle with holy horror, or sometimes some quick temper would strike out from the shoulder, and be quietly removed from the scene of action by gentlemen in blue coats; but, with these exceptions, everything was harmonious, melodious, and good.

At one point a beautiful bouquet was thrown into the Prince's carriage, accompanied by the following lines:

Accept, dear Prince, this humble gift,
 With every kind and loyal prayer;
May Heaven your Highness ever lift
 Above each sad and worldly care.

One prayer among the rest I send;
 Maternal love thus makes me sing,
Though I would not yourself offend:
 May it be long ere you are King.

As soon as the royal cortege passed the regiment in review, owing to the lateness of the hour, it would immediately defile and proceed to the place of dismissal, so that by the time the Prince reached the head of the line the corps at the opposite end had departed for their respective armories.

Long before the cortege reached the hotel, it had become so dark that nothing more than a slim figure in military uniform could be seen of the Prince by the immense multitude that had been waiting in eager expectation of his coming for several hours. This was a cause of great disappointment to tens of thousands, and many of the female portion burst into tears when they found he had gone by without their having seen him.

The concourse in front of the hotel had, however, a glimpse of him as he appeared on the balcony for a few moments soon after his arrival, in acknowledgment of the pæans of welcome which resounded on all sides.

On the following morning, His Royal Highness drove to the University, where he was received by the principals, after which the Chancellor presented an address on behalf of the council. He next visited the Astor Library, then the Cooper Institute, then the New York Free Academy, at each of which places he was received with respectful formality.

A pleasant drive to the Central Park followed next, where the Commissioners did the honors by conducting the party over some of the most favored resorts.

Before leaving, the Prince, at the suggestion of his guides, planted a sapling of oak and another of elm, as emblematical of the two nations. From the park the drive was continued to the rural cottage of His Honor Mayor Wood, where a grand *dejeuner* was served, of which the royal party partook, in company with a number of leading citizens. The Institution for the Deaf and Dumb was visited after this, and here the party were greatly interested by the proficiency displayed by the mutes in composition on the various subjects suggested to them, as also by a young lady, who read a few verses in welcome of the Prince by the usual signs.

The ball given by the committee of four hundred citizens was the great event of the evening. The tickets not being purchasable, the company was limited to the committee and their immediate friends. This was a mistake. In a democratic country like this, an exclusive gathering of the kind ought not to have been tolerated. A high price upon the tickets, and stringent rules as to costume, would have insured, not only as select a company as were there present, but an assembly less composed of old fogies. If the moneyed and venerable Cooperites who had the management of the affair, and who knew as much about dancing as the celebrated pig in the hornpipe, wished to be exceedingly aristocratic, why did they not content themselves with the selection of "ladies patronesses," through whose voucher tickets only could be obtained? If this plan is considered perfectly satisfactory by the nobility of an old monarchical country like England, and in a great city like London, it ought to have satisfied the New York committee of four hundred. As it was, New York did not give the Prince a ball, but a certain number of gentlemen, who subscribed a certain amount of money with which to do the thing handsomely. It was a pity, after all their pains, that the floor over the parquette should have fallen in just as the dancing was about to commence. Either the committee or the carpenters had made a bad job of it there. This and the fall from the front tier to the floor of two large flower vases were the mishaps of the night. The other drawbacks were the consequent postponement of dancing till the carpenters had propped up the floor, the great crush of spectators around the royal party after the dancing commenced, and the comparative insignificance of the number that danced at all.

The ball, however, had its bright side, as everything must have, especially when it belongs to New York. The dresses and *toilettes* of the ladies could not have been eclipsed in magnificence and elegance by any in the world, while for beauty and the display of diamonds, where could their like be met? I know, from long travel and experience, that the women of the United States, and especially of the Empire City, are matchless in their grace and chiseled beauty, while their exquisite taste in matters of costume is enough to win over those who have to pay their bills into a tacit consent to endless extravagance.

Three thousand of the *élite* were present, and the Academy of Music, in which the ball was given, wore a most brilliant appearance.

A shout outside, followed by repeated cheers, announced the arrival of the Prince, and almost instantly the royal party, dressed in full evening costume, entered the room by a side door. There was no cheering, but a simultaneous motion of the crowd evinced the anxiety of the company to see their distinguished guests. There was no rush forward. A few ladies stepped gracefully upon the chairs near them to overlook the throng, but the rest of the company retained their positions with well-bred composure, the spectators in the upper tiers rising, not from curiosity, but in honor of the Prince. The royal party remained standing before the sofas at the extremity of the stage, beneath the pavilion, and as soon as they had taken their positions, the bands struck up the stately anthem, "God save the Queen," following it by the more triumphant strains of "Hail Columbia." The first effect of the scene upon the senses was so dazzling as to render it impossible to separate any distinct or individual parts. Flowers reposing in folds of fleecy lace, lace rising and falling in rich foam-like waves, jewels paling before the fire of bright eyes, or flashing back radiantly from velvet backgrounds; gold and silver glittering in the transparent tarlatane fabrics so thickly embroidered with the same precious substance that they looked like cloth of gold; silver brocade, fair and shining, looking kindly on the stiff and stately moire; flowers, ribbons, jewels, feathers, and the odor of a thousand parterres, all mingling with the lights, the music and the graceful moving throng.

While the royal party were observing the company and the decorations of the room, a sudden rustle and movement of the crowd backwards announced that some accident was about to happen, and in a moment after one of the flower vases upon the front tier fell with a great crash to the floor, scattering its roses upon the people standing by, but fortunately injuring no one. There was a moment's confusion, and then the company, prudently returning from the neighborhood of the vases, remained silent, while the committee presented the Prince with an order of dancing.

Scarcely had the Prince taken his card when another flower vase fell, and the moment afterwards a portion of the dancing floor gave way with a great crash, fortunately injuring no one, however. As the crowd retired, frightened, to various parts of the floor, it gave way beneath them. This was three times repeated, two persons being precipitated to the stage beneath, but not being injured. The floor rather sank than fell, the props beneath it being insufficient to sustain the weight of the throng.

For some moments the greatest confusion ensued; many determined to leave, and a rush was made for the door, but the real nature of the accident being discovered, the company resumed its composure. The Prince was immediately conducted into the supper room, whither a great number of the ladies and gentlemen followed him. The remainder either promenaded, took seats in the parquette, or gathered around the pit, about twenty feet square, which showed the extent of the damage. The promenade and the music diverted the attention of the company, who were kept off the dancing floor as much as possible; the police instantly surrounded the opening with a rope, which they guarded so that no one should pass. As many carpenters as could be crowded into the hole immediately set to work to put up new supports, and those who left in the first fright and confusion, either returned or stopped at the door, and gradually recovering their good humor, the company seemed to remember the proverb, wittily quoted by one of the fairest ladies present,

"A bad beginning has a good ending,"

and that Shaksperean adage retorted by a rival wit and beauty,

"All's well that ends well."

And so passed the time during which the repairs were progressing, in conversation, promenading and flirtations, and patiently awaited the time when dancing should begin. Only the patience and good humor of the company prevented this accident causing this grand ball, so anxiously expected, and so splendidly prepared, from being a complete *fiasco.*

The floral display at the Academy was truly magnificent. Countless flower-pots with their odorous freight, in endless variety, filled up a great part of the space known as the dress circle. There was a cosmopolitan gathering of the brightest and most beautiful from all quarters of the globe. There was no corner of the earth—unless it be the frozen regions of the north—that had not its representative in the clusters that shone from the eighty or one hundred large, handsome vases which ornamented the proscenium, independently of the myriad of flower-pots of a more homely kind. The Continent had its representatives in the floral conclave; but the far greater number were the rich exotics of a more southern clime. There were the beautiful Delphinum Formosum, the Gladiolus and the Salvia Splendens, side by side with the Bignonia from the antipodes and the Astra Fortuni from the Himalayas; while, overtopping all, with its odd-looking red and yellow flower, nodded the sugar-loaf head of the Fritoma Uvaria from the far and dusky regions of Southern Africa. Every step, every glance, brought some new and strange variety to the eye. Bignonias were in great and pleasing variety, mingled with specimens of the Antirrhinum Majus, or Snapdragon, with its snout-like, fragrant blossom; the Granadilla, or Passion Flower of the West Indies, starry and violet rayed, and the sweet Alyssum Maritimum of Old England. The number and variety of Dahlias were positively immense. Their native soil of Mexico never grew such Dahlias as those which lent their magnificent size and every charm of rich and gaudy color to the scene, from the deep crimson, beside which the beautiful Erithrina, or Coral-tree, was pale, to the faintest yellow that the variegated little Phlox of North America could ever possibly manage to get up. Tuberoses were also in great abundance—all alike in their exquisite fragrance and spotless white. The vast building was filled with the odor of this motley multitude of flowers.

But nothing could surpass the bouquets which the New York florists got up for the ladies who were to attend the ball. The majority were but of few colors;

all, or nearly all, with a large Camelia in the centre, which is a rare flower at this season; then a few Tuberoses, fringed by some scarlet flower, or the feathery, violet Eupatorium; then, perhaps, a circle of white Rose-buds, and the whole bound in a frame of evergreens, finishing with a deep fringe of white silk. Some had the Prince's crest and others the letters A. E. worked in flowers. There was nothing gaudy or showy about them; all were simple, though, of course, differing in design one from the other; and it was this simplicity of arrangement that made the exquisite elegance of these bouquets so apparent.

Now "Music arose with its voluptuous swell, and eyes looked love to eyes which spake again," while

> ——Away, like children delighted,
> All things forgotten beside, they gave themselves, to the maddening
> Whirl of the dizzy dance, as it swept and swayed to the music,
> Dreamlike, with beaming eyes and the rush of fluttering garments.

It must have been very delightful to you, Miss Mason, to dance the first waltz with the Prince; and oh! Miss Augusta Jay, and Miss Fish, and Miss Helen Russell, and Miss Van Buren, how divine you must have felt when the royal sleeve encircled your slender forms. Happy maidens! Thrice happy Prince!

On the next day His Royal Highness visited General Scott at his residence, after which he drove to Brady's Photographic Gallery, Barnum's Museum, and other places.

In the evening there was a grand torch-light procession of the firemen, who mustered five thousand strong. The engines and other apparatus were beautifully decorated, and the sight was the finest of the kind ever witnessed. The Prince and suite stood on the balcony of the Fifth Avenue Hotel while it filed past. Hour after hour, mile after mile, the gorgeous phalanx wound its slow length along, suffusing the sky with the lurid glare of rockets, snakes, Prince's plumes, and much beside, and dazzling the eyes of the half million that beheld it with the blaze of Drummond lights, here and there softened by the mellow tints of variegated lanterns. The crowd that assembled to witness this glitter and glory of the night, was only second to the crowd that thronged the streets on the day of the landing. Madison Square disclosed a sea of human heads, lighted by the fitful gleam of fireworks, and from the first appearance till the departure of the royal party, cheers floated with wave-like undulations of sound on the cool night air.

On Sunday morning His Royal Highness attended Trinity Church, and on the following one took his departure by the Harriet Lane for West Point, with an affectionate "godspeed" from the whole population.

CHAPTER XXV.

The Run up the River to see the Prince—The Trip of the Harriet Lane—Excitement of the Ladies—The Review at West Point.

I WAS one of the crowd that traveled by the eleven o'clock train that morning from New York to Garrison's, the station opposite West Point. We passed the Harriet Lane, sailing against a sharp, fresh breeze, and all eyes were directed towards her from the cars.

Onward, beneath the Palisades, through the waters of the shining river, the dark and tiny form of the steamer glided swiftly on its way.

No sooner had the train come to a full stop at Garrison's than there was a grand rush of a thousand or two towards the ferry steamer. The race was to the swift, and two or three ladies, clasping the hands of their worse halves, fell, and, I grieve to say, were made anything but happy in consequence, besides incurring the loss of passage by the boat, which only saved itself from sinking by moving away from the wharf when the decks had been covered with a layer of humanity one deep. She had to return for the balance.

I have, fortunately, long legs and a disposition to run when there is no other enemy than time present, so I flew with the wind, and succeeded in getting a place second to none, although, in point of space occupied, General Scott, who stood beside, had somewhat the advantage, for among dwarfs he would be a pyramid, and we would have to travel to Patagonia to see his equal, odd giants excepted.

We landed at the wooden slip, or pier, under the beautiful cliffs of the beautiful river, at about two o'clock, and the view that here unfolded itself was without parallel in the history of the spot.

Men, women, and children diversified the cliff-sides by sitting or standing wherever there was foothold in cavities or on ledges, while a double line of people had formed all the way down the steep path, from the road fronting the hospital to the water-side, up which the Prince and suite were to ride on those steeds which were already impatiently pawing the ground near the pier.

Beyond, on the hill-summit, in the roadway, on the tops of hotel omnibuses, and elsewhere, thousands were gathered for the purpose of witnessing what they could of the landing and the horsemen as they passed by.

Major Delafield and his lieutenants were on horseback at the river-side, when, at a quarter to three, the Harriet Lane arrived. The royal party disembarked, and boom went the first of the thirty-three guns which constitute a national salute.

Excitement now quickened, and women's hearts—aye, and men's, too—beat faster at the thought of seeing the heir apparent to the throne of England, as much for his mother's sake as his own.

"Here he comes! Here he comes!" was the watchword, as he appeared in sight, riding in plain costume abreast of the military figure of the commandant of the post, Major Delafield, the suite, and American staff officers following in the rear, and the blue and gold uniforms of the latter contrasting with the mixed civilian dress of the visitors.

Such a crowd of people was never seen in the quiet and picturesque precincts of West Point before, nor did a brighter day ever lend lustre to old October, and make the forest gorgeous with the rainbow glories of decay. It was cold, but invigorating, and there was an elasticity in the atmosphere highly conducive to enjoyment, so the spirits of the twenty thousand ran high and all went merry.

There was an escort of dragoons in honor of His Royal Highness, which, when he had entered the house of the commandant of the post, to which he rode direct, drew up in single line, facing the gateway.

Here a presentation of the officers of the staff and others took place by the Major, the Prince shaking hands after the American fashion with each.

The twenty thousand, meanwhile, loitered in front, where the review-ground afforded them plenty of room for moving about, if their curiosity did not impel them to struggle for a front place among the multitude.

After this, which lasted nearly an hour, came the review, the cadets, nearly three hundred in number, having taken up position in a double line in the centre of the plateau, with the engineers and pieces of artillery a hundred yards in the background, and the dragoons, an insignificant force, attending to police duties about the field. Some of these latter were mounted, and others afoot, but they were for the most part equally impudent in enforcing order. They laughed and jested with the crowd, and curveted their horses about in the immediate vicinity of the spectators' toes, for the pleasure of seeing the multitude sway backward.

The plateau, surrounded by a cordon of swelling hills, with here and there a tower, a spire, and a dome, looked splendid in the sunlight, although a bleak wind swept across the expanse, and made every one long for an overcoat if they hadn't one, and button up closely if they had.

The number of troops on the ground was little more than three hundred and fifty, and the review of these commenced by the Prince walking side by side with Major Delafield down the front line and up the second. The suite and staff officers followed. This over, the royal party returned to the front rank of the field, and took up a standing position. The word of command was then given, and the band of cadets struck up slow time, when the march, in which the sappers, with their artillery, took part, was taken up once round. The next round was to quick time, and the third round to double quick time. This was tedious, but well executed in a military point of view.

The party then re-entered the house and partook of luncheon.

I have often found, and sometimes to my cost, that darkeys, and especially darkey hotel-waiters, entertain large expectations. This was conspicuously the case at Cozzens' Hotel, West Point, when, at half-past five, after the review His Royal Highness rode up to the door and dismounted. Those of the ebony complexion were on the alert, in full anticipation of holding my lord's horse and wisping my lord's coat, and waiting upon him at dinner, and otherwise being brought into such immediate contact with him that perquisites of no insignificant amount would be inevitable. But to their sorrow the sequel told them that my lord's own servants would do for him whatever was wanted, and that all the darkeys had to do was to help them.

It would have done my Aunt Sally or anybody's Aunt

Sally good to have seen the rush of her sex towards the spot where Albert Edward alighted on the occasion I have just alluded to, and to have heard such criticisms from their lips as "He's perfectly charming," "Lovely," and "Dear fellow."

It was a matter of much disappointment to many that he had declined dancing in the evening in the large room of the Academy, and some of the ladies were so intent upon having what they called a hop that they presented themselves in person at the drawing-room door of His Royal Highness for the purpose of tendering an invitation to him to come out and dance with them in the adjoining room. This they did, trusting to Providence for a band. But their wishes were not realized. The Prince remained quietly in his dining-room in company with his suite and several of the staff officers who had dined with him, till a game of ten-pins was suggested, after playing which in the bowling alley he went quietly to bed.

At half-past ten on the next morning the royal party drove to the wharf, near the hotel, where lay the steamer Daniel Drew. Several of the military officers were present to see them off, and to these the Prince spoke a kind adieu. The band then struck up the beautiful air of "Home, Sweet Home," which was played with touching pathos, the steamer meanwhile departing on her journey. It was a farewell dirge which almost brought tears to the eyes of those who listened to its magic strains.

Onward glided the vessel within view of the loveliest of the Hudson scenery. Onward past towns and villages, hills and valleys, ever picturesque and romantic, towards Albany.

The steamer was met a few miles below the city by another, having on board the Mayor and others, and at half-past four o'clock she reached the wharf. There the scene was one of grandeur and animation.

The Twenty-fifth and Seventy-sixth Regiments (one

foot and the other cavalry) were on the spot, and had so much difficulty in keeping a space clear for the disembarkation that they were compelled to present bayonets and stand with those weapons pointed at the crowd.

The procession was taken up to the City Hall, in open carriages—the Mayor being seated beside the Prince, and the dragoons acting as an escort, while the infantry followed in the rear.

The whole population of the capital of the Empire State appeared to have turned out and to have gathered at the windows and on the roofs of the houses.

The masses surged after the carriages as they passed, and loud were the pæans of welcome.

It was another glorious sight for the future King of England to gaze upon, another link forged in the chain of international friendship, another wild outburst of genuine good-feeling on the part of the great American people. Welcome those joyous shouts, those waving banners, those delighted eyes, that take part in the noble tribute to a noble cause! There is exultation here, there is fellow-feeling and respect; but these soar above adulation. They are the outpourings of a free and generous, a friendly and an independent people, who hail Victoria's son as they would a brother.

The entry into the Capitol on the hill was succeeded by Governor Morgan making a round of presentations, after which the party entered the Congress Hall Hotel, opposite, where quarters had been taken for them by the courier.

In the evening His Royal Highness and suite dined with the Governor at his residence and so ended the proceedings of the day.

CHAPTER XXVI.

The Departure from Albany—Progress *en route*—The Grand Reception at Boston—An Immense Crowd—The Military Display—The Illuminated Parade, etc.

FROM Albany on the hill to Albany at the water-side, and thence across the Hudson to the Western Railway Station, the Prince and party proceeded on the next morning under an escort of cavalry and infantry. A fragment of the crowd which had gathered in front of the Congress Hall, accompanied them in an irregular troop, and the line of procession was margined with spectators, who cheered and waved their hats and handkerchiefs in a kind farewell.

The Mayor and other authorities took leave of Victoria's son, and at a quarter to nine o'clock the royal train and the State car, which was beautifully embellished, moved away amid the acclamations of those assembled.

Thus ended another of those ovations which have lent lustre to the New World journey of Albert Edward, the beloved. Away sped the locomotive, through valley, over hill, past mirror-like water and woodland, towards Boston. The stay at Springfield, where the train arrived at twenty minutes past twelve, was limited to five minutes; nevertheless, two colonels of the local army entered the royal car, and, presenting the letter of introduction from the Governor of Massachusetts to Lord Lyons, welcomed the Prince to the State, and afterwards accompanied him to Boston. The multitude at the station, including the Mayor, were enthusiastic in their cheers, and it was a matter to them of extreme regret, that His Royal Highness made so short a stay.

When Longwood was reached, the train stopped at the Cottage Farm Station of the Boston and Worcester Railroad, three miles from the city. Here the royal party were joined by the Mayor of Boston and the City Government.

Over the mill-dam there poured a crowd of thirty thousand, which, however, quickly thinned, leaving only the respectable portion to witness the cortege as it passed by. Everett, Winthrop, and Lawrence were among the number on the spot.

The carriages of the Prince and suite moved forward under an escort of the First Battalion of Light Dragoons, consisting of more than two hundred men, the ladies waving their handkerchiefs in a half frantic state of excitement, and joining in chorus with the men, to which the Prince responded by raising his hat and bowing to the crowd. "God save the Queen" was being, meanwhile, played by the band.

Although the procession moved forward at a quarter to four, it was as much past five before it reached Bowdoin Square. I was astonished to see the well-dressed and evidently polite people that lined the streets, especially through Longwood (the name revives my recollections of St. Helena), and pleased to see the fraternal interest they manifested in behalf of the future King of England.

Here he is! Hurrah! was an almost incessant cry, as the Prince's carriage came within view.

Boys, babies, and old women, blushing and blooming girls, and gray-haired men, were alike mingled in the mass, but all united in the one grand sentiment of welcome to the heir apparent to the throne of England, the babies perhaps excepted.

The bright eyes of fair women beamed from a thousand windows, and over the five miles of the line of route their presence graced the way.

I may live long, but I shall never again see such a series of ovations as I did from the arrival of the

Prince of Wales at Halifax up to the present time, and of which this was nearly the last. I would not have missed the sight of them for any money, and yet I am no worshiper of a throne.

Mile after mile the gray of the infantry and the blue and white of the National Lancers, brightened the procession towards the Revere House.

The people of New York, and wherever else the Prince passed through, know enough of the character of these boundlessly cordial receptions, to dispense with my descriptions, which would be but a glimmer compared with the sunlight of the reality.

At Longwood Bridge the crowd grew denser, and carriages and horses almost blocked the way, while the trees were populated with grown men and small boys, who had about the best view of all, besides indulging in the pastime of plundering the apple-trees of their fruit.

The procession quickened its pace as it advanced, and the crowd of followers quickened theirs also, to the tune of passing plaudits.

On went the cavalcade through the main street of Roxbury, the enthusiasm increased, and thousands of handkerchiefs, waved by female hands, kept time to the cheers of the men. There was a snow-storm of cambrics, a thunder of applause, but the latter only rent the air at intervals. There were moments when the Prince moved by almost amid silence. But moments are not hours, and it is these that make the *summum bonum*, the *ultima thule* of such an ovation, and they were well. New York alone excelled, and to it all may cry "Excelsior," but its like is elsewhere unreachable.

I do not profess to elevate every stretch of the human neck into the dignity of history. It is enough to say that all were eager and that nearly all saw. Flags waved before their eyes, and the scene was one of the most inspiriting character.

Past the State House and the Common the cavalcade dragged its slow length along, for here the pace slackened, and so on to the Revere House, the multitude becoming vaster as the hotel was neared. The crowd was here so dense that His Royal Highness, after entering at the side door, came out upon the balcony and acknowledged their cheers, the greatest excitement and most intense enthusiasm venting itself in cheers, meanwhile prevailing. After this, some presentations took place, including Mr. Everett, and then the party remained in quiet till eight P.M., when dinner was served. Kossuth and Jenny Lind respectively produced an excitement in Boston, but nothing was ever seen equal to the present event in its highly respectable precincts, which are, nevertheless, said to have at least five distinct smells.

In the evening the grand procession of the Bell and Everett party took place, and kept up the excitement to boiling point.

For two hours before the procession started, it gathered and came together like the pieces in a puzzle map. Lines of men, with flaming red and white lanterns, came from all wards and all directions, and formed on the Common, their red shoulder scarfs giving them a showy appearance in the glare amid the darkness.

I saw them pass the Revere House, while His Royal Highness came forward to witness the pageantry of the nocturnal scene. Bells tinkled, bells resounded like church knells, rockets flew, crimson lights exploded sunflower-like, cheers swelled on cheers, host succeeded host with the imposing aspect of an army, and the glittering, lustrous, gleaming procession marched on its way, club succeeded club, for more than an hour. Mounted police headed it, and horsemen and carriages, the latter filled with flag bearers, and the lancers brought up the rear.

Illuminated bells and transparencies occurred at

intervals, while the line of route itself was here and there decorated with colored lights, flags, and devices.

Immense enthusiasm prevailed, and "all went merry as a marriage bell."

The usually quiet city of Boston was no longer itself. To use popular language, it was turned upside down, under the combined influence of the Prince of Wales and politics. The people did all possible honor to their illustrious guests. Many of them closed their stores, notwithstanding the unusually large traffic consequent on the presence of tens of thousands of visitors, which showed a self-sacrifice of the most genuine character. The Bostonians are unostentatious and undemonstrative in their show of cordiality, but they are none the less well-meaning than those who make a more boisterous and jubilant display.

The Revere House was, of course, the centre of attraction from an early hour on the following morning, and the Hon. Edward Everett and others called upon the Prince before noon, as also did Ralph Farnham —the hero of Bunker Hill—and his daughter, all of whom were kindly received by His Royal Highness.

The crowd increased in the neighborhood of the hotel as the day advanced, till, at half-past twelve, when the Prince made his appearance through a side door, it was with difficulty kept within the prescribed limits by the mounted and foot police, who lacked civility more than energy.

He was in full colonel's uniform, with the ribbon of the Garter conspicuous across his breast. The Duke of Newcastle, Lord Lyons, and others of the suite, were in plain morning dress.

A burst of cheering greeted him as he stepped into the open carriage in waiting, after which Colonel Reed, of the Governor's staff, took his seat beside him in uniform.

The drive was direct to the State House, where the Mayor and other municipal authorities, had previously assembled to receive him, together with several hundreds of ladies and gentlemen, who filled the Representatives' Hall and Senate Chamber.

As the three or four carriages containing the royal party drove up to the Common, which was densely packed with people—save in the avenues and other places, where the police had kept a space clear—the people unavoidably presented some obstruction to the progress of the cortege; but, after a few moments' delay, the human mass was cleaved in twain, and the horses bounded forward.

As His Royal Highness alighted, there was a good deal of cheering, not only from the multitude on *terra firma*, but from those high up on the balconies of the State House, from the centre of which drooped the flag of England, while at either side hung the flags of the United States and Massachusetts respectively.

The Cadets were here drawn up to receive him, and their band struck up the music of "God save the Queen." Colonel Reed conducted His Royal Highness into the presence of Governor Banks, when he was introduced as "the Prince of Wales," upon which the Governor welcomed him, following which he conducted his illustrious guest through the Representatives' Hall and Senate Chamber, all there present rising as he entered.

Ten minutes had hardly elapsed when they passed down the steps to the Common, where His Royal Highness mounted the horse, Black Prince, in waiting for him, and, with an escort of military, rode forward to the review.

10*

CHAPTER XXVII.

The Review—The Musical Festival—The Grand Ball—The Visit to Harvard College and Bunker Hill—The Departure for Portland—The Embarkation—The last Farewell to America.

It was a fine sight as His Royal Highness appeared on the Common, to hear the cheers and watch the excitement of the tens of thousands of men, women, and children there assembled. The review commenced at two, by the Prince riding slowly past the different companies, commencing at the right of the line, and concluding at the extreme left, when he once more took position in front. During this time the swell of music from the military bands resounded on all sides. The marching salute was now given, and the companies proceeded once round the line. The two thousand five hundred soldiers looked splendid in the sunlight, and as they resumed their positions they were complimented as worthy even to rank with the superb militia of New York—the finest in the world. A drive back to the State House and a collation in the ante-room on the northwest corner of the building immediately succeeded, after which the royal party returned to the hotel. The next great event of the day was the Musical Festival at the Music Hall, which was beautifully refitted, and decorated for the occasion. The singers consisted of twelve hundred boys and girls of the Boston schools, who were arranged on amphitheatric seats in two divisions. The girls who filled one of these were nearly all dressed in white frocks, and contrasted pleasingly with the sombre mass of the other sex.

Every tier was densely crowded with ladies and the pit with gentlemen, by the time the Prince and party arrived at a quarter past five. Their entrance was the signal for a prolonged and enthusiastic burst of cheering, not only from the children, but the entire audience, and quite a snow-storm of white handkerchiefs fluttered in the air for whole minutes.

Then the massive organ pealed out the loud full tones of "God save the Queen," upon which the whole audience rose and the twelve hundred sang in unison with incomparable effect—

God bless our Fathers' Land!
Keep her in heart and hand
    One with our own!
From all her foes defend,
Be her brave People's Friend,
On all her Realms descend,
    Protect her Throne!

Father, with loving care
Guard Thou her kingdom's Heir.
    Guide all his ways:
Thine arm his shelter be,
From him by land and sea
Bid storm and danger flee,
    Prolong his days!

Lord, let War's tempest cease,
Fold the whole Earth in peace,
    Under Thy wings!
Make all Thy Nations one,
All Hearts beneath the sun,
Till Thou shalt reign alone,
    Great King of Kings!

I joined with the multitude in enthusiastic applause when the children sat down again, and after that I listened to their renderings of Mendelssohn, Beethoven, Mozart, and the Old Hundredth Psalm, with as much interest as their anxious mothers in the gallery. They did well, and at the close, soon after six, when the Prince rose, the acclamations were renewed, and exultation and delight beamed in every countenance.

And now a word for the ball in the Theatre, at which I was present a few hours later. It was a grand, full gathering of the *élite* of New England in honor of the representative of Old England. It was a crush certainly, but a glorious crush that gave it the highest *eclât.* There was no vulgarity there. Beauty and diamonds dazzled the eye at every glance, and the costumes generally were strictly *à la mode.*

The Boston theatre seemed to have doubled its size, so immense was the space which was crowded with "fair maidens and brave men." Even after the Academy of New York, with its magnificent *coup d'œil* of light, flowers, and beauty, the Boston ball-room did not seem second rate or *fadê;* but, on the contrary, so unique and original were the designs, and so admirably were those designs carried out, that even the suite of the Prince were delighted, and acknowledged that, in the matter of ball-room decorations at least, the fertility of human invention is wonderful. The Boston ball-room was about the same shape as that of the Academy, and was formed in the same way, the parquette and stage being floored over. The smaller size of the house, however, gave the Bostonians the advantage in a cosy, comfortable, enjoyable feeling which very great rooms always lack, and without which a great ball is simply a great nuisance. One felt at home immediately upon entering the building, and prepared to enjoy himself as naturally as if the affair had been a private party.

Broad double stairs led from the entrance of the building to the reception room, which was rather tawdrily furnished, with red, blue, and white hangings and wreaths of flowers, and which presented no special decoration, except a large British coat of arms, supported by American flags, and suspended opposite the entrance. Near this reception room was the committee room, furnished in the style of, and as richly as, any private parlor. The Prince had the saloon of the theatre for his dressing and retiring room. The saloon was repainted, decorated and furnished in drawing-room style, and was provided with a splendid mirror and all the appliances of the toilet. The other dressing-rooms were very handsomely and conveniently furnished, but presented no special point for description. Having thus hastily glanced through the dressing-rooms, let us proceed through the newly painted corridors, carpeted with green baize, to the centre of attraction and beauty—the theatre itself.

Entering the room from the doors directly opposite the stage, the eye, dazzled by the light from a thousand burners, failed at first to take in the full beauty of the scene. The private boxes were hidden by groves of evergreens, from the deep shades of which peeped pure white statues, as if the wood-nymphs were observing the display and were eager to join in the dance. Those groves flanked the entrance to the stage, and above them were crimson curtains, rising in beautiful folds to the proscenium drapery, which was formed of an immense American flag, most gracefully arranged. The roof of the marquee was painted in arabesque work, in eight varied colors, with fantastic designs, and from this ceiling were suspended three chandeliers, of a style similar to the arabesque designs. Falling from the ceiling to the side walls were crimson curtains, relieved by gold bands, and sloped and lapelled in Turkish style, producing a most beautiful and novel effect. The side walls were painted in imperial purple, with ornamented squares, and relieved by panels framed in gold and painted in lighter colors and more varied designs. From each of these panels —four on either side of the marquee—depended side chandeliers, in ebony and gilt, under which, upon ornamented pedestals, were vases of natural flowers, from Ever's gardens at Brighton. Between these chandeliers were large pier glasses, gilt frames and flower wreathed, and the reduplication of these mirrors seemed to increase immeasurably the size of the room. In the corners, at the extremity of the tent, were also pier glasses, half concealed by common curtains, and just beyond them were evergreens and flowers, forming beautiful supports to the back scene, and relieved by statues of Ceres and Hebe.

Looking from the entrance of the marquee towards its extremity, the effect was bewildering. Besides all these decorations, which the reader must frame into a picture for himself, the eye was attracted by many little details—a stripe of gilt, a happy flourish of the crayon, which cannot be described upon paper, but which aided the general effect. Then immediately opposite, half hidden by trees and flowers, among which a white fountain bubbled up its crystal waters, falling again in diamond drops beneath the brilliant lights, an immense picture of Windsor Castle frowned splendidly and completed the *tout ensemble*. From the turrets of the magnificent castle floated the royal standard. Around were trees, picturesquely arranged and grouping with the real evergreen in the foreground, while by a happy fortune the artist had succeeded in catching that hazy, misty, half clouded sky peculiar to English landscapes. All of the royal party recognized at once the fidelity of this picture, and repeatedly expressed their admiration not only of the artist's skill, but of the good taste which thus beautifully and unostentatiously suggested the presence of the Prince and connected his home with his appearance here. Seats, covered with green cloth, were arranged around the marquee, and the royal party were seated upon velvet sofas.

Turning towards the entrance of the marquee, and looking out upon the body of the theatre, the *coup d'œil* was surprising, and each detail only heightened the pleasure of the first impression. From the ceiling, richly frescoed and painted in gold and white, hung a large chandelier, an inverted dome of gaslights and glass, glittering and blazing indescribably. This and side brackets around the walls gave sufficient light for a dozen such halls, and brought every detail of the decorations into full view. The theatre had three tiers, each of which was differently adorned. Objection might be taken to the motive of the decorations —which was mainly gilt and color—and might have found fault with the gaudiness and lack of simplicity which characterized the affair, but it is certain that everything which could be done with this style of adornment—and it is capable of magnificent effects when intrusted to good hands—was accomplished in the ball-room. From the uppermost tier, gilded pillars, with arches connecting them, supported the roof, and these were left undecorated, except by slight draperies of red, white, and blue flags. The front of this upper tier was covered with a hanging of crimson cloth, fringed with blue, and a blue border, draped in festoons and studded with gilt stars, ran along the upper edge of the balustrade. Each of these festoons was held by a bouquet of natural flowers, from which depended a long blue banneret, ending in a gilt ball, which hung below the balustrade and over the tier below. The second tier was hung with orange colored cloth, fringed with blue and festooned with crimson and wreaths of flowers. At equal distances along the front were shields alternately bearing the Prince of Wales' feather, and the mottoes, " Justitia," " Concordia," " Amicitia," and other Latin inscriptions. Each of these shields was placed upon a blue hanging, with golden stars, and was supported on either side by the British and American flags. The first or lower tier was hung with royal purple velvet, edged and relieved by gold lace, and so festooned and draped as to reveal, at equi-distances, the gilded figures which adorned the front of this circle. The dancing floor was slightly raised above the level of the dress circle, and was inclosed by white drapery, edged with blue and orange cloth. Directly opposite the stage and rising from the first to the third tiers was the royal box, handsomely draped with crimson fancifully embroidered with gold lace, and the whole surmounted by a dome of blue velvet, with outlines and ornaments in gold lace. Upon the front of the box was the Prince of Wales' feather. Above it, where the draperies met, were the crown and arms of England, and upon the summit of the dome was a spread eagle, in gilt. The entrances to the dancing floor, as, indeed, to every other portion of the house, were hung with curtains of purple velvet. If from this description the reader can imagine the immense theatre; the dancing floor inclosed as by a pavilion; each tier differently but richly decorated, and crowded with superbly dressed ladies; the royal box all aglare with light, and rich in gilt, purple, and azure; the frescoed ceiling, with its pendent dome of light; the marquee, with its groves, flowers, mirrors, and arabesque ceiling, its multiform and varied decorations, and its view of Windsor Castle, seen as if from out some immense window; if he can imagine this scene, and then crowd it with a galaxy of both sexes, whil eover all the lights stream their brilliant radiance, and mirrors and jewels flash back and reduplicate the rays, and the soft, sweet swell of the music bears with it the light moving throng in a bewildering maze of beauty, then he can form some idea of the appearance of the Boston theatre at the Prince of Wales ball.

The Prince arrived at half-past ten and opened the ball with Mrs. Lincoln, the wife of the Mayor.

I have a dim idea that Mrs. Governor Banks, and Mrs. Lieut. Wise, and Miss Crowinshield, and Miss Lissie Amory, and Miss Carrie Bigelow, and Miss Lyman, and the most lovely girl I ever saw—name unknown—were among the others who had the felicity of dancing with him afterwards, in consideration of which I have hereby immortalized them.

The supper arrangements were excellent, and the spirit of the ball made glorious the night to all who reveled in its splendor. It was a grand wind up of the festivities of the grand tour of the New World. It shed lustre upon the Bostonians as the receptions which His Royal Highness met with in all the other cities he visited, with the two exceptions of Kingston and Belleville, shed lustre upon their inhabitants also, and it will be a source of pride to them and their posterity hereafter to read the record of their deeds in the history of our time.

It was half-past three when His Royal Highness, after dancing the entire programme of seventeen dances, left the ball-room, the band meanwhile playing "God save the Queen," and the eyes of the company glancing full upon him till he disappeared.

Friday dawned bright and fair, and a crowd, as usual, assembled in front of the hotel where royalty resided. Soon after noon the wish of the multitude was gratified by a sight of the Prince as he stepped into an open barouche in company with the Mayor of Cambridge, who with the members of the Committee of Arrangements of the City Government had come to escort him thither.

The Duke and Lord Lyons sat on the opposite seat, and the remainder of the suite with Governor Banks, Mayor Lincoln, and Hon. Edward Everett entered other carriages, and all drove towards Harvard University. There was a general shout intended for a cheer, and this was continued with varying vigor by those assembled on the sidewalks along the line of route to Cambridge, where the enthusiasm rather increased than diminished. British and American ensigns were suspended across the street at the Cambridge end of the bridge, and in Broadway the children of the Cambridge schools appeared in gala dress on either side of the street. No sooner did the cortege appear in sight than these, to the admiration of their mothers, commenced waving white handkerchiefs in the air. The speed of the royal carriage was slackened into a walk, and as it passed between the juvenile lines the clapping of hands became furious, and one young lady of the number stepped forward and handed the Prince a bouquet, which he took with a graceful bow and a smile that to the girl was a prize.

The young ladies of the high school were assembled further on, and from these came a shower of floral bunches, while people cheered from the housetops, balconies, and windows, in a hearty welcome to the illustrious visitor.

When the party neared the college grounds they found the undergraduates in the order of seniority drawn up to receive them, while, as they entered, the Germania Band struck up " God save the Queen" with excellent effect, and the concourse of ladies and gentlemen there gathered lifted their voices in a joyous chorus of welcome, to which the white handkerchiefs of the former kept time.

Between the lines of students, who numbered more than four hundred in all, the party passed up the main avenue to the library, while the aspirants in law, physic, and divinity cheered warmly their young fellow-student of Oxford. Here he was met by President Felton, and taking his arm he was conducted to the hall, and introduced to Ex-Presidents Quincy, Sparks, Winthrop, and Walker, with whom he entered freely into conversation. He afterwards spoke to the Hon. Charles Sumner, and on being introduced to Dr. Holmes, with whose name was coupled the authorship of the ode entitled " Our Fathers' Land" sung by the school children at the festival of the previous day, he manifested much interest.

The Faculty, Trustees, and other officers, were also here introduced to him. The Librarian then showed the visitors round, and among other curiosities pointed out the first Indian Bible printed in America. After a stay of twenty minutes, the party signed their names in the visitors' book, and left the building.

They were met outside by the students, who had formed in a hollow to receive them.

The President conducted the Prince between lines of the latter, who had formed to keep back the crowd, from this to Boylston Hall, and thence to the University Building, the students still lining the way, and the mass of spectators following. The law school was next visited, and here the students of that department cheered enthusiastically.

The Prince then expressed a desire to see one of the students' rooms, and one was shown him accordingly, no doubt to the intense gratification of its occupant.

The " Academic Groves" meanwhile resounded with the pleasant music of the band in attendance.

The carriages were here re-entered, and the party drove away to the observatory, amid the cheers of the rising lights of the American Athens, the Tremont of its settlers, while the bells of the adjacent church played a sweet and merry peal in concert with the band, and brightly shone the sun over the classic ground.

While the Prince was looking through telescopes, and reading the results of heavenly observations, the sons of *Alma Mater* formed themselves into a circle and sang "Auld Lang Syne," after which the Band played " Fair Harvard" with such effect as to elicit a general clapping of hands.

After the lapse of half an hour the carriages were seen returning. A hasty visit to the Agazzi's Museum followed, and then, passing back to Harvard Hall, the visitors alighted and proceeded to partake of a collation. The whole company present at this numbered nearly a hundred. Here the guiding lights of the home of the Puritans were enabled to make casual allusion in their conversation with the royal party to their city's thrilling traditionary and historical associations, its literary and educational facilities, which begun with the publication of its first newspaper in

1704, more than seventy years after its first settlement, and much beside.

With the termination of the luncheon the visit to the college terminated.

There was a grand chorus of cheers from the students and concourse in the yard generally as His Royal Highness stepped into his carriage, and the cortege moved away towards Mount Auburn, followed by a troop of men, women and children in carriages, on horseback and afoot.

The party were met at the chapel within the gates by two of the trustees, who pointed out the statues of Adams, Story, and Winthrop, after which the Prince, in the presence of a large number of spectators, planted an English elm and purple ash in the ground fronting the chapel.

The Necropolis was not much explored by the party, as, without further delay, they re-entered their carriages and drove away, the Mayor of Boston having now taken the place of the Mayor of Cambridge beside His Royal Highness.

And now for Bunker Hill, and heigh-ho for Charlestown. When the party alighted at the gate leading to the monument they encountered a crowd which impeded their progress towards the small house at the entrance to the structure which somebody explained to the Prince was commemorative of the battle fought on the spot. He was also told that by ascending three hundred steps reaching to its summit he would enjoy a most delightful prospect embracing an extensive sweep of land and water, hill and dale, and a charming panorama of Boston and the long bridges, which shoot from it like the arms of a huge wind-mill. "But," said the Prince, "it's nearly dark," which was accepted as a sufficient reason for his not scaling the height. He, however, signed "Albert Edward" in the visitors' book, and those with him having followed suit the party made an observation of the statue of Warren, and the interior of the base of the monument, after which they returned to their carriages and drove to the city, where they visited the Athenæum Library, and the rooms of the Historical Society, and Public Library, founded by Joshua Bates of London, reaching the latter, in which a large number of ladies and gentlemen were assembled, at few minutes past seven.

He remained here only a few minutes and then drove to the residence of Mayor Lincoln, who introduced his family and friends, and thence to the Revere House, from which he did not emerge till half-past nine on the following morning, when he entered an open carriage and drove with his suite, the Mayor, Governor Banks, and others, under an escort of eighty men of the National Lancers, accompanied by a band in full pipe, to the Eastern Railway Station. Of course there was a great crowd assembled at the hotel, and a mixed assemblage followed the cortege to the station. Meanwhile, a grand rush was being made upon the apartments just vacated by the royal party at the Revere by ladies and gentlemen curious to see the recent abode of royalty.

The station was gay externally, with long lines of flags drooping over its entire front. Symbols of the United States were relieved by a representation of the Victoria Bridge, "the Pride of Canada," while the entrance was spanned by an arch hung with British and American flags, and inscribed with the words "Welcome to the Prince of Wales."

The interior of the roof was decorated with the flags of all nations. More flags adorned the sides, and red and green cloth covered that part of the floor over which the visitors were to pass.

Think me not trivial in enumerating these things; they were delicate expressions of a great national feeling, and trifles give us the key to mighty truths as often, and not seldom more truly, than imposing deeds.

A solid wall of people surrounded the station, while

every window, roof, and fence commanding a view of the approach to, or interior of, the building was occupied.

When the royal cortege arrived there was a general cheer from the assembled masses, which did one good to hear.

The royal train started at ten minutes to ten, amid the renewed cheers of the people, and a salute of thirty-three guns, the Prince having previously taken a kind leave of the Captain of the Lancers, and presented a valuable breastpin to the man who had supplied and driven the royal barouche.

A pilot engine ran two miles ahead of the royal train, which consisted of three cars and a mail and baggage van, all new, and drawn by a locomotive also new. The appearance of the train was extremely handsome. The car nearest the engine was fitted up with an elegance that has never been equaled on any other line. Costly sofas, covered with velvet plush, stood in the place of ordinary seats, and a sprinkling of luxurious easy chairs, a floor with a beautiful carpet, displaying green flowers on a crimson ground, two centre-tables (one of which was ornamented with a chastely gilded stand, bearing a delicious bouquet, a silver ice-pitcher, with gold-lined silver goblets, and two net-work silver-point baskets, laden with luscious bunches of grapes and other fruits), a ceiling of sky-blue silk, plaited and studded with silver stars, draperies of crimson and gold silk damask, and the fine lace curtains of the windows, everything being new, and of the choicest description, gave to the car an air of regal splendor and perfect comfort. The cost of the material and labor in fitting this car was four thousand dollars.

A retiring room was situated at the front end of the car, and this was furnished with a desk, reclining chair, and other conveniences. The Prince of Wales' plume and motto, with the arms of Maine, New Hampshire, and Massachusetts, were placed in panels at the opposite extremity of the car, outside of which a semicircular stand, draped with crimson velvet hangings, was built for the purpose of enabling His Royal Highness to present himself to the crowds expected to line the way.

Everything that possibly could have been done to reach the acme of luxury and ease was done, and that regardless of expense.

At every station on the line of route a crowd had gathered, and decorations were displayed. At Salem the Mayor was in waiting, and on the arrival of the train he stepped into the Prince's car, and welcomed him in a neat speech, a salute being meanwhile fired from Castle Hill, and all the church bells set ringing. Eight or ten thousand people filled the air with their cheers as the train moved slowly away.

At a quarter to two the train arrived at the Grand Trunk Railway Terminus at Portland, under a salute of thirty-three guns from Bramhall Hill. An immense crowd had gathered at the station, where the Mayor, Admiral Milne, and others, were in waiting to receive His Royal Highness, as also the whole of the First Regiment, the Norway Light Infantry, the Lewiston Light Infantry, and the Auburn Artillery, with their bands. These acted as an escort to His Royal Highness through the city to the Great Eastern wharf, the place of embarkation.

The concourse on the hill overlooking the latter place was immense for so small a town as Portland, and could only be accounted for by the large number of visitors from Canada and the neighboring district, who had come to "see him off," as they said. Vehicles of the bathing-machine type were there by the hundred, and the scene was one of extreme animation.

Nothing of uncommon interest occurred during the drive. There was, of course, the usual flutter of handkerchiefs, and sounds of kindly greeting were heared as the cortege passed along the streets.

There was a salute from the First Regiment as His Royal Highness alighted from his carriage to walk down the hill, passing under a triumphal arch on the way, and there were cheers and eager looks. But the touching part of the day's proceedings lay in the leave-taking on the platform at the foot of the stairs. It is enough to say that the eyes of more than one or two of the illustrious visitors glistened with moisture from the well of feeling. Before them lay the ships which were to bear them back to fatherland. The harbor, surrounded by land save at the narrow entrance, displayed the flags of England and America fluttering from the ships at anchor, and the steamers, heavy laden with excursionists anxious to witness the sailing of the royal barge, and the first movement of the fleet.

The day was clear and sunny, but cold and with a fresh breeze blowing from the east, which rippled the surface of the water.

"Good by, good-by," said the Duke with unusual pathos at the same time clasping my hand warmly, "good-by," said His Royal Highness, and at a quarter past three they entered the Hero's boat and rowed away from the shore. A loud, long, glorious cheer followed them across the water.

This was the farewell between the eldest son of Queen Victoria and the last of thirty millions of kinsmen whose affectionate love he bore back with him to his native land to strengthen his throne and reunite the hearts of both peoples for all time. Farewell!

And now there boomed the royal salute from the guns of the Nile, the Hero, the Ariadne, the Styx, and the Flying Fish, the yards of which were manned by their cheering crews. From the city and Fort Preble similar salvos were also fired, and the air resounded far and near with the roar of cannon.

What more can I say? It is for the imagination to

fill up the picture, which was one of unrivaled interest.

We watched the receding boat till it became lost to the view through an intervening vessel; then we had another glimpse of it as, a mere speck on the water, it neared the Hero, for the latter lay two miles away and the water was somewhat troubled.

It was within ten minutes of four when the Prince's standard was run up to the maintop of the Hero, which was the signal for another salute from the two vessels of the North American squadron—the Nile and Styx.

A solitary gun was fired from the Hero soon after this. It was the signal to weigh anchor. Accordingly at half-past four the fleet started, the Hero leading, and the excursion steamers hovering round, while the thousands that crowded their decks uttered a long farewell.

Through the gap leading from the harbor to the ocean passed the noble vessels one by one, exchanging salutes as they went with Fort Preble.

Onward they careered on their watery way till they became mere pencilings on the horizon, and were finally lost in night.

CONCLUDING REFLECTIONS.

It is hardly necessary for me to remark that the royal tour, which in the foregoing narrative I have chronicled with cosmopolitan impartiality has been a great success both to the reigning family and government of England, the people of the British Provinces, and their neighbors of the United States. With the exception of the Orange difficulties in Upper Canada, the progress of the Prince of Wales, from his first landing on American soil to the day of his final departure from it, was marked with a series of the most flattering demonstrations, not only from those he will one day in the ordinary course of nature and by the constitution of his country be called upon to govern, but from the free people of a great and friendly power, which although differing in system from his own aims at a like result—the priceless boon of liberty. Wherever he went on British soil the inhabitants displayed their loyalty to the throne and their affection for the Queen and that son who came among them as her representative. At every city, town, and village through which he passed one at least, and frequently half a dozen, addresses of devotion and welcome were presented, and as promptly replied to. I should have felt much satisfaction in printing the whole of these, for they did equal credit to the head and heart, but the space they would occupy is more than I could afford, and official documents of that kind are, after all, not very lively reading.

The prepossessing appearance and social qualities of the Prince were of immense assistance in fanning the fire of his popularity, and his fondness for dancing aroused the interest of the ladies to a very high pitch indeed, aye and of the men too, for what father or brother would not like to see his daughter or sister dance with the future King of England? I knew of several official gentlemen who traveled part of the way round with His Royal Highness, taking their daughters or other lady relatives with them, merely in order that they might have the chance of being selected as the Prince's partners, or even of enjoying the only less delightful honor of dancing in the same set with him. Many are the complaints that I have heard from those who were disappointed in their expectations of an introduction to him—that great object of feminine ambition. Many blamed, and probably with good reason, the members of the local ball committee, who, it is said:

> Sought not his taste to please,
> Asked not his wishes,
> While all around him stood
> So many misses:
> Belles at the right of him
> Belles at the left of him
> Belles all in front of him
> Young and full grown;
> While that committee set,
> All around went to get
> Friends of their own.

The graver import of his visit was, however, in strengthening the popular feeling of attachment to the mother country. This result was equally achieved in the British Provinces and the United States, in the one case binding the Colonies closer to the parent land, and in the other, securing more firmly the general interests of the two great sections of the Anglo-Saxon race, as represented by Great Britain and the United States. The sentiment expressed on several occasions by Lord Lyons, the British Minister at Washington, who accompanied His Royal Highness from the landing at Quebec to the departure from Portland, and whose already high popularity was widened by the excellent manner in which he performed the duties which devolved upon him during this time in his official replies to various American citizens, and particularly the Chicago Committee, was extremely gratifying to the people of the United States. So, also, was the following letter from His Grace of Newcastle to the Mayor of Boston, which is so emphatic and true to the feeling in America as to hardly need comment:

"I cannot say with what kindness the Prince has been received in those cities which he has yet visited in the United States. If each individual had been instructed what to do, the whole people could not have shown greater delicacy of feeling and consideration for the position he occupies in England, though without the slightest surrender of their own claims to independence of action. They have all looked upon him as a guest, and resolved to treat him as such, but without overdoing the character of host.

"In return, of course, every effort has been made, and shall continue to be made elsewhere, to gratify the amiable curiosity of our good cousins to see the son of a Queen whom they love and respect almost as much as we do."

It may well be said in England that such words are more than mere words, and that all such real kindnesses on the one side, and prompt acknowledgments on the other, are sure to bear good fruit in all future relations between the two nations.

To the Prince, personally, the tour must have been one of no less pleasure than profit, although it was a task which few in any other position would have had either the boldness to undertake, or the industry to accomplish within so short a period. He has been thereby versed in the school both of nature and human nature, to which a voyage across the Atlantic was a good introduction, and another back again a satisfactory wind-up. It is true that he endured no small amount of hard work during his travels, extending over more than five thousand miles and performed in less than three months, between his first landing in

America and his final departure, but to a youth with such excellent stamina, and such a flow of good spirits and love of adventure as he proved himself possessed of, it must have been most cheerfully endured, while the positive enjoyment with which it was mingled made the effect only similar to that of dancing with the lovely of the land at a ball all night.

Nature in the New World opened to his view vistas of stupendous lakes, and rivers to which those of Europe are as rivulets, vast prairies, the grandest cataract under the sun, and a country, not only majestic in its physical, but in its social aspect. He has visited great cities that only a few years ago were great wildernesses, and he has been enabled to glance, although hastily, at the moral and political phenomena of popular sovereignty which has earned for the United States the reputation of being the school of statesmen and the study of philosophers. He has observed the general prosperity of the people, a consequence of their indomitable energy, industry, and perseverance, their intelligence and free institutions. What other such splendid example of the advantages of self-government could he have had than was here afforded him? There was nothing so much calculated to imbue his mind with wide and generous sympathies with his fellow-creatures, and to inspire him with a noble confidence in the destiny of that great republic—that glorious Union which from one extremity of the globe to the other, is no less the wonder than the envy of mankind, and the unexampled progress and prosperity of which commands universal respect throughout the entire realm of civilization. Such a great and valuable lesson to one, in such a position, is certain not to be otherwise than productive of the most happy results in every way, especially when coupled with the many pleasant associations of his visit.

The next prominent event in his history may be a voyage to India, where the prestige of royalty is so great that he would be certain to meet with a splendid reception. The effect of which upon the native population could not fail in being highly conciliatory and beneficial to British interests. Australia is so remotely situated that the chances in favor of the Prince of Wales visiting its shores are few. But I can vouch for the delight the colonists would feel at even the prospect of such an event, and I can imagine the magnificent sequel. It is highly probable, nevertheless, that Prince Alfred or one of his younger brothers will, at no distant period, make his appearance

"By the long wash of Australasian seas."

In a former part of this work I have made allusion to a very probable occurrence, namely the formation of all the British North American Colonies into an United Confederacy, extending from Canada on the east, to British Columbia on the west, and St. John's, Newfoundland, to the Red River Settlement. The project here held out is one the merits of which I could illustrate at considerable length, but I shall content myself with a few words. There is, I am convinced, from personal inquiry, a strong popular feeling in the Provinces, favorable to such a consolidation. Indeed I may call it a popular aspiration. In the Red River Settlement the people are sadly in want of a government, and British Columbia, a highly promising country, is by its isolation just as much in want of an Atlantic connection, as Louis Napoleon, when he became Emperor of France, was of a royal one. The North American Colonies combined have a population of more than four millions—a number, considering also the abundance of their public works, and their advanced civilization, well capable of forming a powerful empire, capable at any time of withstanding aggression.

The pride of having a national name and a national character on a wider scale than the present, may have much to do with the popular sentiment in favor of such an organization. The hope of increased dignities arising from an extended government, and the prestige of a greater name may also contribute to the impulse. But for me, it is enough to say that it exists, and I have every reason to believe that the policy of the Home Government inclines in this direction, and only requires time to reach its maturity. Before concluding these reflections, I must say a word for the people of British America, of whose hospitality and kindness generally I have the most lively recollection. If by my impartiality I have disappointed some of them, they must refer the matter of that disappointment to its proper cause—my entire freedom from local prejudices. Any man may be proud in claiming Canada for his home or birthplace, and if my footsteps ever wander in that direction again I shall feel unmingled satisfaction.

SUMMARY OF THE PRINCE'S TOUR.

THE visit of the Prince of Wales to the British Provinces and the United States is one of those great historical events which will be handed down to posterity for all time, and be treasured up by the peoples of the two nations forever.

The first inception of the Prince's visit, it may be remembered, was from the Canadians themselves, who petitioned the Queen to send one of the royal family, as she herself would not be able to attend, to inaugurate the opening of the Victoria Bridge at Montreal. It certainly was never contemplated that the heir apparent would be selected for that purpose—popular expectation being satisfied with some smaller personage. It pleased the Queen, however, to send the young Prince of Wales himself to visit the Western possessions of his imperial mother, and at the same time to pay a visit to the United States. Never has monarch arrived at so wise a determination; for the lessons to be derived from the visit of the young Albert Edward to America can hardly fail to impress the future King Edward the Seventh in such a manner as to lead to the full recognition of the rights of the people, throughout his illimitable dominions, on which, according to popular tradition, the sun never sets.

It will be remembered that, in accordance with this arrangement, President Buchanan wrote an autograph letter to the Queen, inviting the young Prince to visit Washington and the United States in general, in his passage through the most interesting portions of the continent. The letter of the President and the reply of the Queen to her "good friend," were published simultaneously in the American newspapers, and ran thus:

LETTER FROM THE PRESIDENT TO THE QUEEN.

To Her Majesty Queen Victoria:

I have learned from the public journals that the Prince of Wales is about to visit Your Majesty's North American dominions. Should it be the intention of His Royal Highness to extend his visit to the United States, I need not say how happy I should be to give him a cordial welcome to Washington.

You may be well assured that everywhere in this country he will be greeted by the American people in such a manner as cannot fail to prove gratifying to Your Majesty. In this they will manifest their deep sense of your domestic virtues, as well as their convictions of your merits as a wise patriot and constitutional sovereign. Your Majesty's most obedient servant, JAMES BUCHANAN.

Washington, June 4, 1860.

THE QUEEN'S REPLY.

Buckingham Palace, June 22, 1860.

My Good Friend,—I have been much gratified at the feeling which prompted you to write to me, inviting the Prince of Wales to come to Washington. He intends to return from Canada through the United States, and it will give him great pleasure to have an opportunity of testifying to you in person that these feelings are fully reciprocated by him. He will thus be able, at the same time, to mark the respect which he entertains for the Chief Magistrate of a great and friendly State and kindred nation.

The Prince of Wales will drop all royal state on leaving my dominions, and travel under the name of Lord Renfrew, as he has done when traveling on the Continent of Europe.

The Prince Consort wishes to be kindly remembered to you. I remain ever, your good friend, VICTORIA R.

In this affair the Queen did herself honor in honoring the United States, by announcing that in passing the frontiers which divide the British Provinces from the States, His Royal Highness would drop all royal state, and assume the lowest title to which he could lay claim—the rather uncouth one of Baron Renfrew, derived from a small Scottish town, situated in a county of the same name, with the addition of "shire" at the end, making up the rather uneuphonious name of "Renfrewshire." Many and rich were the jokes of the London papers on the assumption by the Prince of this rather out-of-the-way title, and Mr. *Punch* distinguished himself by suggesting Sir Edward Chester, Duke of Cornwall, Mr. Guelph (pronounced Welf) and a whole lot of other nomenclature. But the Queen and the Prince, and their advisers, were deaf to all these suggestions, and as Baron Renfrew it was arranged that the Prince of Wales, Duke of Cornwall, and a whole host of et ceteras, too numerous to mention, was to be distinguished in the United States, and as Baron Renfrew he traveled accordingly.

And now to the summary.

JULY.

10. The Prince of Wales and suite, consisting of the Duke of Newcastle, the Earl of St. Germains, General Bruce, Major Teesdale, Captain Grey, Dr. Acland, and others, embark on board the steamship Hero at Plymouth.

23. The Hero, with the Prince on board, accompanied by the Ariadne, enter the port of St. John's, Newfoundland, and cast anchor, at seven o'clock P.M., under a royal salute. In consequence of a heavy fall of rain, the royal party sleep on board the Hero.

24. Landing of the Prince, under a royal salute from the Citadel, the vessels of war Ariadne and Flying Fish, and the French war steamer Sesostris. The yards of these vessels are all manned, and the Prince is received by Governor Sir Alexander Bannerman, and driven to the Government House, under an escort of volunteer troops, accompanied by a procession of the several patriotic and trade societies.

25. The great ball at St. John's. Newfoundland.

26. The Prince holds a levee, after which he embarks for Halifax, Nova Scotia.

30. Arrival of the Prince at Halifax at ten o'clock A.M., under a royal salute and in the midst of a violent rain-storm. He is received by Lord Mulgrave, the Governor, the Mayor, and Corporation, with an address, to which he makes a suitable reply.

31. Review of troops in the midst of a drenching rain. In the evening, a grand ball is given in the Provincial Building, which is opened by the Prince with Lady Mulgrave.

AUGUST.

1. A regatta takes place during the day, which is succeeded by a display of fire-works in the evening.

2. The Prince leaves Halifax for Windsor by special train, at seven o'clock A.M., amid great demonstrations of loyalty, where he arrives at half-past eight. He then embarks on board the Styx for St. John's, New Brunswick, where he arrives at half-past ten o'clock P.M., after a pleasant run in the Bay of Fundy. He is welcomed with a royal salute at St. John's, and receives an address from the Mayor and Corporation, to which he responds.

5. His Royal Highness attends Divine service in the Cathedral.

6. He attends a ball given in his honor, at which six hundred persons are present.

7. Leaves St. John's for Prince Edward's Island.

9. Lands at Charlottetown, Prince Edward's Island, from the Hero, after a pleasant passage. The Hero is accompanied by the Nile, the flagship of Admiral Sir Alexander Milne, the Cossack, Valorous, and Flying Fish, and the French Commodore's ship Pomona. The royal party are received at the wharf by the government officers and the public functionaries, the clergy,

members of the bar, and the most prominent citizens. He is escorted to Government House by a volunteer force. In the evening he is present at a ball at the Colonial Buildings.

11. Leaves Government House and proceeds to the Colonial Buildings, where he receives an address from both branches of the Legislature, to which he replies; after which he leaves for Gaspe, under a salute from the ships of war.

12. Arrival at Gaspe Bay amid great excitement and a general outburst of loyalty; the houses are illuminated, the Governor goes on board the Hero, and has an interview with the Prince.

13. The Prince's standard is hoisted, and receives a royal salute from Fort Ramsay. On leaving the harbor the Hero runs aground, but is got off without injury. At half-past one o'clock P.M. the squadron makes sail.

14. Meeting of citizens in New York, at which it is agreed to invite the Prince to a dinner at the Academy of Music on his arrival in the city.

15. His Royal Highness lands at Saguenay, the houses of which are handsomely decorated with flags, and where the Hero again runs aground, but floats two hours after. Lord Lyons arrives from Washington and joins the royal party. The squadron again sails for Quebec, passing Ha-Ha Bay and other points of interest on the route.

18. Arrival at Quebec. The Prince lands amid great enthusiasm, and is received by the Mayor and Corporation, members of the Cabinet, and the Anglican and Roman Catholic bishops and clergy. The squadron receives a royal salute. The royal party, in the midst of a down-pour of rain, proceed, under a military escort, to the residence of the Governor. The day is turned into a general holiday. The evening closes with an illumination.

19. The Prince attends Divine service at the En-

glish cathedral, after which he pays a visit to the Heights of Abraham, and views General Wolfe's monument, and the place where Montgomery fell. The fortifications were also inspected, and one can almost imagine that the royal youth recalled to mind the delectable quatrain in which a poet thus described the ascent of General Wolfe to the Heights of Abraham:

> He marched without dread or fears
> At the head of his bold grenadiers;
> And what's most remarkable, nay, very particular,
> He climbed up rocks that were perpendicular.

20. He pays a visit to Chaudiere Falls, and receives a delegation from Rhode Island, inviting him to visit that State.

21. He formally takes up his residence at the Parliament House, where he holds a levee and receives addresses and deputations in the Council Chamber, on which occasion he confers the honor of knighthood, by the accolade, on the Hon. Narcisse Belleau, Speaker of the Legislative Council, and the Hon. Henry Smith, Speaker of the Assembly.

22. Ball given by the citizens, which the Prince attends. He falls with his partner while dancing, but recovers himself in a moment. Brilliant display of fire-works, during which a stage falls, and seriously injures several persons.

23. His Royal Highness leaves Quebec for Montreal, in the steamer Kingston. On their way up the royal party stop at Three Rivers, where the Prince receives a royal salute from the Royal Artillery. The landing is handsomely decorated with evergreens. The Prince is received by the Mayor and Corporation, the clergy, public officials, and citizens generally. A State dinner is given, which the Catholic bishops refuse to attend, because the Prince in his reply to their address did not style them "my lords" or "gentlemen."

24. His Royal Highness arrives at Montreal, amid the thunders of cannon and every demonstration of loyalty. In consequence of a heavy down-pour of rain, the illuminations, which were arranged to take place this evening, were postponed to the following night. The Prince announced that he would not land publicly till next day, though it is supposed that he landed privately, and slept that night at the residence of Sir W. F. Williams. Much ill-feeling existing between the French and the English inhabitants—the former outnumbering the latter in their display of national flags. In loading a gun to fire a salute, three sailors belonging to the Flying Fish and one belonging to the Valorous are killed by a premature discharge.

25. His Royal Highness disembarks at ten o'clock A.M., and a grand military, civic, and clerical procession is formed, by which the Prince is escorted to the Crystal Palace, which he inaugurates formally. He then proceeds to the Victoria Bridge, which he opens with due solemnity. [This was the principal object of the Prince's visit to Canada.] The Boston Fusileers take part in the reception—a compliment with which the Prince is much gratified. The ceremonies close with a grand *dejeuner.*

26. The Prince attends Divine service at the Protestant Episcopal cathedral, and hears a sermon from Bishop Fulford. Great crowds inside and outside the church.

27. Indian games, at which the Prince and suite attend, and are much amused. The New York Committee wait on the Prince, and tender him an invitation to a grand banquet. The Prince accepts the invitation, but prefers a ball, which is subsequently acceded to by the general committee. The great Montreal ball takes place to night, in the building specially erected for the occasion. Gorgeous decorations, and a brilliant display of wealth, beauty, and fashion. The ball cost about $40,000.

28. Great musical festival, at which about eight thousand persons are present.

29. His Royal Highness visits Logan's, where he reviews fifteen hundred volunteers. From there he proceeds to Lachine, where he witnesses a number of Indians at their games and canoe races. He extends his trip to Caughnawaga, and returns to Montreal.

30. Visits Sherbrooke, ninety miles from Montreal, and several places of interest intermediate. At St. Hyacinth he is escorted by two hundred Jesuit priests to their college, where he receives an address in French and English. At Brampton Falls he inspects some of the largest saw-mills in America. At Sherbrooke he restores to his rank in the navy a Mr. Felton, who was signal midshipman to Lord Nelson at Trafalgar, and who had been unjustly dismissed the service. At half-past six P.M. he returns and attends the people's ball, but does not dance.

31. Leaves for Ottawa.

SEPTEMBER.

1. His Royal Highness arrives at Ottawa, the little city fixed upon by the Queen herself (in council, of course,) as the future capital of the Canadas, though the Canadians themselves, who chose the Queen as the umpire in the matter, seem disposed to repudiate the arrangement, where he is greeted with the same enthusiasm which met him throughout the route. He there lays the corner-stone of the new Houses of Parliament with much solemnity.

2. The Prince attends Divine service at Christ Church.

3. He rides in an open carriage to the little village of Aylmer, *en route* for Kingston. Arrives at Brockville at eight o'clock P.M., and is escorted through the town by a firemen's torch-light procession—the first

the Prince has ever seen, and at which he is surprised. Troubles are apprehended at Kingston, from the determination of the Orangemen to erect Orange arches and organize processions of the order, with their obnoxious banners and other paraphernalia, at which the Roman Catholics take offense. The Duke of Newcastle, to avoid a collision, which may be attended with effusion of blood, sends word on to Kingston that he will not allow the Prince to pass through any arch decorated with party devices, nor take part in any demonstrations in which party symbols are used.

4. Arrival at Kingston, amid great excitement, in consequence of the firm attitude of the Duke of Newcastle. Stormy meeting of the City Council. The Mayor informs the Council that the Prince will consent to land if the contemplated Orange procession is given up, but not otherwise, which is far from satisfactory. Third Grand Master Cameron orders the Orangemen to give up the position they have assumed, but he is met with the response of "No surrender." The Prince remains on board the steamer; but his suite, with the exception of the Duke of Newcastle and the Earl St. Germains, disembark.

5. The Orangemen continue obstinate and the Prince refuses to land, causing great excitement. The "Marseillaise" is insultingly played opposite the steamer. The Prince offers to receive the address of the Mayor and Corporation on board, but the City Council pass a resolution refusing to present it anywhere else but on shore. The Magistrates, however, present an address on board, which is received and replied to by the Prince, regretting that circumstances should have prevented him from landing. The Orangemen hold out threats to follow the Prince to Toronto, or wherever he might go.

6. Arrival of the royal party at Belleville, where similar riotous demonstrations await them as at Kingston, in consequence of which the Prince refuses to

land, and passes on to Cobourg, where there are no signs of Orangeism. The Prince lands, and is received with every demonstration of loyalty, and he attends a ball in the evening.

7. The Prince takes a special train from Cobourg at ten o'clock A.M., and arrives at Peterboro, crossing Rice Lake on a steamer. He is received at Peterboro by a procession. From Peterboro he departs for Port Hope, which he reaches at two P.M., where there is another procession, by which he is conveyed to the Court House, where he partakes of a *dejeuner* and receives addresses from the civic functionaries. From Port Hope he proceeds to Whitby, where he arrives at three o'clock. Leaving this latter place, he reaches Toronto at half-past six P.M. Here he finds that the Orangemen had submitted, and have but one arch remaining, which the Prince and suite carefully avoid during their stay in the city. The Prince lands, and is received with deafening cheers. He receives an address from the Corporation, and is escorted to Government House, which he reaches at nine P.M. The city is brilliantly illuminated.

8. This morning the Prince holds a levee, and in the evening he attends a ball given by the members of the bar. An angry correspondence takes place between the Duke of Newcastle and the Mayor, on the subject of the solitary arch.

9. The Prince attends Divine service, carefully avoiding the arch in his way to and fro. Large multitudes collect around the church. In the evening the Duke of Newcastle and the Governor, while taking a walk, are grossly insulted for advising the Prince against passing through the arch.

10. Starts for Collingwood, ninety-five miles' distant, by special train. On passing the town of Aurora, and other places on the route, Orange arches are seen erected. Arrival at Collingwood.

11. The Prince joins a yacht club, lays a corner-

stone of the Queen's statue, and plants a tree in the Botanic Gardens. He pays a visit to the University and the Normal School, holds a levee, receives addresses and attends a ball in the evening.

13. Arrives at London, where he is received with the utmost enthusiasm and respect.

15. His Royal Highness leaves London by special train on the Great Western Railroad, and arrives at Woodstock. In a pavilion at the Mayor's residence he receives several addresses, and then leaves for Paris, where he changes his cars for those of the Buffalo and Lake Huron Railroad. At Brantford he finds a line of little girls, who strew flowers in his way. He receives addresses from some Indians. At Fort Erie, after receiving an address, he embarks in a steamer for Chippewa. His Royal Highness arrives at Niagara Falls, and spends some time in examining this stupendous work of nature. He witnesses Blondin's performances on the rope stretched across the boiling gulf.

16. He attends Divine service at Chippewa.

17. Arrival at Queenstown Heights, and reception of an address from the veterans of 1812.

18. The Prince is received at Hamilton by several hundred farmers with every demonstration of loyalty.

19. He receives several addresses, and visits the Central Public School, where he is again addressed by the trustees in presence of four thousand children. In the evening His Royal Highness attends a ball, given in a building specially erected for the occasion, adjoining the Anglo-American Hotel.

20. Visit to the Provincial Exhibition, where His Royal Highness is addressed by the President of the Agricultural Society. He takes lunch at Dunburn Castle, the residence of Sir Allan McNab, after which he leaves for Detroit, Michigan, by the Great Western Railroad, at two o'clock P.M., passing the frontiers between the Canadas and the United States. His

Royal Highness is supposed to have dropped all royal state, and to have assumed the comparatively modest style and title of Baron Renfrew. He arrives at Detroit in the evening, where he experiences, among democratic Americans, as enthusiastic a reception as any that greeted him through the provinces of monarchical England. There is a general illumination and torch-light procession, and he is escorted to his hotel by multitudes of citizens, all vieing with each other to do honor to Victoria's eldest son.

21. The morning is passed in a series of visits to the most notable places in the city, and a glad welcome meets the Prince everywhere. He leaves for Chicago, Ill., at ten o'clock, which he reaches in the evening, when the reception he met at Detroit is duplicated.

22. The Prince visits several objects of interest in company with Mayor Wentworth, especially the grain elevators, which he views with surprise. He remains in the balcony of the hotel for some time at the request of the people, who evince their anxiety to see him by their immense numbers. He is astonished at the account given him of the rapid growth and present prosperity of Chicago. He leaves for the prairies, and arrives at Dwight Station in the evening, where he has a rehearsal of next day's sport before supper.

23. His Royal Highness attends the Presbyterian church at Dwight.

24. Shooting of prairie chickens. Not much sport.

25. Leaves Dwight for Stewart's Grove, where the royal party have better sport, quail shooting. Return to Dwight.

27. The royal party leave Dwight for St. Louis, Mo., where they arrive early in the evening, and meet with an enthusiastic reception.

28. The royal visit to the Agricultural Fair, at which one hundred thousand persons are present

Grand ovation to the Prince. The royal party evince their judgment respecting cattle and horses.

29. The Prince and suite arrive at Cincinnati, Ohio, and visit the piggeries. The evening winds up with a ball, given by the Porkopolitans to the Prince, who is as popular as everywhere else on his route.

30. The royal party attend Divine service at St. John's Church, when Bishop McIlvaine preaches the sermon.

OCTOBER.

2. The Prince reaches Pittsburg, Pa., where he is enthusiastically received by Mayor Wilson and the Corporation, and the citizens generally. The Mayor addresses the Prince. His Royal Highness is surprised at the magnitude of the factories in Pittsburg, which he and his suite call the Manchester of America. The evening winds up with an illumination and a serenade to the Prince, who leaves for Harrisburg, where he arrives at eleven P.M. All along the route he receives shouts of welcome, and at Harrisburg he is favored with a serenade.

3. The Prince drives to the Capitol, accompanied by his suite, at nine A.M., where he receives an address from Governor Parker. From Harrisburg he departs for Baltimore, where he is met at the depot by the City Council—a band playing "God save the Queen." Leaving Baltimore by special train, the royal party reach Washington at four P.M., amid thunders of artillery. The Prince is received by General Cass, who conducts him, under an escort, to the White House, where he is presented to President Buchanan, by whom he is introduced to Miss Lane. At six o'clock the President gives a grand dinner in honor of the Prince's arrival.

4. The Prince and suite visit the National Capitol,

and other objects of interest. At noon the President holds a levee, at which he introduces the Prince to the notabilities. The Prince then visits the Patent-office, after which he accompanies Miss Lane to Miss Smith's Institute for Young Ladies, where he has a game of ten-pins. In the evening the President entertains the *corps diplomatique* at dinner, at which the Prince is present, which is followed by a reception by Miss Lane, and a grand pyrotechnic display.

5. At ten o'clock this morning the Prince and suite embark on the Harriet Lane, and proceed to Mount Vernon, where they visit the tomb of Washington—a touching incident destined to be of historical interest. The Prince plants a young horse-chestnut-tree, in commemoration of the occasion. In the evening a dinner is given by Lord Lyons to the royal party.

6. The royal party embark again on board the Harriet Lane and land at Acquia Creek. Thence they proceed by rail to Richmond, Va., where they are most enthusiastically received.

7. The Prince and suite attend Divine service, after which His Royal Highness pays a visit to the Governor, with whom he drives out to view the different objects of interest in the city and suburbs.

8. Arrival at Baltimore, where the Prince receives the usual ovation.

9. His Royal Highness arrives at Philadelphia in the midst of the election excitement, which diverts attention from the royal party somewhat, and renders the reception of the Prince less enthusiastic than it would otherwise have been.

10. Great operatic entertainment at the Academy of Music in honor of the Prince, at which the *artistes* from New York take the leading parts. Immense enthusiasm.

11. The Prince and suite leave Philadelphia for New York by the Camden and Amboy Railroad. The Harriet Lane, which had been placed at the disposal

of the Prince by the President, leaves the Battery with the Committee of Reception to meet His Royal Highness at Perth Amboy, where the royal party embark. The Prince is saluted by the batteries and shipping as the Harriet Lane steams up the bay, amid the cheers of the immense multitudes on shore and on board the different vessels. His Royal Highness lands at the Battery, where he is received by Mayor Wood, who welcomes him to New York, and presents him to the members of the Common Council present. He then assumes his colonel's uniform, and, at the request of General Sandford, to whom the Mayor introduces him, he reviews six thousand volunteer troops of the First Division, at Castle Garden; after which he proceeds up Broadway, in a handsome barouche, drawn by six superb black horses, amid the acclamations of a vast multitude, numbering several hundred thousand. At the City Hall the Prince received a marching salute. His Royal Highness then proceeded up Broadway to the Fifth Avenue Hotel, amid the plaudits of the crowd.

12. He visits the New York University, the Deaf and Dumb Asylum and other institutions, and takes lunch with Mayor Wood, after which he pays a visit to the Central Park, where he plants an oak and an elm tree. In the evening a magnificent ball is given to the Prince by the citizens of New York, in the Academy of Music, which is gorgeously decorated with flowers for the occasion. Early in the evening part of the flooring of the ball-room gives way, creating much excitement and alarm, but, happily, without injuring any one. The breach is repaired, and, after an elegant supper, the Prince opens the ball with Mrs. Governor Morgan, and dances till a late hour on the following morning.

13. His Royal Highness visits General Scott, after which he pays a round of visits to several places, including Barnum's Museum. In the evening there is a grand firemen's procession, in which five thousand

firemen, bearing torches, take part. The engines and other apparatus are beautifully decorated; and, in fact, it is pronounced to be the largest and most brilliant procession of the kind that has ever taken place in the city.

14. The royal party attend Trinity Church, the streets leading to which are lined with people, and the vicinity crowded. After service they partake of luncheon with Mr. Archibald, the British Consul. Sermons on the Prince are preached, in their respective places of worship, by the Rev. Mr. Frothingham, Unitarian, and the Rev. Mr. Harris, Methodist. The evening is stormy, and the Prince stays within doors.

15. They leave for West Point, in the Harriet Lane, and on their arrival they have a grand reception, after which the Prince reviews the cadets. The Prince inspects the Academy, and finishes the evening with a game of ten-pins.

16. Departure for Albany, up the Hudson, where the Prince is received by the civil authorities and the people. In company with Governor Morgan, he visits the State Capitol and other places of interest.

17. Off for Boston, which is reached in the afternoon. The Prince is escorted by a troop of cavalry to his hotel. Vast crowds line the way and express much anxiety to see the Prince.

18. This is a gala day. The principal public buildings, hotels, some private houses, and the shipping in the harbor, are handsomely decorated with flags and streamers. In the afternoon the Prince, in full uniform, with staff, accompanied by Governor Banks and his staff, reviews two thousand five hundred troops on the Common. The sight is witnessed by thirty thousand persons. After the review the vast multitude form a procession, and escort the Prince through the principal streets to his hotel.

19. The Prince visits Harvard College, Mount Auburn Cemetery, Bunker Hill and the Charlestown

Navy Yard, and the Public Library in the evening. He attracts large crowds wherever he goes.

20. He leaves Boston for Portland, Maine, where he is received by the Governor of the State, the Mayor of the city and a respectable body of military, together with almost the entire population, by whom he is escorted through the principal streets to the place of embarkation, where he goes on board the Hero, under a royal salute, and almost immediately after the squadron sails for Old England.

THE HISTORICAL PRINCES OF WALES.

In the hereditary halo surrounding the title of Prince of Wales there is much calculated to involve the detail of the historian. Identified as the dignity has been with English story for more than five centuries, few readers even of that story are cognizant of the powers or events nearly allied to the honorary designation of the regular heir to the British throne, and who may not discover in the following brief summary of the lives and deaths of the nineteen Princes of Wales, preceding the present and twentieth, something to ponder over and repay the perusal.

The first Prince of Wales (of English connection) was Edward of Caernarvon, eldest son of King Edward the First—born at the castle where he derived his appellation, at the moment his father was consummating the conquest of the Welsh people. An old legend, as likely to be true as false, has been handed down to us in respect to this Prince, to the effect that the Welsh refused up to the latest moment to accept a Prince apart from one who was their own countryman, and could speak no language except their own—a difficulty which the adroit Edward soon disposed of by presenting to his new subjects his own infant, born only the previous night in Caernarvon. This Prince afterwards became King Edward the Second, and is noted in history as one of the weakest and most unfortunate of monarchs who ever held the English sceptre. Hurled from place and power, he was confined in the lowest dungeons of Berkeley Castle, and there murdered by a process as unnatural as it was horrible.

The second Prince of Wales was son of the above

unhappy king, but very unlike him in disposition and the glory of his reign. The name of Edward the Third fills a brilliant page in English history, as does that of his son, known as the "Black Prince," the most successful of generals and the most accomplished of warriors, who, we are told, was the first to adopt the three ostrich feathers, with the motto "*Ich Dien*," as a cognizance, and who, much to the sorrow of his own countrymen, died before he could attain the dignity held by his parent, and which must have devolved on him had he been spared a few years longer.

As though for the purpose of showing how imbecility is reflected in the same family, and of contrasting one Prince of Wales with his immediate predecessor, Richard, afterwards the second king of that name, and son of the "Black Prince," took up the motto dropped by the latter. A man of indecision and weakness, he was the victim of courtly cabals, and, it is recorded, was starved to death. His cousin and successor on the throne, Henry, of Lancaster, had a son, who, perhaps more than all the other Princes of Wales, has claimed the respect and admiration of subsequent generations. Who, at all familiar with the Shaksperean muse needs to be reminded of the madcap Harry, boon companion of fat Jack Fallstaff, royster in general in his youth, but afterwards, when the "awful round of sovereignty" had clasped his brow, the illustrious hero of Agincourt and chivalrous gentleman of Europe. Again: in connection with the title of Prince of Wales, we come to a duplicate and a contrast as well of character. The son of the dead monarch is crowned in Paris when only nine months old. This Prince also has been portrayed by Shakspeare, who, in the amiable yet vacillating Henry the Sixth, has shown us a man to pity more than to admire or condemn.

Passing over a few years, we come to another Prince of Wales, as valiant as his grandfather and as unfortunate as his father We speak of the young Edward, who, it is said, was stabbed on the battle-field of Tewkesbury, by "Dukes Richard, Clarence, and the rest."

After this Prince comes the eldest son of Edward the Fourth, of York—numbered among the monarchs of England as Edward the Fifth—who, according to general belief, was murdered in the Tower of London, at the instigation of his uncle, afterwards Richard the Third.

Many years pass and many changes take place before the title of Prince of Wales is again taken up—in the present instance by Arthur, son of Henry the Seventh. This Prince dies in his father's lifetime, and leaves his dignity to his brother Henry, afterwards Henry the Eighth, of no very enviable memory. Henry's son is the next Prince of Wales—a title he becomingly bears until his ascension to the throne as Edward the Sixth. Mary and Elizabeth follow ; and as neither has progeny, the title of right belonging to the hereditary heir apparent to the English throne remains in abeyance until the coming of the Scottish James, on whose accession to the throne left vacant by Elizabeth, his eldest son Henry assumes the dignity of Prince of Wales ; and after him, he dying young, his brother Charles, subsequently King Charles, who was beheaded in 1649. The eldest son of this unfortunate monarch was, of course, Prince of Wales during his father's life, and Charles the Second when he died. He left no legitimate offspring, and was succeeded by his brother, the Duke of York, as James the Second. James it is well known, was obliged to fly from England, taking with him his wife and infant son (Prince of Wales), afterwards known as the Chevalier St. George, in whose behalf the so-called "Rebellion" of 1715 was concerted, and whose son, Charles Edward, was commonly called the "Pretender."

The Guelphs taking possession of the English throne in 1714, the next Prince of Wales was the son of the first George, and on the death of that monarch, George the Second. He had a son, Frederick, who, in 1727, became, in his turn, Prince of Wales, and who, dying early, left the title to his son George, afterwards third king of that designation on the English throne, which he ascended in 1760. Two years afterwards he had a son, who, according to usage, was created Prince of Wales by patent, when a few days old. This personage became Regent in 1812, and King in 1820, and was, in his time, noted for the splendor of his living. Dying in 1830, he was succeeded by his brother, the Duke of Clarence (William the Fourth), who, having no legitimate offspring, left, on his decease in 1837, the right, title, and dignity to his niece, the Princess Victoria, of Kent, of whom the Prince of Wales, Albert Edward, is the eldest son. His Royal Highness was born on the 9th of November, 1841, at Buckingham Palace, London.

The materials which in future days will be at hand to enable a biographer to write a history, or part history, of his life are not yet to be found. The deeds of his youth and the achievements of his manhood and maturity are yet to be enacted. At present he can only be congratulated on the splendid prospect he has before him, and as the fortunate possessor of a wide field for good.

His visit to America has naturally caused great interest, partly on account of its being the first visit ever paid by a Prince of Wales to the great republic, but more particularly by reason of the universal respect entertained by the American people for his mother, Queen Victoria. It has been the fate of few women placed in so elevated a position to receive so widespread a reputation for the womanly virtues, and it would seem as though she had determined to train her children with as much care as she had been trained herself.

The titles of the Prince of Wales are, Duke of Saxony, Prince of Saxe Coburg Gotha, Duke of Cornwall and Rothsay, Earl of Chester, Carrick, Dublin, Baron Renfrew, and Lord of the Isles. These titles he derives partly by inheritance and partly from creation, from the circumstance of King Edward I. having, in politic concession to the Welsh chieftains, created his heir "Prince of Wales," a few days after his birth, which took place in Caernarvon Castle. This was the unhappy Edward II., who was so barbarously murdered by Mortimer in Berkeley Castle. A few days after he was created Earl of Chester, which title has been retained up to the present time. The Scottish titles of the Prince are derived from Robert III., in whose reign they were vested in the heir apparent of the Crown of Scotland. His Irish titles were conferred on the present Prince of Wales by Queen Victoria, on the 10th of September, 1849, in commemoration of her visit to Ireland. In the House of Lords he is known as the Duke of Cornwall.

Dod, the great authority on all these questions, thus defines the rank and position of the Prince of Wales: "The Prince of Wales has ever been regarded as the first subject in the realm, the nearest to the throne, the most dignified of the Peers of Parliament, and though not exercising any political power beyond his vote as a legislator, yet regarded by all men as the most eminent person in the State next after the sovereign."

The education of Albert Edward has been conducted under the immediate supervision of the Queen. In the languages, classics, natural philosophy, mathematics, jurisprudence, and other branches, His Royal Highness has had the most eminent professors of the day.

On the 9th of November, 1858, the Prince of Wales, having on that day completed his seventeenth year, was appointed colonel in the army.

Having thus fairly entered upon the duties of manhood, His Royal Highness determined upon pursuing his studies, for a time at least, at home. Accordingly, after a brief visit to his illustrious sister at Berlin, the Princess Frederick William of Prussia, he proceeded on his journey to Italy. On his way thither he performed the first public act of his life, by presenting colors to the 100th or Prince of Wales' Royal Canadian Regiment of Foot, then stationed at Shorncliffe, near Folkestone.

The Prince arrived in the Eternal City in the latter part of January, 1859, and, having spent some time in exploring ancient and modern Rome, proceeded quietly and unostentatiously to his studies. Before doing so, however, he paid a visit to the Pope. His appearance at the Vatican is worthy of note, inasmuch as a Prince of the blood-royal of England had not made a similar visit for some centuries. Agreeably to the expressed wish of Her Majesty, the reception was conducted with little ceremony. His Holiness rose on the entry of the Prince, and, coming forward to the door of the apartment to meet him, conducted him in the most affable manner possible to a seat, and entered into conversation with him in French. Col. Bruce was the only other person present at the interview, which was brief, and limited to complimentary expressions and subjects of local interest, but perfectly satisfactory to all parties. On the Prince rising to take his leave, the Pope conducted him again to the door with the same warmth of manner which he had testified on receiving him. The stay of His Royal Highness in Rome being interrupted by the outbreak of the war in Italy, he traveled to Gibraltar, and from thence to Spain and Portugal. He returned to England on June 25, 1859.

On his return he took up his residence at Oxford to pursue his studies, and on the 9th of July last he embarked with his suite at Davenport, on board the Hero ship of war, and sailed for America on the following morning.

In person the young Prince has rather a short slim figure, which is always displayed to the best advantage in trim fitting garments of the latest style. He has his mother's profile, and in order to see the contour of his face, it is only necessary to look at the effigies of the Queen upon an English sixpence.

The manners of the Prince of Wales would form a good model for any youth to follow. Modest, unassuming, courteous, and agreeable to all, he makes hosts of friends wherever he goes.

THE ROYAL PARTY.

THE DUKE OF NEWCASTLE.

HENRY Pelham Clinton, fifth Duke of Newcastle, is a Statesman and Peer of the British Empire, and Secretary of State for the Colonies. He was born on the 22d of May, 1811, in London, and is descended from the ancient family of the Barons Clinton, who inherited in 1756 the Dukedom of Newcastle, under the name of Lord Lincoln. He was educated at the University of Oxford, and as soon as he became of age he took his seat in the House of Commons, to which he was constantly re-elected until 1851, at first for the borough of Nottingham, and then for that of Falkirk. At this latter date he took his father's seat in the House of Lords, and continued to support the policy of the conservative party, of which he is a moderate representative. He differed with the old tories on the double question of the endowment of the Catholic clergy and the reform of the tariffs, for which he voted. He was appointed Lord of the Treasury in 1834, in connection with the first Cabinet of Sir Robert Peel; in the second Peel Cabinet of 1841 and 1846 he held the still higher post of first Commissioner of the Woods and Forests. In 1846 he was for some time Secretary in Chief for Ireland.

In 1852 the Duke of Newcastle formed a part of the Aberdeen ministry, and after having discharged the duties of the Colonial Office for some time, he was made Secretary of War in June, 1854, a most important position at that period, in consequence of the Russian war. The campaign had hardly opened when loud complaints arose on all sides against the insufficient and unsatisfactory manner in which the ministry had provided for the necessities of an army on the march. The Duke defended himself in Parliament with a great deal of spirit, and yet with moderation, and afterwards Lord John Russell attributed the errors with which the Duke had been charged to the numerous interruptions which had prevailed in a badly organized ministry. The Duke of Newcastle, however, being greatly dissatisfied, resigned his port-folio into the hands of Lord Panmure in February, 1855. A commission of inquiry was then appointed, which did not justify any of the accumulated charges against the Duke. He spent the autumn of 1855 in visiting the Crimea and all the military posts of the Black Sea. By his marriage with the only daughter of the Duke of Hamilton, from whom he publicly separated since 1850, he has five children. The eldest, Henry Pelham Alexander, Count of Lincoln, was born in 1834.

Although the natural and easy manner in which the Prince has accommodated himself to the circumstances in which he has been placed may in a great measure be set down to the genial and amiable impulses of his own nature, it must not be forgotten that he has been all the time under strict tutelage, and that it is more to the judgment and tact of his advisers than to his own unfettered discretion that are due the admirable propriety and freedom from all that was likely to shock democratic prejudices that marked his progress on the American shores. It is but right that the Mentor to whom the popularity of the British Telemachus is in a great measure owing should have his fair share of the credit attaching to the conduct of his royal charge. It is not generally known, and it is time that the fact should be stated, that on His Grace the Duke of Newcastle devolved by Queen Victoria the entire responsibility of her son's actions during his visit to America. Among the whole British aristocracy, a wiser or more judicious selection could not have been made. The career of this nobleman, from his first entrance on public life, has been marked by an uprightness, a soundness of judgment, and a comprehensiveness of views, which have singled him out as one of the most patriotic and estimable of living British statesmen.

When Lord Lincoln, he was one of the first to give his adhesion to the free trade theories of Sir Robert Peel, convinced that in their adoption lay the only permanent foundations of the prosperity of his country. When that great man was made the incessant object of bitter persecutions by the party whom he had conscientiously deserted, Lord Lincoln was one of the small but gallant band of statesmen who adhered to his fortunes, and who, after his death, esteemed it their greatest pride to have been numbered among his followers. But it is not in his public life only that the Duke has displayed those rare qualities which have earned him universal respect. The course which he pursued on coming into possession of his father's title and estates offered an equally striking example of the justness of views and lofty disinterestedness which seem to be the leading qualities of his character. In his address to the tenantry of the Clumber estates, Notts, delivered in December, 1851, he gave expression to sentiments and intentions which did equal credit to his head and heart. In the first place he informed them that the custom that had prevailed of demanding the rent immediately after harvest would be discontinued, as he felt that the practice was prejudicial to the tenant, by compelling him to thresh out his corn at a time when it was not fit for market, and disposing of it at a considerable loss to himself. Then, after prefacing the announcement by an allusion to certain abatements of rent made by his father, he stated that he had come to the conclusion that, as a claim for such reductions had been made, he thought the fairest course was to have all the farms upon the estates revalued, which had accordingly been done by his orders, and the result was the reduction of the rent of a large proportion of them, while the few that were raised he had decided upon leaving at their old rental. Considering the heavy sacrifices which these concessions entailed on a landlord who had a princely rank to maintain, they manifest a conscientious regard for his obligations and duties towards his tenantry, which is but rarely to be met with among the class to which he belongs.

With the same disregard of time-honored prejudice, the Duke in several instances practically annulled the obnoxious and stringent game laws, so long the detestation of English tenants. During his visit to Niagara Falls, in company with the Prince, report says, he met one of his old tenants, now engaged in a flourishing business, and the recognition was so marked and cordial that the bystanders were led to inquire in regard to the circumstances of the former acquaintance between the parties. It appears that some years ago the game preserved by the Duke made such sad havoc with the crops of his tenantry that the nuisance became unbearable. Filled with indignation, one of the tenants—the gentleman in question—started for the Duke's residence, and seeing, but not recognizing, His Grace standing near the lodge, and very roughly dressed, he requested his landlord to open the gate.

This the Duke did, and the man rode up to the house. There he found no Duke, but plenty of beef and ale, which English hospitality furnishes to the poorest visitor. After waiting awhile he started for home, more indignant, but not quite as sober, as ever. Again he met the Duke, again requested him to play the part of porter, and, again consenting, the Duke, by adroit questionings, led the man to ventilate his grievances. Pleased to find a sympathizer, the tenant grew eloquent upon his losses, and finally left for home, slightly relieved at having been able at least to talk of his griefs. When he arose the next morning he found the gamekeepers and neighboring tenantry busy in destroying the game which had played such pranks with his grain, and besides this present relief, he received permission to repeat the destruction as often as the game became troublesome. Most English noblemen would—indeed, most English noblemen do—allow their tenantry to get along as they may, and carefully protect, from even a stick or stone, their fine but destructive preserves.

The manly and straightforward conduct of the Duke in Canada, on the occasion of the Orange disturbances, is fresh in the recollection of the public. A timid and vacillating man would never have been equal to the emergency; but the bold and determined stand taken by the noble Duke has doubtless tended to prevent the loss of many valuable lives.

The Duke of Newcastle is tall, with a decided inclination to corpulency. He has large, finely formed features, and allows his beard, to grow upon his face, naturally without trimming or arrangement. The Duke stands very erect, and has an air and manner which instantly announce the high-born gentleman, and, when in uniform, his appearance is especially *distingué* and imposing. The firm, independent, honest, open character of the man inspires his whole form. From these very qualities—the qualities that appeal most to Americans—he stands hardly second to the Prince in popular favor, and at almost every place which the party visited cheers for the Duke succeeded those for the Prince. This was the case even in Canada, where the Orangemen, after exclaiming vehemently against him whom they had never seen, fell in love with His Grace as soon as he appeared personally among them, were completely captivated by his mingled firmness and kindness, and enthusiastically applauded the very man against whom they had professed to entertain the bitterest hostility. For a statue of honest, manly independence, no form, after that of Washington, could be more expressive than that of the Duke.

THE EARL OF ST. GERMAINS,

One of the most polished noblemen of the Court of St. James, and for some time Lord Lieutenant of Ireland, and at present Lord High Steward of Her Majesty's household, belongs to an ancient family which flourished for several generations in the county of Devon before it removed into Cornwall, and in the beginning of the fifteenth century, Walter Eliot, one of his ancestors, was returned among the gentry of that shire. The Earl is named Edward Granville Eliot. He was born on the 29th of August, 1798, and was married on the 21st of September, 1824, to Jemima, daughter of the late Marquis Cornwallis. His ancestor, Sir John Eliot, was member of Parliament for the county of Cornwall in the reign of Charles the First. This gentleman, a strenuous opponent of the Court, was appointed by the House of Commons one of the managers of the impeachment of the Duke of Buckingham, for which, with Sir Dudley Digges, the other manager, he was committed to the Tower, but soon afterwards released. In 1628, Sir John Eliot, with other members of the Commons, was again sent to the Tower for refusing to answer before the Privy Council for unparliamentary conduct, and on the 29th of May, in that year, an information was exhibited in the Star Chamber against Sir John and his companions for their undutiful speeches, and they were sent to the Tower, where Sir John died on the 29th of November, 1632.

The Earl of St. Germains is tall and slightly built. He is gray haired, and extremely pleasant looking. He dresses well, and seems to take a pride in the arrangement of his *personnel.*

Indeed, the Earl, in his attention to his costume, and in his jaunty air, resembles not a little Lord Palmerston, of whom it has been said that he grows younger with age. With his handsome form, set off by the best made of frock coats, or the full dress uniform of the members of Her Majesty's household, his hat jauntily set on one side, his cane lightly held or tapping his brightly polished boot, St. Germains looks every inch the Earl, and, at a distance, looks rather like the brother than like the father of the Hon. Mr. Charles George Cornwallis Eliot, who accompanied him during the greater part of this tour; as also Viscount Hinchinbrooke, eldest son of the Earl of Sandwich, and grandson of the Marquis of Anglesey, the honored military companion of the Duke of Wellington.

Both these gentlemen were on terms of intimate friendship with His Royal Highness, and traveled with the suite.

MAJOR GENERAL THE HON. ROBERT BRUCE.

Major General the Hon. Robert Bruce, brother of the Earl of Elgin, and son of that illustrious peer so well known as the collector of those splendid Grecian antiquities denominated "The Elgin Marbles," is in his forty-eighth year, and is one of the finest-looking men of the day, with peculiarly attractive and cordial manners. He occupies the position of "Governor" to the Prince of Wales, and in this capacity he resides with him, and accompanies him upon his travels.

General Bruce is tall and well built, his hair and whiskers gray, his mustache dark, his forehead round, full, and dome-like, his complexion pure and transparent, his eyes dark hazel, his dress the perfection of neatness and good taste. He is probably the most cultivated gentleman of the suite, and his mind and manners are equally polished. General Bruce was the only person present during the memorable interview between the Prince and the Pope of Rome, and indeed, accompanied the Prince during his first Con.

tinental tour. His Royal Highness could not have a better "guide, philosopher, and friend." Equally at home in the drawing-room, the field, and the library —equally well versed in the etiquette of court and camp, and as scholarly as he is accomplished—General Bruce appears the model gentleman, while his goodness of heart, his instant recognition of merit in every station, his suavity and his affability, make him no less loved than admired.

—

DR. ACLAND, M.D.

This gentleman, a distinguished member of the University of Oxford, and of great literary and scientific attainments, is the Prince's physician. He is tall and stoutly built, and has full light-colored side whiskers, and high forehead.

—

MAJOR TEESDALE.

This brave officer is one of the Prince's equerries, and distinguished himself at the siege of Kars, in the defense of which he took an active and prominent part, under Gen. Williams. He wears several medals of honor. He is handsome, having a face of the Teutonic type, and light curly hair and mustache.

—

CAPTAIN GRAY.

Captain Gray, who is also distinguished for bravery, and who wears several medals of honor, ranks equally with Major Teesdale as an equerry of the Prince. Captain Gray is tall, stoops slightly forward, and is distinguished by his closely cut hair, his long, heavy side whiskers, his brilliant dark eyes, fine complexion, and high color.

THE ROYAL QUARTETTE.

(INTENDED TO BE SUNG ONLY BY THE COMPOSERS.)

" *Welcome, Laddie, for your Mither's sake.*"

Much has been said and done sin' the Prince cam' here,
To mak' him kind welcome and gie him guid cheer;
But the best thing seen or said on land, stream, or lake,
It was, " Welcome, laddie, for your mither's sake."

Oh! light be the heart o' him wha designed it,
Calm as the feeling which nestles behind it;
Be his head ever clear, may his soul have no ache,
Wha welcomed the " laddie for his mither's sake."

'Tis as chaste as the gem which slumbers in light,
As clear to the mind as the sun to the sight;
The hand o' him wha said it I'd cheerfully shake,
Wi' a " Welcome, laddie, for your mither's sake."

As simple an' sweet as the breath o' a bairn,
An' sparklin' an' pure as the dew on the chairn;
Oh! dead were the soul that the sense were slow to take
O' that " Welcome, laddie, for your mither's sake."

A charm's in the word that's found in no other,
From lowliest life to exalted Queen Mother;
True feeling was his who such sentiment could make;
May his hope be in heaven " for his mither's sake."

AT THE GRAVE OF WASHINGTON.

The soft rays of the autumn sun
Fell goldenly on land and wave,
Touching with holy light the grave
That holds the dust of Washington.

A sacred Presence brooded round,
A halo of divinest flame;
The memory of the mighty name
That makes Mount Vernon hallowed ground!

A stately, silent group was there—
    The nation's Ruler, crowned with years,
    And England's Prince, amid his peers,
Uncovered in the reverent air.

Beneath the old ancestral trees
    They walked together, side by side,
    In sun and shadow, close allied,
Linked in the happy bands of peace.

Two friendly nations met in them,
    Two mighty nations, one of old,
    Cast in the same gigantic mould,
Shoots from the sturdy Saxon stem.

They gathered round his holy dust,
    The wisest of the many wise
    That shaped our early destinies,
And fought our battles, sternly just.

Like brothers, at his grave they stood,
    And gloried in his common name
    Forgetting all things but his fame,
Remembering only what was good!

'Twas gracefully and nobly done,
    A royal tribute to the free,
    Who, Prince, will long remember thee,
Before the grave of Washington!

In the golden sun of the early October,
  By the wide Potomac's yellow flood,
At the tomb of the great world's noblest sleeper
  A group of strangers silent stood.

Full many a foot the path had trodden—
  And ever with slow and careful tread,—
The path sweeping down from the house to the river,
  That passes the tomb of the mighty dead.

Full many an eye through the iron grating
  Had looked on the marble coffer gray
Where a nation, half a century younger,
  Laid the gem of their pride in dust away.

All nations, and colors, and habits, and races,
  Had made it a spot of pilgrim tryst,

Paying homage to valor, and wisdom and goodness—
No blood and no climate can ever resist.

But here was a group from the Isle of the Ocean—
The rocky isle of our fathers' birth—
The isle whose drum-beat circles and startles
The echoes of morning over the earth.

And one was a boy, with the hair of a Saxon,
The bright blue eye of the German land,
Who will hold some day, if the fates are propitious,
The sceptre of George the Third in his hand.

Behind him were men of the proudest title—
The feudal lords of English boast,
Standing ever around the royal scion
As the great ships guard their native coast.

Victoria's son—high Albert Edward—
He had stood already, in year's so few,
On many a spot, made famous in story—
On Naseby, and Barnet, and Waterloo—

The spots where a dynasty tottered and trembled,
Or a rebel baron in ruin fell,
And where, over the startled and shuddering Europe,
Rang out the great Corsican commoner's knell.

But never, I ween, on a spot so pregnant
With varying thought, stood the boy before;
And what must have been the mingled color
That his young reflection silently wore?

Before him the dead lay—helpless, but mighty;
Around him was stretching an endless chain
Of hills, and plains, and crowded cities,.
And rivers down laughing to the main.

This golden land had once been a jewel
That flashed and glittered in a Britain's crown,
His own great grandsire had ruled and lorded
Wherever the visitor's foot came down.

The man that was dead, in the century faded,
Had won a wreath for his manly brow,
That a hundred years have budded and brightened;
Did the royal boy remember how?

PADDY'S ODE TO THE PRINCE.

(WRITTEN IN NEW YORK.)

O Mighty Prince! it's no offince,
Your worship, that I mane ye,
While I confiss, 'twas as ra-al bliss,
A moment to have sane ye!

That you should see the likes o' me,
The while I stud adjacent,
I don't suppose, although me clothes
Was mighty clane and dacent.

But by my troth, and Bible-oath!
Wid all my Irish shyness,
I've passed the word wid many a lord
Much taller than your Highness!

Ah! well—bedad, no doubt ye had,
In token of allagiance,
As good a cup as ye could sup,
Among thim black Canajans:

But wha'-d'ye think of Christian dhrink,
Now tell me that, me tulip!
When through a straw your Highness saw
The flavor of a julep?

And what is more, we've got galore,
Such oysters—none can bate 'em;
Ye'll bliss the day ye crossed the say,
When ye sit down to ate 'em.

There's craythers rare and mighty quare
In Barnum's great Muzaum,
By land and wather, and for a qua'ther
Your Highness may survey 'em.

Thim haythen chaps, the nayger Japs,
Wid all their grate expinses,
Just tuk their fill, and left a bill
At which the paple winces.

Fernandy Wud has decent blood,
And illigant morality;
And ye may sware our mighty Mayor
Will show his horse-pitality.

The soldiers are all at his call,
Wid captains to parade 'em;
And at the laste, ye'll get a taste
Of dimmocratic fraydem!

But plase to note, ye'er not to vote—
A privilege, by Jabers,
Ye could'nt hope, were ye the Pope,
Until ye've got the papers!

Well, mighty Prince, accept these hints;
Most frayly I indite 'em;
'Tis luck indade, if ye can rade
As aisy as I can write 'em!

And when the throne is all ye'r own
At which ye're daily steerin',
With all the care that ye can spare,
Remember poor ould Erin!

THE NEW YORK BALL TO THE PRINCE, OR THE BELLES HE DANCED WITH.

'Twas a grand display, was the Prince's ball,
A pageant or fête, or what you may call
A brilliant corruscation;
Where ladies and lords of noble worth
Enchanted a Prince of royal birth,
By a royal demonstration.

Like Queens, arrayed in their regal guise,
They charmed the Prince with dazzling eyes,
Fair ladies of rank and station—
Till the floor gave way, and down they sprawled
In a tableaux style, which the artists called
A floor-all decoration.

At the Prince's feet like flowers they laid,
In the brightest bouquet ever made,
For a Prince's choice to falter—
Perplexed to find, where all were rare,
Which was the fairest of the fair
To cull for a Queenly altar.

But soon the floor was set aright,
And Peter Cooper's face grew bright,
When, like the swell of an organ,
All hearts beat time to the first quadrille,
And the Prince confessed to a joyous thrill
As he danced with Mrs. Morgan.

Then came the waltz, the Prince's own—
And every bar and brilliant tone
Had music's sweetest grace on;
But the Prince himself ne'er felt its charm
Till he slightly clasped with circling arm,
That lovely girl, Miss Mason.

But ah! the work went bravely on,
And meek-eyed Peace a trophy won
By the magic art of the dancers;
For the daring Prince's next exploit
Was to league with Scott's Camilla Hoyt.
And overcome the Lancers!

Besides these three he deigned to yield
His hand to Mrs. B. M. Field,
Miss Jay and Miss Van Buren
Miss Russell, too, was given a place—
All beauties famous for their grace
From Texas to Lake Huron.

With Mrs. Kernochan he "lanced,"
With Mrs. Edward Cooper danced,
With Mrs. Belmont capered;
With fair Miss Fish, in fairy rig,
He tripped a sort of royal jig,
And next Miss Butler favored.

And thus, mid many hopes and fears,
By the brilliant light of the chandeliers,
Did they gayly quaff and revel;
Well pleased to charm a royal Prince,
The only one from Old England since
George Washington was a rebel.

And so the fleeting hours went by,
And watches stopped—lest time should fly—
Or that they winding wanted;
Old matrons dozed and papas smiled,
And many a fair one was beguiled
As the Prince danced on, undaunted.

'Tis now a dream—the Prince's ball,
Its vanished glories, one and all,
        The scenes of the fairy tales;
For Cinderella herself was there,
And Barnum keeps for trial fair,
The beautiful slipper deposited there
        By His Highness the Prince of Wales.

SYNOPTICAL VIEW

OF

H. R. H. the Prince of Wales' Tour in America.

1860.	LEAVE	1860.	ARRIVE AT	Miles.
July 10,	Plymouth, England,...	July 23,	St. John's, N. F.,...	—
" 26,	St. John's, N. F.,......	" 30,	Halifax, N. S.,....	900
Aug. 2,	Halifax,..............	Aug. 2,	St. John's, N. B.,..	120
" 7,	St. John's, N. B.,......	" 9,	Charlottetown, P. E. I.,..........	250
" 11,	Charlottetown,........	" 12,	Gaspe,..........	200
" 13,	Gaspe,...............	" 15,	Quebec, C. E.,....	650
" 20,	Quebec,..............	" 20,	Chaudiere Falls and back.......	30
" 23,	Quebec,..............	" 24,	Montreal, C. W.,..	170
" 29,	Montreal,.............	"	Chaughnawaga and back,..........	180
" 30,	Montreal,............	"	Sherbrooke and back,..........	50
" 31,	Montreal,............	Sept. 1,	Ottawa...........	180
Sept. 3,	Ottawa,..............	" 4,	Kingston.........	101
" 6,	Kingston,............	" 6,	Cobourg,.........	90
" 7,	Cobourg,.............	" 7,	Toronto,.........	70
" 10,	Toronto,.............	" 10,	Collingwood,.....	95
" 13,	Collingwood,.........	" 13,	London,..........	25
" 15,	London,..............	" 15,	Niagara Falls,....	126
" 18,	Niagara,.............	" 18,	Queenston,.......	10
" 18,	Queenston,...........	" 18,	Hamilton,........	25
" 20,	Hamilton,............	" 20,	Detroit, Mich.,....	150
" 21,	Detroit,.............	" 21,	Chicago, Ill.,.....	284
" 22,	Chicago,.............	" 22,	Dwight,..........	70
" 25,	Dwight,..............	" 25,	Stewart's Grove and back,......	30
" 27,	Dwight,..............	" 27,	St. Louis, Mo.,....	212
" 29,	St. Louis,...........	" 29,	Cincinnati, O.,....	340
Oct. 2,	Cincinnati,..........	Oct. 2,	Harrisburg, Pa.,..	615
" 3,	Harrisburg,..........	" 3,	Washington, via Baltimore,.....	123
" 5,	Washington,..........	" 5,	Mount Vernon and back,..........	34
" 6,	Washington..........	" 6,	Richmond, Va.,...	130
" 8,	Richmond,...........	" 8,	Baltimore, Md.,...	150
" 9,	Baltimore,...........	" 9,	Philadelphia,.....	98
" 11,	Philadelphia,.........	" 11,	New York,.......	90
" 15,	New York,...........	" 15,	West Point,......	51
" 16,	West Point,..........	" 16,	Albany,..........	99
" 17,	Albany,..............	" 17,	Boston, Mass.,.....	200
" 20,	Boston,..............	" 20,	Portland, Me.,....	187
" 20,	Portland for England,.			
	Total distance traveled,..................			5134

THE RETURN HOME.

It is not less a source of pleasure and relief to the Americans, both of the United States, and British Provinces, than it must have been to the people of England, who individually regard him almost "as one of the family," to hear of the safe arrival, after a voyage of unusual length and severity, of the Prince of Wales at home.

We learn that the royal squadron experienced head winds and bad weather during the entire passage from Portland, and that although it did not anchor at Plymouth till the 15th of November, it was within a day's sail of England on the 6th, when a heavy gale retarded any further progress. At this time provisions on board the fleet were running short, so that, during the last few days at sea, the royal party were compelled to live solely on salt and preserved food. However, on landing, none of them appeared the worse for the change; and what has become a proverb tells us that "All's well that ends well."

It will be heard with satisfaction that the Duke of Newcastle, the able Mentor of the Prince, is to receive the Order of the Garter, which has just become vacant by the death of the Duke of Richmond. No one, we should judge, is more worthy of this new honor than His Grace, whose visit to this country will be always pleasantly associated with that of His Royal Highness.

The effect of the brilliant and hearty receptions which the Prince met with in the United States is making itself felt from one extremity of Great Britain to the other, and there is no more conspicuous evidence of this than in the altered and extremely congratulatory tone of the English press towards their transatlantic cousins. Instead of remaining studiously silent about them, or regaling Jonathan with an occasional sarcasm or display of hostility, the leading English journals now come forward with lengthy articles in which the praises of the great republic are sounded in the most friendly manner possible.

This is all the more gratifying when we know it to be only a faint expression of the popular feeling in England. Almost every true Englishman feels himself just now, with regard to the Americans, in the position of one who had sent his best friend, his grandson, or his brother, as the case might be, with a very warm letter of introduction to a distant cousin, who had entertained him well beyond expectation; while, to add to this feeling, there is the grand and absorbing influence of an exchange of international courtesies between two of the greatest nations of the earth, whose people are bound together by the ties engendered by an affinity of race, an affinity of language, and the most intimate commercial relations.

We can hardly overestimate the good results, not only direct, but indirect, which will accrue to both countries—for have they not a common interest?—from the happy auspices under which the eldest son of Queen Victoria sojourned among the American people. There is no knowing how soon—although, for his mother's sake, we wish it may be long—that young man may be called upon to ascend the throne, which, by the accident of birth, he inherits; and there is hardly a limit to the power of kings, be it for good or evil. His visit to the New World will have enlarged his ideas and enlisted his sympathies in behalf of its inhabitants. He will be less influenced by prejudices than are many of his countrymen, and be a far wiser man than was his great-grandfather, George III., but for whose tyrannical policy with regard to the old thirteen colonies, what are now the United States might still have been

British territory. It was that very tyranny that defeated itself and gave birth to independence; and what was England's loss was America's gain.

Mark the difference between the reign of the third George and now. Then the people were proclaimed rebels; now they have just occupied the friendly position of hosts in entertaining his great-grandson. The corresponding change of feeling involved in this is no less remarkable. When the Prince of Wales was in the United States he viewed the great American section of the Anglo-Saxon race with no envious, no ungenerous emotions. He simply saw a great people, having institutions in common with his own, and all trying to give him as hearty a welcome as they could, and to make his short stay in this country as agreeable as possible, sparing neither purse nor labor to do him honor—and all this without the slightest toadyism or in the least overdoing the thing. How, therefore, can his impressions of his visit be other than of the most lively and endearing character? The same feelings prevail among the Americans, and will endure. A compliment to the Prince of Wales such as that paid by the people of the United States is a compliment to the Queen and the whole British nation, which will not easily be forgotten, and will have more effect in softening whatever asperities may in the future arise on either side than all the diplomacy in the world.

Meanwhile, the glorious welcome he met with abroad has only been exceeded by his welcome home, and the inhabitants of every town and village in the British provinces he has visited will feel themselves bound closer to the parent land than before his coming, and similar will be the effect upon the popular and individual mind wherever else he may wander through those dominions, upon which, it is the glory of England to say, the sun never sets.

www.ingramcontent.com/pod-product-compliance
Lightning Source LLC
LaVergne TN
LVHW020242110826
845151LV00003B/1014

* 9 7 8 1 4 2 5 5 2 8 9 3 5 *